VICTORY
THROUGH
SURRENDER

Confessions of a Prisoner of Grace

A 365-Day

How-To Guide

VOLUME ONE

Tim Tremaine

7710-T Cherry Park Dr, Ste 224
Houston, TX 77095
713-766-4271

Cover design: Harvest Creek Ministry by Design, www.harvestcreek.net

ISBN: 9781648302640

Dedication

To my wife Dottie, and our son, Chase
To our son Taylor, and his wife, Laura
To our granddaughter, Selah

CONTENTS

INTRODUCTION

With this book, I hope to help answer the question, How? How do we walk the Christian walk, live the Christian life, every day successfully? The short answer to the question is, we can't. But Jesus can, and will, live His life through us if we let Him. Together, we will walk through centuries of Christian devotional thought regarding the subject of living a life of absolute surrender to God.

When I took a course on Spanish for law enforcement officers years ago, one of the first phrases we learned (and one of few I remember) was "*manos arriba*!" Hands up! Raising your hands over your head is the universal symbol of surrender. Raised hands in worship should signify our surrender to the God in whom we place our trust and to whom we offer our allegiance. But what does surrender mean and how does surrender work? That is the focus of this book.

As a police officer for almost 33 years, I know a little about confessions. You investigate the crime, figure out the facts, present the facts to the suspect, and attempt to get a confession. When the suspect confesses, he is saying "I'm guilty, I did it." In a religious context, confessions are often associated with sin; however, throughout church history there have been confessions of faith as well. When believers in Jesus Christ make a confession of faith, we are saying, "I can't do it, but I believe You can." Living a life of absolute surrender to God is a confession of faith. I will model for you how to use Scripture as confessions of faith to assist you in living the surrendered life, assisted by the Spirit-filled writings of men and women throughout the centuries.

There are two contexts in which most people typically think about the concept of surrender. One is a criminal surrendering to the law and the other is a soldier surrendering when he has lost, or given up, the fight. When a criminal surrenders to the law, he becomes a prisoner of the state and loses his freedom. When a soldier surrenders to an enemy, he becomes a prisoner of war and loses everything he has. When a believer surrenders to God, he gives up everything he has, to gain everything God is, thereby, becoming a *Prisoner of Grace*. I hope you will take this journey with me and discover the joy and simplicity of living a life of absolute surrender.

Although I have been a Christian for over 50 years, I always struggled in this area. The Lord changed my life by teaching me that surrender, in its simplest form, was saying "Yes, Lord" to Him about everything in life. Whatever He says, whatever He wants, my response is "Yes, Lord." I had a glimpse of this life 40 years ago and came closer to it 20 years ago but missed both times. Don't wait that long to understand who you are really supposed to be – a *Prisoner of Grace*. Start today to win the **Victory Through Surrender**.

The humble shall see this and be glad; And you who seek God, your hearts shall live.
For the Lord hears the poor, And does not despise His prisoners.
Psalms 69:32-33

For this reason I, Paul, the prisoner of Christ Jesus for you Gentiles— if indeed you have heard of the dispensation of the grace of God which was given to me for you...
Ephesians 3:1-2

HOW TO USE THIS BOOK

Were you to pick up this book and flip through the pages, you might think this is a devotional based on the layout. But that it not quite accurate. I refer to it as a "confessional – journal - anthology." It involves something you speak, something you write, and something you read. The purpose is not just to teach lessons, although I have included a few and I trust you will learn something along the way. The purpose is to model for you how to live the Christian life in complete surrender to God and trust in God through daily confessing the truths of His Word. The *Confessions* sections, not unlike confessions of faith throughout history, are based on Scripture as well as the Spirit-led words of other faithful men and women through the centuries.

These confessions are prayers, in the sense that you are talking to God, but not in the sense that they are requests, petitions, or intercessions. They are more like proclamations, declarations, or affirmations of truth. They will sound and feel like praise but are really your faith responses to truth. I have my own God-given filter that takes in truth and finds a way to speak it out that is meaningful to me. Maybe I can communicate in a meaningful way to you. I am not re-interpreting Scripture or making a new translation, although it might sound like it. I simply want to model for you how you can take the truths in Scripture, accept them, incorporate them into your life, verbalize them as faith confessions, and let God transform you through them.

The approach is more like; "Since these things are true, therefore I will respond like this." I encourage you to read the Scripture passage first, then read the confession. I am sharing the style the Lord has given me and the styles I have found with other people. There is space at the end of each week to journal what you learn or write your own confessions and prayers.

God is always the primary audience, but not the only audience. You will be speaking to yourself as well. There is something powerful and wonderful about hearing the truths of God in your own ears spoken by your own voice. These confessions are not simply to be read. They are to be read *out loud*. You can recite them privately or as part of a group or congregation. But the point is, speak them *out loud*. Get them out of your brain and into the air. The powers of the air, the enemy with which we war every day, will also be an audience to your confessions. The strongholds you battle are like the walls of Jericho. But the walls did not fall from silent prayer and worship, they fell at the shouts of obedience! So, give voice to your devotion.

Spirit-filled words based on God's truth are powerful and effective when spoken into our atmosphere, sounded forth into the heavenlies, and endorsed by the awesome "Yes!" of the Lord Jesus Christ. The concept of words, the spoken word, or The Word is very important in the economy of God. Throughout the history of man, God has spoken to His people and given them words to speak. Phil Driscoll, the great trumpeteer and general in the worship army of God, says that "words are process starters." He refers to 1 Corinthians 14 where it talks about words having significance. Speaking the truth to God, to yourself, and to others is an important and powerful part of the process of sanctification.

These confessions are not just made at the beginning of the Christian walk when a person is born again. Confessions of faith need to be made throughout our life as we grow in the Lord and learn how to trust Him and depend on Him and wait on Him every day. The walk of holiness, obedience, and surrender requires a continual confession of faith. Not that we have to be saved over and over, in terms of our regeneration, but in terms of working out our salvation on a daily, hourly, moment by moment basis. It's walking by the Spirit, step-by-step, less of me and more of Him, toward the goal of maturity and the fullness of Christ in our life.

Men and women of faith have been teaching these principles for centuries and I will highlight many of them in the *Insight and Encouragement* sections. When I read books, I often highlight, underline, or make notes, then I go back and type up those notes creating a synopsis of the book for my future reference. Throughout the book, I will share synopses, adaptations, and excerpts of other books that God has used over the years to help me along the way. Many are condensed or adapted for clarity and space purposes, but I strive to remain true to their message. I also include some insights that the Lord has given me. I hope they are helpful as well.

I have also included a number of poems and old hymns, written out in poem form, in the *Hymns and Poems* sections. Reading those great hymns of old as poems, underscores that the saints of old had a pretty good handle on what it means to live the life "hidden with Christ in God." At times, the voice of the selection is changed from third to first person. Like the *Confessions* section, these too are meant to be spoken *out loud*.

The believers referenced herein span the centuries and represent a wide range of theological perspectives and backgrounds. Just because I have used someone as a resource for this book does not mean that I agree with everything they ever said or wrote. It simply means that, in this instant, I and others have found some truth in what they wrote regarding the subject at hand – living the surrendered life. You may not like everything I have shared and that is ok. These are examples that spoke to me and helped me along the way. They are tools, part of the "how to" of living the Christian life. My hope is to demonstrate the consistency of the message and experience throughout the ages of the church era. Some will speak to you where others will not and that is ok too.

I encourage you to use my examples to "prime the pump" of your own faith confessions. Use mine until your thought categories are developed by the Holy Spirit to create your own. The purpose is to further your relationship with Him and teach you how to submit to that relationship in total surrender as a true disciple of Christ. If you question whether this is necessary, read and meditate on Luke 14. I trust you will gain a fuller appreciation for the effort.

My hope is to encourage you by illustrating that this message, this process, this effort has been consistent throughout the centuries of the Church era. I have left most of the language as I found it in the source, so there will be some language you may not be familiar with. But I trust there will be many who speak to you in a way you can receive that will transform your life and walk with the Lord.

While researching the book, I came across a few books from the recent and distant past that follow a similar format. These resources (listed in the Bibliography) were a great source of encouragement and material for me. I am very grateful to those who "plowed the row" ahead of me: John Baillie, A. W. Tozer, Charles and John Wesley, Richard Foster and James B. Smith, and John Shepperd.

Four times along the way, we take a break from the daily devotional format and spend a week delving into a particular subject. I hope you will be blessed by these expanded studies. They are meant to bring a deeper understanding and appreciation of Biblical topics that are crucial for living the surrendered life. Most weeks have a topic or a featured author so if you want to hear from a particular person or need to address a particular area you can jump around to those pages. Indexes are provided in the back. At the first of every month (or 30-day section), I include a short personal story about my background, successes, and failures living the Christian life. I hope these testimonies will be a blessing and encouragement to you.

Most of the selections are about one-page in length. Some are shorter, a few are longer. Once in a while I insert a longer multiple day study. The order of the days is not important. I have tried to use each of the three sections almost every week for variety, but you are welcome to switch the order around as needed. If time is short one day, pick a day with a shorter section. Periodically, I will interject a note or comment on a page. These "Author Notes" are in brackets to identify them as mine.

Week One talks about salvation. Everything begins at new birth. Confirm and affirm your adoption into the family of God before you move on. Week Two begins with a two-page adaptation from the first book God lead me to after my 10-hour "road trip encounter" with Him. This was the beginning of my journey into the surrendered life. Week Two Day Two follows with the Surrender Prayer I developed after that. The prayer has been revised and amended from time to time, but I have prayed it every day since. I invite you to join me on this amazing journey. Use my prayer until you can formulate your own.

Pray your Surrender Prayer at the beginning of *each day*. **Read** that day's devotion or confession as early in the day as you can. **Journal** whatever the Holy Spirit speaks to you as a record of what God speaks into your life. This is not just information for you to learn, it is a lifestyle for you to live.

A PERSONAL WORD

I shared bits and pieces of this journey with family and church friends along the way. One day, my eldest son and I were discussing the whole concept. As I encouraged him to surrender a certain area that was presenting a challenge to him, his response was, "It can't be that easy [just saying 'I surrender']." I thought about that for a couple of days then sent him this reply by email.

"Thank you for your honest feedback in our discussion the other day. That helped me understand something I was missing in my presentation of the concept of surrender and how to do it. You were correct when you said it can't be that easy. It is not easy, but it is simple. I forget that others do not have the context I have for working this out day to day. In a sense, I have been trying to figure this out for decades but, practically, I have three years of experience working on living out this concept. There have been some very difficult times and hard decisions. But the process itself has been easy because God does the heavy lifting all the way. The more I have learned to live this life, the more I have wanted less of what the world has to offer and more of what the Lord has to offer. I spend hours most days in reading, listening to worship music or sermons, praying and writing, not because I have to, but because I want to.

"While the New Testament does not use the word 'surrender,' we use it to describe what Jesus talks about in Matthew 16:24 (Luke 9:23; Mark 8:34) '*If anyone desires to come after Me, let him deny himself, and take up his cross, and follow Me.*' Luke adds the word 'daily,' which is appropriate because this is a daily, sometimes hourly, process. The whole passage in Luke 9 is powerful. Luke chapter 14 takes it further and three times says, 'If you do not bear your cross (or forsake everything you have) you cannot be My disciple.'

"Paul says it another way in Romans 6. We are not to present ourselves to sin for unrighteousness but to God for righteousness (v. 13). Because we are the slaves to whomever we present ourselves (v. 16), we should present ourselves to God as 'slaves of righteousness for holiness' (v. 19). In Romans 12:1, Paul says we should present ourselves as living sacrifices, holy and acceptable to God. So, when I talk about surrendering to God, I'm talking about presenting myself to Him in obedience to His word, to acknowledge that Jesus is Lord and live accordingly.

"That's what the process of surrender is. We die to ourselves daily by presenting ourselves to God for righteousness. When we do that, He responds by accepting our 'surrender' and starts working out that righteousness in our lives. It is a simple process. It works just like salvation. What did you have to do to be saved? Believe the Word, accept Christ by faith, and ask Him for forgiveness and salvation. Surrender is the same. Believe His word (He said we must take up our cross and die to ourselves, so it must be possible to do), act on His word by praying a prayer of surrender (just like you prayed a prayer for salvation), then receive it through the power of the Holy Spirit.

"Learning how to live a life of surrender is like learning how to be filled with the Holy Spirit and live a life totally dedicated to Jesus as Lord. When you are filled with the Spirit, you cannot be filled with yourself. What comes out of you will be based on His character ("the fruit of the Spirit"), not yours and you will do things based on His abilities ("the gifts of the Spirit"), not yours. You can tell when you are not filled with the Spirit because what comes out of you will be the opposite of His fruit (anger, impatience, harshness, etc.). When I sense this happening, I immediately ask the Lord for forgiveness (and the person I wronged if there is one), and I surrender again to Him asking to be filled again with Him. It is simple, but not easy. The good news is that it does get easier with time and practice. There are many things I struggled with in the past that I have not had to struggle with again (or at least not as much) since I began to surrender those areas to the Lord. The blessings from learning how to live this way are too many to count. Marriage, finances, work, ministry, you name it, and it has gotten better!

"I hope this explanation helps. It has helped me to have to find a way to get my thoughts across in a more understandable way. Have a conversation with God about it. Share with Him your questions and frustrations and concerns. Let the Holy Spirit speak to you. He wants us to get this more than we do, and He will 'move mountains' so that we can get it, if we simply ask.

Love, Dad"

This is volume one of two. Combining both volumes will give you one year of devotions focused on living a life of absolute surrender. You might wonder, why do we need to spend an entire year studying one concept? As I told my son, the process is simple, but it is not easy. The purpose of this book is to help you work through some of the most difficult hurdles in living the surrendered life. This won't just be a one year study. You and I will be working on this the rest of our lives. This is a process, a journey that will only end when you see Jesus face to face. It takes time, practice, and perseverance to succeed. There is no end to the insights God wants to reveal to us along the way. Experts say it takes anywhere from 18-254 days to establish a new habit. This is more than a habit – it's a way of life, a way of thinking, a way of processing and implementing Kingdom realities into earthly circumstances. Stick with it. You will not regret it.

I leave you with this verse: *He who has My commandments and keeps them, it is he who loves Me. And he who loves Me will be loved by My Father, and I will love him and manifest Myself to him* (John 14:21). Obey, and Jesus will show up!

MONTH ONE

I have a notoriously bad memory, much to the chagrin of my family. Much of my childhood and most of my adult years just are not present with me. I have absolutely no recollection of my senior year in high school. Imagine that! (No, I did not drink or do drugs.) I suppose to some degree, that's just the way I'm wired. Perhaps it is because I simply do not dwell on the past. I rarely bring up war stories from my past career (although I will include a few in pages to come) or talk much about the "remember when" stories. Perhaps it was my attitude toward work. When the day was over, I was done with it, whether the day included fights or car chases, homicides, or hangnails. But there are a couple of days from my childhood that I do remember: the day I was saved and the day I was baptized.

I am what we used to call a "cradle roll Baptist." My parents were in ministry, so I have been going to church since inception. I grew up in the church and never left. It was the afternoon of January 16, 1965. I don't know how many times my dad and I talked about salvation. I had heard dozens of sermons on the subject, no doubt. That afternoon, as I recall, I brought up the subject and told my dad I wanted to be saved. We talked for a while so he could be sure I understood, to the best of my young ability, what it meant to be saved and how that could happen. The specifics of the conversation are not in my memory bank, but I remember the scene. We were in Dad's upstairs office at the church. It was a Sunday afternoon. When the time was right, we knelt together next to the wingchair and he led me in the sinner's prayer. I meant every word of that prayer. Later that night, when the invitation was offered (we used to have a time at the end of every service where people were invited to stand up and walk to the front for prayer, or to make a decision for Christ, or to join the church), I went forward and shared my decision with the church.

The next Sunday night I was baptized. Our church was a typical Baptist church of the day. The baptistry was elevated behind the pulpit and above the choir loft. I can remember looking out at the congregation as I stood in the water thinking how high up and far away from the people we were. When I went back as an adult, I realized it wasn't really that high up or far away. But to a boy's eyes it was like looking down from a mountain. I know not everyone has clear memories of the day they were saved. Some cannot even put a date to it, and that's ok. But the knowledge that on a particular day, at a particular time, you prayed and asked Jesus to forgive you of your sins and come into your heart is an important part of our faith pilgrimage. If you have not had that day, I pray the first few pages of this book will help bring you to that day or confirm in your spirit that day has happened.

Many who come to the Lord early in life have a crisis of faith later on or begin to wonder if they really did get saved back then. I had that experience in college. Failure and temptation can cause a person to question their salvation and that's what I did. I finally decided I need to settle the matter, to drive a stake in the ground and be able to say without a doubt, Jesus lives in my heart. Sitting in my second floor dorm room, I wrote out my sinner's prayer, signed it, dated it, and posted it on my wall to serve as a remembrance like those stone altars in ancient days. I still believe I was saved when I prayed in my dad's office all those years ago but reaffirming that decision in college was also an important step in my pilgrimage. Now, I reaffirm my salvation and surrender to the Lord every day. That's what this book is about: ***daily absolute surrender***.

WEEK ONE   **Confession about Salvation**   **DAY 1**

I believe Your Word is true about my salvation. I confess that:

- I am a sinner and fall short of the glory of God, I was dead in my sins and trespasses, without hope and without God in the world. (Romans 3: 23; Ephesians 2:1-2, 12)
- for my sake, God made Jesus who knew no sin, to be sin, so that in Him I might become the righteousness of God. (Romans 8:3-4; 2 Corinthians 5:21; 1 Peter 2:22-24)
- God sent His son to redeem me so that I could be adopted as a son of God and be able to call God, my Father. (Romans 8:15; Galatians 3:26; 4:4-7)
- Jesus is the crucified, resurrected one and only son of the living God. (Mark 1:11; John 1:18; 3:15-17)
- the gift of God is eternal life in Jesus Christ, who came not only to give us the hope of heaven when we die, but an abundant life while we still live. (John 10:10; 14:1-3; Romans 6:23)
- there is no other name given among men whereby I must be saved. (Acts 4:12; 10:43; 1 Timothy 2:5)
- the only way to God is through His son, Jesus Christ. (John 14:6; 11:25-26; 1 John 5:20)
- at the name of Jesus, every knee shall bow and every tongue confess that Jesus Christ is Lord. (Romans 14:11; Ephesians 1:21; Philippians 2:9-10)
- the only way to live the abundant new life hidden with Christ in God is to totally and completely yield and surrender myself to His will. (Mark 8:34-37; Galatians 2:20; Colossians 3:3)

Briefly write out your salvation story on the next page as a remembrance of God's grace in your life. If you are not saved or unsure, write out your personal confession of faith now and receive the gift of the Holy Spirit. Even if you have been a church member or church-goer for years, if you are asking Jesus Christ into your heart for the first time now, share this decision with your church group and request believer's baptism. It is humbling to make this decision public, but you are not alone. Many people who have grown up in the church and just assumed they were Christians, acted like Christians, but never had a real relationship of faith with Jesus, have gone before you and survived!

Record your testimony of faith here. DATE:

_____

_____

_____

_____

_____

_____

_____

_____

_____

_____

_____

_____

_____

_____

WEEK ONE   *HYMNS and POEMS*   **DAY 2**

What Will You Do With Jesus?

by A. B. Simpson (1843-1919)

Jesus is standing in Pilate's hall--
Friendless, forsaken, betrayed by all;
Hearken! what meaneth the sudden call!
What will you do with Jesus?

Refrain:
What will you do with Jesus?
Neutral you cannot be;
Someday your heart will be asking,
"What will He do with me?"

Jesus is standing on trial still,
You can be false to Him if you will,
You can be faithful thro' good or ill:
What will you do with Jesus?

Will you evade Him as Pilate tried?
Or will you choose Him, whate'er betide?
Vainly you struggle from Him to hide:
What will you do with Jesus?

Will you, like Peter, your Lord deny?
Or will you scorn from His foes to fly,
Daring for Jesus to live or die?
What will you do with Jesus?

"Jesus, I give Thee my heart today!
Jesus, I'll follow Thee all the way,
Gladly obeying Thee!" will you say:
"This I will do with Jesus!"

https://hymnary.org/text/jesus_is_standing_in_pilates_hall_friend

WEEK ONE   *INSIGHT and ENCOURAGEMENT*   **DAY 3**

The Life That He Lived

by Major W. Ian Thomas (1914-2007)

Have you accepted Christ as your Redeemer? Do you know that for His dear sake your sins are forgiven? You may know this just as soon as you say, "Thank you, Lord! Be it unto me according to Your Word! Redeem my soul, cleanse my heart, and wash me in the Blood of the Lamb; the Lamb of God that taketh away the sin of the world!" To know your sins are gone is joy indeed! The record cleansed, and reconciled to God, heaven is now your home; but is that all you need? It is where you must *begin*, but it is not all you need! Does the knowledge that your sins have been forgiven, *in itself*, impart to you any new capacity to live a different kind of life? The answer obviously is – No!

There may have been created within you a genuine desire to serve God, out of a sincere sense of gratitude to Christ for dying for you; you may be impelled out of a sense of duty as a Christian, to seek conformity to some pattern of behavior which has been imposed upon you as the norm for Christian living; you may be deeply moved by the need of others all around you, and holy ambitions may have been stirred within your heart, to count for God; if however, all that has happened is that your sins have been forgiven, because you have accepted Christ as the Savior who dies for you, leaving you *since* your conversion only with those resources you had *before* your conversion, then you will have no alternative but to "Christianize" the "flesh" and try to teach it to "behave" in such a way that it will be Godly!

That is sheer impossibility! The nature of the "flesh" never changes, no matter how you may coerce it or conform it; it is rotten through and through, even with a Bible under its arm, a check for missions in its hand, and an evangelical look on its face! You need something more than forgiveness, and what you need is the *big news* of the Gospel! This is the very heart of the message, for the life that Christ live, qualified Him for the death that He died, then the death that He dies qualified you for the life that He lived!

The moment you are redeemed through the atoning death of Christ upon the cross, you receive the Holy Spirit within your human spirit. You have "passed from death to life" – raised from the dead – and the Life which has been imparted to you by the Holy Spirit is the very Life of Christ Himself. *'But God, being [so very] rich in mercy, because of His great and wonderful love with which He loved us, even when we were [spiritually] dead and separated from Him because of our sins, He made us [spiritually] alive together with Christ.'* Ephesians 2:4-5 AMP.

The life that the Lord Jesus Christ lived for you nineteen hundred years ago – condemns you; but the life that He now lives in you – saves you! The Christian life is the Life which He lived *then*, lived *now* by Him *in* you.

Excerpted from *The Mystery of Godliness*. Carnforth, Lancs., Great Britain: Capernwray Press, 1981. Pp. 119-121 (Emphasis his.)

WEEK ONE   *INSIGHT and ENCOURAGEMENT*   **DAY 4**

Is There Any Other Explanation for You but Christ?
by Major W. Ian Thomas (1914-2007)

The Christian life can only be explained in terms of Jesus Christ, and if your life as a Christian can still be explained in terms of *you* – *your* personality, *your* will-power, *your* gift, *your* talent, *your* money, *your* courage, *your* scholarship, *your* dedication, *your* sacrifice, or *your* anything – then although you may *have* the Christian life, you are not yet living it.

If the way you live your life as a Christian can be explained in terms of *you*, what have you to offer to the man who lives next door? The way he lives his life can be explained in terms of *him*, and so far as he is concerned, you happen to be "religious" – but he does not! "Christianity" may be *your* hobby, but it is not his, and there is nothing about the way you practice it which strikes him as at all remarkable! There is nothing about you which leaves him guessing, and nothing commendable of which he does not feel himself equally capable without the inconvenience of becoming a Christian!

It is only when your quality of life *baffles* the neighbors that you are likely to *impress* them! It has got to become patently obvious to others that the kind of life you are living is not only *highly commendable*, but that it is beyond all *human explanation*! That it is beyond the consequences of man's capacity to *imitate*, and however little they may understand this, clearly the consequence only of God's capacity to *reproduce Himself* in you!

In a nutshell, this means that your fellow-men must become convinced that the Lord Jesus Christ of whom you speak, is essentially Himself the ingredient of the Life you live!

Thus, to walk is to experience with Paul the Apostle: *'I know how to be brought low, and I know how to abound. In any and every circumstance, I have learned the secret of facing plenty and hunger, abundance and need. I can do all things through him who strengthens me.'* Philippians 4:12-13.

Without this kind of faith, it is impossible to please God (Hebrews 11:6), for without this kind of faith, it is impossible for God to reproduce His character in you – and that is Godliness! True Godliness leaves the world convinced beyond a shadow of a doubt, that the only explanation for you, is Jesus Christ – to whose eternally unchanging and altogether adequate "I Am!" your heart has learned to say with unshatterable faith, "*Thou art!*" That is really all you need to know!

Excerpted from *The Mystery of Godliness*. Carnforth, Lancs., Great Britain: Capernwray Press, 1981. p. 24f. (Emphasis his.)

WEEK ONE   **Confession about Salvation**   **DAY 5**

Read Psalms 118

Thank you, Lord, for you are good and your love endures forever. When I cried to the Lord in distress you answered me and set me free. Since you are with me, what can anyone do to me? You are my helper, and I will look in victory on my troubles. It is better to rely on the Lord than to rely on men or governments. When trouble surrounds me on every side, in the name of the Lord I will cut them off. I was about to lose everything, but God helped me. God, you are my strength and my song and my salvation. I will fill my home with shouts of joy and victory. I will survive your discipline and live to proclaim what you have done for me. You will make the path of righteousness possible for me because you answer me and save me. You are my God. You are shining your light on me. I will thank you and lift up your name in praise. You have made today, and I will rejoice and be glad in it.

WEEK ONE *HYMNS and POEMS* **DAY 6**

The Welcome to the King

by Frances Ridley Havergal (1836-1879)

Midst the darkness, storm, and sorrow
One bright gleam I see,
Well I know the blessed morrow
Christ will come for me
Midst the light and peace and glory
Of the Fathers home,
Christ for me is watching, waiting--
Waiting till I come

Long the blessed Guide has led me
By the desert road;
Now I see the golden towers--
City of my God.
There amidst the love and glory,
He is waiting yet;
On His hands a name is graven,
He can ne'er forget.

There amidst the songs of heaven--
Sweeter to His ear
Is the footfall through the desert,
Ever drawing near.
There, made ready are the mansions,
Glorious, bright and fair;
But the Bride the Father gave Him
Still is wanting there.

Who is this who comes to meet me
On the desert way,
As the Morning Star foretelling
God's unclouded day?

He it is who came to win me,
On the cross of shame
In His glory well I know Him,
Evermore the same

Oh! the blessed joy of meeting,
All the desert past!
Oh! the wondrous words of greeting
He shall speak at last!
He and I together entering
Those bright courts above,
He and I together sharing
All the Fathers love.

Where no shade nor stain can enter
Nor the gold be dim,
In that holiness unsullied
I shall walk with Him
Meet companion then for Jesus,
From Him, for Him made,
Glory of God's grace for ever
There in me displayed.

He who in His hour of sorrow
Bore the curse alone,
I who through the lonely desert
Trod where He had gone.
He and I in that bright glory
One deep joy shall share
Mine to be forever with Him
His that I am there.

Tim Tremaine

Coming to the King, 1886. The Gutenburg Project EBook, 2004. p. 19-21.

WEEK ONE   *INSIGHT and ENCOURAGEMENT*   **DAY 7**

True Repentance

Johann Arndt (1555-1621)

Repentance, or true conversion, is the work of the Holy Spirit, under the influence of which, man, through the *law*, acknowledges his sin, and the wrath of God provoked against it; and earnestly mourns over his offences; and then, understanding, through the *Gospel*, the grace of God, by faith in Christ Jesus, he obtains the remission of his sins. By this repentance, the mortification or crucifying of the flesh, and of all carnal lusts and pleasures, is carried on; together with the quickening of the Spirit, or the resurrection of the new man in Christ. Under the exercise of repentance, therefore, the old Adam, with his corruptions, dies within us; and Christ lives in us, by faith (Gal. 2:20); for we must be aware that these two are inseparably connected. The resurrection of the spirit follows the mortification of the flesh; and the quickening of the new man, destroys and annihilates the old man; the ruin of the one, is the life and resurrection of the other. "Though our outward man perish, yet the inward man is renewed day by day." 2 Cor. 4:16. We are, therefore, enjoined to "mortify our members which are upon the earth" (Col. 3:5); and to "reckon ourselves to be dead indeed unto sin, but alive unto God, through Jesus Christ our Lord." (Rom. 6:11).

Let us, however, inquire why the flesh is thus to be mortified; and why the whole body of sin is at last to be destroyed. It has been remarked that, by the fall of Adam, man became earthly, carnal, and devilish; without God, and without love: for being without God, he was also without love. Man was now turned from the love of God to the love of the world, and especially of himself; so that in every situation, and under all circumstances, he now studies, favors, flatters, counsels, and applauds himself; and provides only for his own interest, honor, and glory. All this is the consequence of Adam's fall; who, while meditating how he might erect himself, as it were, into *a god*, was involved, together with all his posterity, in the same awful sin and perdition. This depravation of human nature must of necessity be entirely removed; and this can be effected only by serious repentance; by Godly sorrow; by a faith that apprehends the remission of sin; by the mortification of sensual pleasure; and by the crucifixion of pride and self-love.

For true repentance consists not in putting away gross and open sins only; but it requires that a man should enter his heart, and search into its inmost recesses. The secret parts, the windings and the turnings of iniquity are to be laid open; in order that the returning sinner may be thoroughly renewed, and, at length, be converted from the love of himself, to the love of God; from the love of the world, to a life of spirituality; and from a participation of earthly pomps and pleasures, to a participation, through faith, of the merits of Christ. Hence it follows, that a man must deny himself (Luke 9:23); that is, he must mortify his own will, and suffer himself to be entirely led by the will of God. The cross of Christ... consist(s) in mortifying the flesh, with its sinful propensities; in turning away from the world to God; in an inward and constant secret sorrow for our sins; in a daily dying to the world, and living to Christ by faith; in following his steps with sincere lowliness and humility; and in confiding only in the grace of God in Christ Jesus.

Excerpted from, *True Christianity*. Philadelphia: Smith, English, & Co., (unk). p. 92-96.

Record your insights, revelations, and meditations from this week. DATE:

_____

_____

_____

_____

_____

_____

_____

_____

_____

_____

_____

_____

_____

_____

Absolute Surrender

By Andrew Murray (1828-1917)

The condition of God's blessing is absolute surrender of all into His hands. There is no end to what God will do for us, and to the blessing God will bestow. Are you willing to surrender yourselves absolutely into His hands? To find the secret of the power of that life?

First of all, *God claims it*. It has its foundation in the very nature of God. God cannot do otherwise. Think of God's creation. Is it not all surrendered to God? Can you think that God can work His work if there is only half or part of them surrendered? This one lack of absolute surrender is just the thing that hinders God's working in our lives. Can God work His work every day and every hour unless you are entirely given up to Him? Every one of us is a temple of God, in which God will dwell and work mightily on one condition – absolute surrender to Him.

Not only does God claim it, but *God will work it Himself*. Many fear that absolute surrender implies more than they can do. They think they dare not face the entire giving up of life, because it will cause so much trouble and agony. But God does not ask you to give perfect surrender in your own strength, or by the power of your will; God is willing to work it in you. *"for it is God who works in you to will and to do according to his good purpose."* Philippians 2:13.

Come with your feeble desire; and if you fear that your desire is not strong enough, or you are not willing for everything that may come, or you are not bold enough to say you can conquer everything – I pray you, learn to know and trust your God now. Say: "My God, I am willing that You should make me willing." If there is any sacrifice you are afraid of making, come and prove how gracious your God is. Be not afraid that He will command from you what He will not bestow. ("God does not *command* from you, what He does not *commend* to you." – Author) You have hindered and hindered Him terribly, but He desires to help you to get hold of Him entirely.

Not only does God claim it and work it, but *He accepts it when you bring it to Him*. The Holy Spirit bids you speak it out and yield to Him that absolute surrender. When you bring it, it may, as far as your feelings and your consciousness go, be a thing of great imperfection, and you may doubt and hesitate and say: "Is it absolute?" Remember, there once was a man to whom Christ said, "all things are possible to him that believes." His reply was, "I believe, help my unbelief."

Simply come and say, "Lord, I yield myself in absolute surrender to my God." Even if you think, "I do not feel the power, I do not feel the determination, I do not feel the assurance," *IT WILL SUCCEED*. Have you not learned that the Holy Spirit works with mighty power, while on the human side everything appears feeble?

When you do yield yourself in absolute surrender, let it be in the faith that God does now accept of it. That is the great point, and that is what we so often miss – that believers should be thus occupied with God in the matter of surrender. In humble simplicity say, "God I accept your terms of absolute surrender." Even if silently spoken in your heart, know that there is a God present that takes note of it and at that very moment takes possession of you.

What God claims and works and accepts, *He also maintains*. Perhaps you have gone through cycles of passion for God and seeking consecration, but it soon faded and was gone. When God has begun the work of absolute surrender in you, and when God has accepted your surrender, then God holds Himself bound to care for it and to keep it. Why have you not experienced it? Because you have not trusted God for it, and you do not surrender yourself absolutely to God in that trust.

This life of absolute surrender has its difficulties. In fact, with men it is impossible. In your strength it is unachievable. But it is possible if you understand that it is God who does it in you and maintains it through you. George Mueller lived this life. His "secret" of success was two-fold: he believed he had been enabled by grace to maintain a good conscience before God day by day, and he was a lover of God's word. Complete obedience and unbroken fellowship are key.

First, do what God wants you to do: give up yourselves absolutely to the will of God. Say: "By your grace I desire to do your will in everything, every moment of every day." Do you think that possible? Ask yourself this: What has God promised you and what can God do to fill a vessel absolutely surrendered to Him? 1 Corinthians 2:9-10 says; *"However, as it is written: 'What no eye has seen, what no ear has heard, and what no human mind has conceived' - the things God has prepared for those who love him - these are the things God has revealed to us by his Spirit."*

Second, let God work what He wants to do and only can do. If you say: "I give myself absolutely to God, to His will, to do only what God wants. I give myself absolutely to God, to let Him work in me to will and to do of His good pleasure," God will enable you to carry out the surrender. He will accept it and He will teach you what it means. Have you been praying for blessing in your life? There must be absolute surrender.

No words can tell the sad state of the church of Christ on earth. Just think of the Christians around you. I do not speak of nominal Christians, or of professing Christians, but I speak of hundreds and thousands of honest, earnest Christians who are not living a life in the power of God or to His glory. So little power, so little devotion or consecration to God, so little conception of the truth that a Christian is a man or woman, boy or girl, utterly surrendered to God's will. Let us learn of Paul, "for me to live is Christ" (Phil 1:21).

Accept God's teaching that in your flesh dwells no good thing. Nothing will help you except another life come in. You must deny yourself once and for all. Denying self must every moment be the power of your life. Cast this self-life and flesh-life at the feet of Jesus and trust Him. Don't worry about trying to understand all about it, just come in the living faith that Christ will come into you with the power of His death and the power of His life and the power of the Holy Spirit to make it so.

Adapted from my dad's copy of ***Absolute Surrender and other addresses*** by Andrew Murray. Published by Moody Press, Chicago. Unknown year, but the original price was .50 cents.

WEEK TWO   **Prayer of Surrender**   **DAY 2**

Here is my daily surrender prayer. Borrow it until the Lord gives you your own. Start every day with this prayer and believe that God hears it and accepts it, regardless of your feelings.

My God, I am willing to be made willing (Psalm 51:12). Lord, I yield myself in absolute surrender to you, my God. I accept your terms of absolute surrender. By your grace, I desire to do Your will in everything, every moment of every day. I give myself absolutely to You, to Your will, to do only what You want. I give myself absolutely to you God, to let You work in me to will and to do of Your good pleasure.

I count, reckon, and consider myself dead to sin and alive to God in Jesus Christ my Lord. Help me not to let sin reign in my body so that I obey its evil desires or offer the parts of my body to sin, as instruments of wickedness. I offer myself to You and the parts of my body to You as instruments of righteousness (Romans 6:11-14); in order that in everything, You may be glorified through Christ Jesus my Lord (1 Peter 4:11).

You are my God, apart from you I am nothing (Gal 6:3), I know nothing (1 Cor 8:2), I have knowing (1 Cor 4:7), and I can do nothing (John 15:5). I want to speak what You are speaking and do what You are doing (John 5:19). I am willing to lose what I have, or what I think I have, to gain what You are willing to give. I am putting my trust in You. Show me the way I should go, for to You I lift up my soul. Teach me to do Your will for You are my God. May Your good Spirit lead me on level ground (Psalms 143:8, 10).

This is the foundation for everything that follows. Stay here for as long as you need to, until you sense a breakthrough. Do not read over it lightly and leave. Let God begin to work His work in you. Think about each sentence and let the Holy Spirit speak to you.

WEEK TWO   **Confession about Obedience**   **DAY 3**

Read Psalm 119:73-80

I confess and believe that I am your creation. You made me capable of learning and understanding your commands. I will live with such obvious and evident hope, because I put my faith in your word, that it will encourage and instruct others who seek to live in obedience and faith. Your obedient ones will be happy every time they see me. Your laws and commands are totally right and good. Even my hard times and difficulties demonstrate your faithfulness. Your unfailing, never-ending love will comfort me in times of trial and pain and sorrow just like you promised. I live because you continually display your compassion to me as I continue to delight in your word. Even when the proud and arrogant among the disobedient attack me and falsely accuse me, I will stay focused on your word and your ways. Those who live in reverence and obedience and who understand your laws and precepts will find support and encouragement in me. I will live a blameless life according to your word in order that I bring no shame upon myself or upon your name.

WEEK TWO   *INSIGHT and ENCOURAGEMENT*   **DAY 4**

Disciplined Habits

by E. Stanley Jones (1884-1973)

"Praying the Scripture" is a unique way of dealing with the Scripture; it involves both reading and prayer. Turn to the Scripture; choose some passage that is simple and fairly practical. Next, come to the Lord. Come quietly and humbly. There, before him, read a small portion of the passage of Scripture you have opened to.

Be careful as you read. Take in fully, gently, and carefully what you are reading. Taste it and digest it as you read. In the past it may have been your habit, while reading, to move very quickly from one verse of Scripture to another until you have read the whole passage. Perhaps you were seeking to find the main point of the passage.

But in coming to the Lord by means of "praying the Scripture," you do not need to read quickly; you read very slowly. You do not move from one passage to another, not until you have *sensed* the very heart of what you have a read. You may then want to take that portion of Scripture that has touched you and turn it into prayer.

After you have sensed something of the passage, and after you know that the essence of that portion has been extracted and all the deeper sense of it is gone, then, very slowly, gently, and in a calm manner begin to read the next portion of that passage. You will be surprised to find that when your time with the Lord has ended, you will have read very little, probably no more than half a page.

"Praying the Scripture" is not judged by *how much* you read but the *way* you read. If you read quickly, it will benefit you little. You will be like the bee that merely skims the surface of a flower. Instead, in this new way of reading with prayer, you become as the bee who penetrates into the depths of the flower. You plunge deeply within to remove its deepest nectar.

Of course, there is a kind of reading the Scripture for scholarship and for study – but not here. That studious kind of reading will not help you when it comes to matters that are *divine*! To receive any deep, inward profit from the Scriptures you must read as I have described. Plunge into the very depths of the words you read until revelation, like a sweet aroma, breaks out upon you. I am quite sure that if you follow this course, little by little you will come to experience a very rich prayer that flows from your inward being.

Foster, Richard J. and Smith, James Bryan. *Devotional Classics*. New York: Harper One, 2005. p. 302-303.

WEEK TWO   *INSIGHT and ENCOURAGEMENT*   **DAY 5**

How to Enter In

by Hannah Whithall Smith (1832-1911)

In order to enter into this blessed interior life of rest and triumph, you have two steps to take, – first, entire abandonment; and second, absolute faith. No matter what may be the complications of your peculiar experience, no matter what your difficulties, or your surroundings, or your "peculiar temperament." These two steps, definitely taken and unwaveringly persevered in, will certainly bring you out sooner or later into the green pastures and still waters of this life hid with Christ in God. You may be perfectly sure of this. And if you will let every other consideration go, and simply devote your attention to these two points, and be very clear and definite about them, your progress will be rapid and your soul will reach its desired haven far sooner than you can now think possible.

Shall I repeat the steps, that there may be no mistake? You are a child of God, and long to please Him. You love your divine Master, and are sick and weary of the sin that grieves Him. You long to be delivered from its power. Everything you have hitherto tried has failed to deliver you: and now, in your despair, you are asking if it can indeed be, as these happy people say, that Jesus is able and willing to deliver you. Surely you must know in your very soul that He is, that to save you out of the hand of all your enemies is, in fact, just the very thing He came to so. Then trust Him. Commit your case to Him in an absolute unreserve, and believe that He undertakes it; and at once, knowing what He is and what He has said, claim that He does even now save you. Just as you believed at first that He delivered you from the guilt of sin because He said it, so now believer that He delivers you from the power of sin because He says it. Let your faith now lay hold of a new power in Christ. You have trusted Him as your dying Savior; now trust Him as your living Savior. Just as much as He came to deliver you from future punishment did He also come to deliver you from present bondage. Just as truly as He came to bear your stripes for you has He come to live your life for you. You are utterly powerless in the one case as in the other. You could as easily have got yourself rid of your own sins, as you could now accomplish for yourself practical righteousness. Christ, and Christ only, must do both for you; and your part in both cases is simply to give the thing to Him to do, and then believe that He does it.

Shall I do it out loud for you? "Lord, Jesus, I believe that you are able and willing to deliver me from all the care and unrest and bondage of my Christian life. I believe you died to set me free, not only in the future but now and here. I believe you are stronger than sin, and that you can keep me, even me, in my extreme weakness, from falling into its snares or yielding obedience to its commands. Lord, I'm going to trust you to keep me. I have tried keeping myself and failed. I am absolutely helpless. So I will trust you *utterly* and give myself to you now."

Adapted from *The Christian's Secret of a Happy Life*. Grand Rapids: Revell, 1952. p. 52-54.

WEEK TWO   *INSIGHT and ENCOURAGEMENT*   **DAY 6**

Christians Without Christ
by Major W. Ian Thomas (1914-2007)

Every step you take, every attitude you adopt, every decision you make, everything you do and all you hope to be, is either in dependence upon the God who created you as His own dwelling place, or else the byproduct of the demon spirit of this world, "who now works in the sons of disobedience" (Ephesians 2:2), and who perpetrates his lies through a mindset of self-reliance in fallen humanity.

The Bible calls this attitude of independence a "carnal mind" (Romans 8:7). It is a mind that is set "on the things of the flesh" rather than on "the things of the Spirit" (Romans 8:5). It means exercising the faculties of your personality in ways that are not dependent on the God whose presence alone in parts to you the quality of true humanity that He always intended for you.

The carnal mind can be in the believer just as much as in the unbeliever. Carnal or fleshly Christians have been regenerated by the restoration of the Holy Spirit to their human spirit, but in certain ways they still repudiate the Spirit's legitimate right to reestablish the rule of Christ in their minds, in their emotions, and in their wills. Although they profess Christ as redeemer, their actions and decisions typically are taken for the sake of their own interests and for who they are in themselves, rather than for God's interests and for who He is. Their minds are still the plaything and the workshop of the devil, for the devil is smart enough and cunning enough that he can always persuade countless numbers of professing Christians to try and be Christians without Christ. They are willing to do anything for Jesus sake, but they fail to understand that *His presence* is absolutely imperative to do it, that without Him we are nothing, have nothing, and can do nothing.

To be a carnal Christian is still to claim the right to exercise your own jurisdiction, make your own decisions and plans, choose your own pathway. But you will be useless to God, and you will make it into heaven only "as through fire" (1 Corinthians 3:15).

What kind of a Christian do you want to be? To choose to be a carnal Christian is to choose spiritual oblivion. But if you decide genuinely that Christ must be everything and have everything in your life, if you say in your heart, "I want nothing less than to be all that for which the blood of God's dear Son was shed," then He is ready to lead you into discoveries that can completely revolutionize your whole humanity for time and eternity.

Excerpted from *The Indwelling Life of Christ*. Colorado Springs: Multnomah Publishers, 2006. p. 33-35.

WEEK TWO   **Confession about Perseverance**   **DAY 7**

Read Psalm 119:81-88

I confess and believe that my hope in your word will not be disappointed. When I am totally spent and exhausted, waiting and longing for Your rescue, I will not give up. When my tears have dried up and my eyes cannot focus any longer looking for your promise to be fulfilled, when my cries for comfort go unanswered, when I feel wrung out and shriveled up and out of strength, I will continue to hope and trust in your word. You know the questions I wrestle with in my mind: how long must I wait? When will these difficulties end? How will I escape the pitfalls my enemies have set for me? Nevertheless, I know your word is trustworthy and I will keep believing in you. I will keep asking for your help despite what others may do to me or say about me. These difficulties have almost wiped me out, but I have not forgotten your promises or forsaken your commandments. You will preserve my life according to your abundant love for me. And I will continue to obey everything You have told me to do.

Record your insights, revelations, and meditations from this week. DATE:

_____

_____

_____

_____

_____

_____

_____

WEEK THREE   **Confession about Joy**   **DAY 1**

Read Philippians 3

I will rejoice in the Lord. I will worship by the Spirit of God. I will glory in Jesus Christ alone. I will not rely on anything I can accomplish or achieve in my own strength. I will not depend on heritage, family, education, wealth, religion, or anything else but You. Anything that could have been a benefit to me, in the world's eyes, I gladly surrender and count as worthless for Christ's sake. Nothing is better, nothing is greater, nothing is more desirable than knowing Christ Jesus my Lord. Anything that I lose, I won't miss. Compared to knowing Christ, everything else is as good as trash. Considering any benefit I might have or claim being as worthless as trash is how Christ increases in my life. It's how I can be found in Him with a righteousness that comes, not from obeying all the rules, but from God by faith. I want to know you, Lord, and the power that raised You from the dead, and the fellowship that comes in shared suffering. In this way, I can become like you in Your death, totally surrendered to God's will, and will share in the life of the resurrected One. I will rejoice in the Lord always.

WEEK THREE   *INSIGHT and ENCOURAGEMENT*   *DAY 2*

The Father Abiding in Me Does the Work

by Andrew Murray (1828-1917)

Jesus Christ became man that He might show us: what true man is, what the true relationship between man and God is, and what the true way of serving God and doing His work is. When we are made new creatures in Christ Jesus, the life we receive is the very life that was and is in Christ. It is only by studying his life on earth that we know how we are to live. "As the living Father has sent me, and I live by the Father: so he that eats me, even he shall live by Me" (John 6:57).

Christ did not consider it a humiliation to be able to do nothing of Himself – to be always and absolutely dependent on the Father. He counted it His highest glory because all His works were the works of the all-glorious God in Him. When will we understand that to wait on God, to bow before Him in perfect helplessness and let Him work everything in us, is our true nobility and the secret of the highest activity? This alone is the true Christ-life, the true life of every child of God. As this life is understood and maintained, the power for work will grow because the soul is in the attitude in which God can work in us, as the God who "is good unto them that wait for Him" (Lamentations 3:25).

It is in ignoring or neglecting the great truths that there can be no true work for God. The explanation of the extensive complaint of so much Christian activity with so little genuine result is *God works in us*, yes, but He cannot work fully in us *unless we live in absolute dependence on Him.* The revival which many are longing and praying for must begin with this: the return of Christian ministers and workers to their true place before God – in Christ. And, like Christ, completely depend and continually wait on God to work in us.

I invite all workers, young and old, successful or disappointed, full of hope or full of fear, to come and learn from our Lord Jesus the secret of true work for God. "My Father worketh hitherto, and I work" (John 5:17). "The Father that dwells in me, He does the works" (John 14:10). Divine Fatherhood means that God is all, and gives all, and works all. Continually depend on the Father and receive, moment by moment, all the strength needed for His work. Try to grasp the great truth that because "it is the same God which works all in all" (1 Corinthians 12: 6), your one need is, in deep humility and weakness, to wait for and to trust in His working. From this, learn that God can only work in us as He dwells in us. "The Father that dwelleth in me, He doeth the works." Cultivate the holy sense of God's continual nearness and presence, of your being His temple, and of His dwelling in you. Offer yourself for Him to work in you all His good pleasure. You will find that work, instead of being a hindrance, can become your greatest incentive to a life of fellowship and childlike dependence.

Excerpted from *How to Work for God.* Pittsburgh, PA: Whitaker House, 1983. p. 33-35.

WEEK THREE   **Confession about Endurance**   **DAY 3**

Read Psalm 119:105-112

I confess and believe that your word can and will keep my feet from stumbling. Your word will illuminate my way and show me the path I should take. I have committed myself to following the righteous path by obeying your laws and commandments. I have to admit that life is hard sometimes and there has been some pain and suffering along the way, but you keep me going just like you said you would. I gladly and freely speak out praise to you, My Lord. I trust that my words of praise are acceptable to you and in response to them you will teach me more about your word. During dangerous and precarious times, I will not forget your law. When the enemy set traps for me and tempts me to wander from the path you have shown me in your word, I will not break your rules and stray from that path. Living a life surrendered to your will is my legacy. Nothing brings me more lasting joy than being obedient to your word. I am determined to follow your will and your ways to the very end.

WEEK THREE   *INSIGHT and ENCOURAGEMENT*   **DAY 4**

Starting Out on the Crucified Life Pathway

A. W. Tozer (1897-1963)

Allow me to go out on a limb and state something that I have no way of knowing for sure; it's a shrewd guess based on knowing spiritual laws. That is, simply, that once a person begins this journey of living the crucified life, during the first phase of that journey, you will experience some of the worst weeks of your life. It is at this point that many will get discouraged and turn back. Those who persevere will find that instead of breaking into the clear bright sunshine, just ahead of them are more discouragements, doubts and deceptions.

Instead of lifting you up, this kind of teaching will cast you down. But let me say this: those who have been so discouraged – those who have bumped their foreheads on the ceiling or scraped their chins on the sidewalk – and have gone down in some kind of defeat are the very ones who are getting nearer to God. Those who are unaffected – those who can still be worldly and not mind it – have made the least progress. But those who have found things going against them – those who in their longing and yearning for the crucified life, those who wait for Jesus Christ to lead them and instead wonder if He is discouraging them – they probably don't realize that they are very close to the Kingdom of God.

We read about Adoniram Judson or D. L. Moody and say, "God, I want you to do that to me." We want to tell God how to do it, and at the same time we want to reserve a little bit of the glory and have some areas in our life uncrucified. What we really want is a technical crucifixion. We are very happy to listen to another exposition on the sixth chapter of Romans on how we are crucified with Christ, but few people in reality truly want it.

Unless we put ourselves in the hands of God and let God do with us as He wills, we will be just what we are – mediocre Christians singing happy songs to keep from being completely blue and trying to keep up the best we can. And while we're doing this, we will not be making any progress toward a crucified life and will not know what it is to be one with Him experientially. Our hearts must be cleansed and our true intent must be to perpetually love Him and worthily praise Him. Then we may be filled with His Spirit and walk in victory.

You do not know what it means to look on God and then go away, letting Him have His way with your life. You are afraid of that. You hope He is all right, you believe He gives all right, and you know what the Bible says, "God so loved"; but still you are afraid that if you leave your life in God's hands, something bad will happen.

Excerpted from, *The Crucified Life: How to Live Out a Deeper Christian Experience*. Minneapolis: Bethany House, 2017. p. 137-139.

WEEK THREE   **Confession about Comfort**   **DAY 5**

Read Lamentations 2-3

I confess and believe that in the face of hardship and affliction, I can cry out to the Lord and you will hear me. Though I grieve night and day with many tears, you will hear me. When I cry out in the middle of the night and pour out my soul in your presence, you will hear me. Even when I am bent over with grief and sadness, I will lift up my hands and worship you, and you will hear me, because your compassions never fail. I survive because of your awesome love for me. Your mercies are new every morning. Your faithfulness is so great it is beyond my ability to comprehend. You are all I have. I will wait patiently for you. I will remind myself that you, my Lord and my God, are my only hope. I trust that the Lord is good to those who place their hope totally and completely in you. You are good to those who continually and passionately seek after you. It is a good thing, and it is good for me to wait quietly for your salvation and rescue to come. Even when I feel forsaken, I know it will not last forever. Your compassion and love will never fail me. Even in the depths of despair, I can call on your name and you will hear me. Because I place my trust in you, I will not be afraid.

WEEK THREE   *INSIGHT and ENCOURAGEMENT*   **DAY 6**

Keys to Developing an Intimate Relationship with Jesus
by Ken Kessler (unknown – present)

What are the practical ways to develop an intimate relationship with Jesus? Developing intimacy with Jesus is a lifelong process. It begins at the point of salvation. From there, we are invited to come freely and boldly before His throne of grace. Here are some disciplines presented in the Bible that cultivate this relationship.

Unconditional surrender is spoken of throughout the Old and New Testaments. Jesus said that we cannot be His disciples unless we deny ourselves, take up our cross daily, and follow Him (Luke 9:23). Many other passages speak of similar calls to surrender. Let me illustrate the importance of surrender in the development of intimacy in this way. In the initial stages of the dating relationship, the couple may have many friends with whom they are equally open. But, as the relationship progresses toward engagement, they begin to confide in each other in a much deeper way. As they enter the marriage covenant, their level of intimacy progresses to an even deeper lever, as they become one in body, soul, and spirit. Although the emotional aspects of love are a major reason why the two have become so close, commitment is what actually binds them together. As both parties to the relationship become secure in the other's commitment to them, they begin to open up to the other in progressively deeper ways.

We also see this concept expressed beautifully in the Book of Esther. Esther was selected as a candidate to be the bride of King Ahasuerus. Because of her commitment and surrender to the leading on the king's eunuchs, she said "yes" to every part of the preparation process. Ultimately, this attitude caused her to be selected as queen. Because of her lifestyle, she was given the privilege to come freely into the king's presence and request anything she needed. Just as Esther grew close to the king, we grow more intimate with the Lord as we continually surrender to the will and purposes of God. As we obey His voice, we grow closer to Him.

Throughout the Scriptures, Babylon is presented as a picture of what man is like apart from God. It often represents the independence and rebellion of man. It also symbolizes the ways of the world. In Revelation 18, Jesus tells His Church to come out of Babylon. At the time of His return, Jesus says that the voice of the Bride will not be heard in Babylon any longer. The Church as the Bride of Christ is a picture of how we relate to Jesus intimately.

To grow in intimacy with Jesus, we must develop **a lifestyle of progressive separation from worldly ways**. James says, "Do you not know that friendship with the world is hostility toward God? Therefore, whoever wished to be a friend of the world makes himself an enemy of God" (James 4:4). The Apostle John describes worldly ways as the lust of the flesh, the lust of the eyes, and the boastful pride of life (1 John 2:16). Intimacy with the Lord grows as we separate from the things of the world. As we become those who are in the world but not of the world, our intimacy with God is enhanced.

Separation is a two-fold process. It requires separation from worldly ways, but it also requires a separation unto God. **Separation unto God** is another important key to developing an intimate relationship with the Lord. Exodus 30:30 reads, "You shall anoint Aaron and his sons, and *consecrate* them, that *they may minister as priests to Me*." Before God allows His people to minister to Him, He first calls them to a life of consecration. As we dedicate ourselves to God and His purposes, a deeper level of consecration comes about in our lives. As we embrace deeper levels of consecration, our intimacy with God grows.

After Martha complained to Jesus about Mary's inactivity, Jesus told her that sitting at His feet and listening to His words was the only thing necessary in life (Luke 10:42). He told her that this one thing would never be taken away from her. **Taking time to sit at the feet of Jesus** is an extremely important discipline that helps facilitate a lifestyle of intimacy with Jesus. Waiting on the Lord for Him to speak, with an attentive heart toward His voice, is vital if we want to grow closer to Him. It takes consistent times of sitting at His feet – Bible in hand – reading, meditating, and listening for His voice. We must regularly break away from our busy schedules in order to wait on Him. As we sit at the feet of Jesus, intimacy with God is developed.

Ministering to the Lord is such a broad concept that it encompasses the four previous keys. Ministry to the Lord involves consecration along with the disciplines of worship, prayer, fasting, meditating on the Word, and waiting on the Lord. In many cases, ministering to the Lord is set in the context of the Tabernacle of Moses or the Temple. Ministering to the Lord is associated with progressing from the outer court, where ministry is focused on people, to the inner court, where ministry is focused on the Lord.

The Tabernacle paints a beautiful picture of how we move toward the Holy of Holies and minster to the Lord. Each piece of furniture in the Tabernacle can symbolize an aspect of our relationship with God. The golden lampstand represents the Holy Spirit giving us light and revelation. The table of shewbread is symbolic of the Word of God. The altar of incense typifies prayer and intercession. The Ark of the Covenant in the place of God's glory and majesty. To minister to the Lord effectively, we need the ministry of the Holy Spirit, the Word of God, worship, and prayer. As we practice these disciplines, we will grow closer to the Lord and abide in the presence of His glory.

We also see continuous ministry to the Lord around God's throne. As we glimpse the heavenly throne room pictured in Revelation 4-5, those that are closest to the Lord are continuously ministering to Him through praise, worship, and thanksgiving. Along the same lines, Acts 13 reveals how the early church ministered to the Lord and out of this, the Holy Spirit set apart Barnabas and Saul for ministry. Again, we note the relationship of intimacy to hearing God's voice. Through routine times of private and public ministry to the Lord, we develop intimacy with God that positions us to hear His voice.

Excerpted from *Learning to Hear God's Voice.* Kennesaw, GA: Restoration Times Publications, Inc., 2003. p. 34-39.

WEEK THREE   *HYMNS and POEMS*   **DAY 7**

Surrender

by J. Edwin Orr (1912-1987)

Forgive me, Lord, that I have failed so often,
Striving so hard, yet striving all in vain,
Thinking to conquer self and sinful nature,
Instead of which I taste defeat again.

Things I would do, I long leave unaccomplished;
Things that I hate, I far too often do:
In wretchedness my heart cries for the answer
Who shall deliver me? I wish I knew.

"Then sin some more that Grace may be the greater?"
O Lord forbid! That cannot be the way!
Deliverance there must be found in Jesus,
And victory for me o'er sin today.

Hast Thou a word to help me, Blessed Master,
To show me how to run aright the race?
Or must I wander on alone in twilight
And seldom see the sunshine of Thy face?

"Confess thy sins: the Blood has power to cleanse thee;
Submit thy will, and make it one with Mine:
Accept by faith the joy of promised blessing,
And start afresh to walk in light divine!"

Is it so simple then—to take by trusting,
Just as I did when I was born again?
I see it now, it's in the Cross for asking,
And ask I will, the victory to gain.

I hunger and I thirst for Thee, Lord Jesus!
O quench that thirst within my inmost heart:
Take all my life that I to Thee surrender,
And may the blessing nevermore depart.

Full Surrender. London: Marshall, Morgan & Scott, 1951. p. 3.

Record your insights, revelations, and meditations from this week. DATE:

_____

_____

_____

_____

_____

_____

_____

_____

_____

_____

_____

_____

_____

WEEK FOUR   *HYMNS and POEMS*   **DAY 1**

My Soul Complete in Jesus Stands

by Grace W. Hinsdale (1833-1902)

My soul complete in Jesus stands;
It fears no more the law's demands;
The smile of God is sweet within,
Where all before was guilt and sin.

My soul at rest in Jesus lives;
Accepts the peace his pardon gives;
Receives the grace his death secured,
And pleads the anguish he endured.

My soul its every foe defies,
And cries—'tis God that justifies!
Who charges God's elect with sin?
Shall Christ, who died their peace to win?

A song of praise my soul shall sing,
To our eternal, glorious King;
(I'll) worship humbly at his feet,
In whom alone (I) stand complete.

https://hymnary.org/text/my_soul_complete_in_jesus_stands

WEEK FOUR   **Two-Step Process (part 1)**   **DAY 2**

What's the purpose of an exercise like the one this book represents? Why is it necessary, or if not necessary at least advisable, to learn how to daily surrender oneself to lordship of Jesus Christ? Part of the answer lies in the correct understanding of the meaning of discipleship. Luke chapter 14 makes it abundantly clear that being a disciple of Christ means more than learning Biblical principles and scriptural truths and trying to apply them to one's life. Three times in that chapter Jesus says you cannot be His disciple unless you are willing to do certain things. Read through Luke 14.

Jesus says we cannot be His disciple unless we "hate" every other relationship and even our own lives, unless we bear our cross and come after Him, unless we forsake all we have. So, it is clear discipleship is more than simply learning how to share your faith, learning how to have Christian attitudes, or learning how to live by Biblical principles. Being a disciple of Christ, as the Bible describes it, is not simply an add on to a life, as one might add on the responsibilities of a new job, or a new family member, or a new club membership to what you are already doing in life. To be a true disciple of Christ is a replacement of your life with His.

Experience tells us this process is not automatic, although you can certainly argue it should be. Otherwise there would be no need for discipleship classes, and discipleship books, and discipleship programs. There is a point at which the Christian life begins but there is also a process by which the Christian life continues. During this week's devotions, I want to diverge from our normal weekly schedule and spend some time examining the fact that the Christian life is, in effect, a two-step process. I hope to demonstrate from the

Scripture this two-step process is described in a number of places and a variety of ways, and that this process is absolutely essential to living the victorious, abundant life of obedience and surrender to Christ.

Let's begin by looking at Galatians 3. In verse 11 it says, "the just shall live by faith." It does not say you shall live by faith to become just. You are justified by faith, but you do not earn justification through living by faith. Justification occurs when you are born again then from there you continue to live by faith. Verses 13 and 14 explain our redemption comes through Christ's death on the cross and thereby we receive two things; the blessing of Abraham (that we might become the people of God) and the promise of the Spirit through faith.

Look now at Romans 5. In verse 10 we see the same truth stated in a slightly different way. We were reconciled to God through Christ's death. But there's much more. Having been reconciled, we shall be saved by his life. Reconciliation refers to that point in time when a person is born again, becomes a Christian, is adopted into the family of God, and enters into the Kingdom of God. But we're not saved so that we can just hit heaven and miss hell. The Kingdom of God has broken through into this life. The Kingdom of God is within us and we can live under the dominion of God through Jesus as He lives His life in and through us. Step One is reconciliation or regeneration, being born again. Step Two is the ongoing process of sanctification whereby Jesus lives His life through us. Step One gets you into the Kingdom of God. Step Two gets the Kingdom of God into you. The rest of this week we will examine what else the Scriptures have to say about this two-step process of salvation.

WEEK FOUR **Two-Step Process (part 2)** **DAY 3**

This week we are examining the proposition that the Christian life or the experience of salvation is a two-step process. The first step, referred to as regeneration, is being born again where we accept Jesus Christ as our savior, receiving forgiveness of sins and the gift of eternal life. The second step, refer to as sanctification, is daily walking in newness of life and growing in grace, as we depend on the Holy Spirit to manifest the life of Christ in and through us. Let's look at the scriptures that describe the relationship between regeneration and sanctification. Hopefully, this will lead to a better grasp of what it means to live a holy life and how that can be accomplished.

Read Galatians 5:16-25. In this passage, Paul outlines the difference between someone who is walking in the Spirit or being led by the Spirit, and someone who is walking in the flesh. He contrasts the works of the flesh with the fruit of the Spirit. Paul explains clearly what must be done with the flesh. It must be crucified or put to death. And he makes the statement, "If we live in the Spirit, let us also walk in the Spirit." This brief sentence summarizes the two-step process. *Living in the Spirit* is regeneration. *Walking in the Spirit* is sanctification. It is apparently possible to live in the Spirit and not walk in the Spirit, or Paul would has not given this command. Remember, he is speaking to believers. It seems, at the end that once we are born again, we must make an intentional effort through obedience to continue in the process of sanctification here defined as "walking in the Spirit."

Galatians 3:2-3 seems to be referring to the same process. The phrase "having begun in the Spirit" is a reference to redemption. The phrase "being made perfect" refers to the process of sanctification. Paul is asking the question in the negative, "Are you now being made perfect by the flesh?" The implication is that we are to be made perfect by the Spirit. Step One then, is *beginning in the Spirit*. Step Two is *being perfected in the Spirit*.

The Galatians passage echoes the words of Christ in Matthew 19:16-22; the story of the rich young ruler. Jesus says, in answer to his question, "If you want to enter into life, keep the commandments." In response, the man says, I've done all these things, what do I still lack? "Jesus says to him, if you want to be perfect… come, follow me." For the rich young ruler, following Christ meant ending his reliance on wealth and taking on a lifestyle of generosity. Unfortunately, he refused. But we see the two-step process demonstrated, nonetheless. Step One, *enter life*. Step Two, *be perfect*, "follow Me."

Turn to John 12:24-26. Here Jesus is talking about the illustration of a grain of wheat. The grain of wheat dying in the ground to be able to produce grain is representative both of what Jesus did for us to have eternal life and of what we must do to live that life to the full. He goes on to say, "If anyone serves Me, let him follow Me." Again, we see another description of the two-step process. Step One is *identifying as a servant* which equates to the born again experience or redemption. Step Two is *acting like a servant* by obeying the command to follow Jesus. This equates to the process of sanctification.

WEEK FOUR   **Two-Step Process (part 3)**   **DAY 4**

So far, we've looked at a number of New Testament passages and seen the two-step process described in a number of ways. But there's also an Old Testament example or foreshadowing of this process in the story of the children of Israel leaving Egypt and entering the Promised Land. In Exodus chapter 14, the Israelites are standing by the Red Sea watching the Egyptian army get closer. In fear, they start to mumble and complain to Moses. Moses response in verse 13 was, "Do not be afraid. Stand still, and see the salvation of the Lord, which He will accomplish for you today." The experience of crossing the Red Sea is described as "salvation." This is a picture of the born again experience. We are brought out of the land of the sin and the flesh, redeemed through the red blood of Christ on the cross, saved from sin and death like the Israelites were saved from death at the hands of the Egyptians.

1 Corinthians 10:1-2 refers to the experience of crossing the Red Sea as a baptism into Moses. Just as we are baptized into Christ for salvation, the Israelites were baptized into Moses for salvation. But they did not immediately enter into the promised land of milk and honey. What should have been an 11 day journey took 40 years. They were free, but not obedient. In Joshua chapter 3 we see it took another "baptism" to get the people of God where God wanted them to be. This time the baptism was not through a body of water, it was through the Jordan River. The river is a picture of the Holy Spirit. The desire to return to Egypt cost that first generation entry into the Promised Land. Once that generation was gone, and the desire for Egypt was put to death, the children of God could enter the land of God and enjoy the abundance of God in the presence of God according to the promise of God. That had been God's will all along.

We see something similar demonstrated in the teaching of the Israelites. Leviticus 20:7-8 says, "Consecrate yourselves therefore, and be holy, for I am the Lord your God. And you shall keep my statutes and perform them: I am the Lord who sanctifies you." In this passage, the God who sanctifies gives a two-part command stated in two different ways. First, consecrate yourself or set yourselves apart, which is a picture of redemption. Then he adds the command, be holy. Or in other words, he instructs them to "keep My statutes, and perform them." Combined, the principle is, "Set yourself apart by keeping or remembering My word and be holy by performing it." Deuteronomy 29:9 in essence says the same thing, "Keep the words of this covenant and do them, that you may prosper in all that you do."

King David alludes to the same thing in Psalm 51. We see him crying out to God for mercy, for forgiveness of sin. He says over and over, wash me, cleanse me, purge me, blot out my iniquities. Then in verse 10 he says, "Create in me a clean heart, O God, and renew a steadfast spirit within me." Step One is a clean heart. Step Two is a steadfast spirit. Keeping the word and doing it. Redemption and sanctification. Forgiveness and holiness.

WEEK FOUR   **Two-Step Process (part 4)**   **DAY 5**

As you are beginning to see, the apostle Paul has much to say on this subject and finds a variety of ways to make his point. Three times in the book of Titus alone he refers to this two-step process. In the first verse, he introduces himself as a "bondservant" of God and an apostle of Jesus according to two things: the faith of God's elect and the acknowledgement of the truth which accords with Godliness. So, right away, we see Step One is being made a bondservant according to the faith and Step Two is acknowledging the truth which accords with, or results in, godliness.

In chapter 2 verse 14, Paul is talking about the grace of God that brings salvation and he refers to Jesus as the One who gave Himself for us to do two things; to redeem us from every lawless deed, and to purify for Himself His own people, who are zealous for good works. Step One, redemption. Step Two, purification.

Again, in Titus 3:5-7, speaking of the provision of salvation through the kindness and love of God, clearly states Jesus saved us "through the washing of regeneration and renewing of the Holy Spirit." He goes on to say that after being justified by His grace, the Holy Spirit is poured out on us abundantly through Jesus Christ. Step One, the washing of regeneration. Step Two, the renewing of the Holy Spirit who is abundantly poured out.

Paul uses similar terms to highlight this point in his epistle to the Romans: "Therefore, having been *justified by faith*, we have peace with God through our Lord Jesus Christ, through whom also *we have access by faith into this grace* in which we stand, and rejoice in hope of the glory of God. And not only that, but we also glory in tribulations, knowing that tribulation produces perseverance; and perseverance, character; and character, hope. Now hope does not disappoint, because the love of God has been *poured* _out_ in our hearts by the Holy Spirit who was given to us" (Romans 5:1-5). Step One, we are justified by faith. Step Two, we have access by faith into the grace that is poured out on us by the Holy Spirit.

Paul uses different imagery when writing to the Corinthians, but the principle is the same. "And I, brethren, could not speak to you as to **spiritual** people but as to **carnal**, as to babes in Christ. I fed you with milk and not with solid food; for until now you were not able to receive it, and even now you are still not able; for you are still carnal. For where there are envy, strife, and divisions among you, are you not carnal and behaving like mere men?" (I Corinthians 3:1-3). He states the points in reverse order here. Step One results in a carnal Christian (with rare exception). Step Two results in a spiritual Christian.

Paul is not alone as we have seen. In John's gospel chapter 15, where Jesus is talking about the vine and the branches, He says, "If you abide in Me and My words abide in you…" Step One abide in Christ – new life. Step Two, His words abiding in you – the fruitful life. So, we see very simply, the Christian life has two steps. Step One – _believe in Jesus_. Step Two – _believe Jesus_.

WEEK FOUR **Two-Step Process (part 5)** **DAY 6**

What is the difference between believing in Jesus and believing Jesus? In the first case, we come to know about Jesus. We believe He is who He says He is and did what He says He did. We accept His claims and place our trust in Him to be our Savior. In the second case, we learn what He says we should do and come into agreement with those imperatives to the point that we adjust our behavior to come in alignment with His example and His instruction. Or rather, we come to understand through divine revelation we must surrender ourselves to Him in complete obedience if we are to be pleasing in His sight and reap all the benefits of His promises. When He says you cannot be my disciple unless you forsake everything, we believe Him and follow Him. At this point, we are trusting Him to be our Lord.

If you are like me, the next question that pops into your head is, "How?" That is really what this book tries to address. But there are answers to that question throughout Scripture, if you are honestly looking. The entire book of Ephesians speaks to that. The first three chapters deal with Step One of the equation. The last three chapters focus on the Step Two matters. Ephesians 1:6-7 says "He has made us accepted in the Beloved. In whom we have redemption through His blood, the forgiveness of sins." Since that is the case; Ephesians 4:1 instructs us to "walk worthy of the calling with which you were called," and 5:8 charges us to, "Walk as children of light." The Biblical concept of "walk" implies living life, movement, progression.

This walk is not anything you can accomplish on your own or in your own strength or by your own ingenuity. This walk, this lifestyle, this attitude can only come from and through the Holy Spirit. For "we are debtors—not to the flesh, to live according to the flesh. For if you live according to the flesh you will die; but _if by the Spirit you put to death the deeds of the body, you will live._" (Romans 8:12-13).

Step Two is the baptism of the Holy Spirit. Not in the sense of a one-time event that changes your spiritual condition permanently, but rather a daily immersion in and by the Holy Spirit into the life of Christ so that we can echo with the apostle, "For me to live is Christ." It is the absolute surrender to the Lordship of Jesus, the sanctification or being made holy that comes about through the abiding of the word of God in our hearts and the transformation that comes through the renewing of our minds. Romans 12:1 – *brethren* (Step One) … *present* (Step Two).

All that to say this: "As you therefore have **received Christ** Jesus the Lord, so **walk in Him**" (Colossians 2:6). "He who says he **abides in Him** ought himself also to **walk just as He walked**" (1 John 2:6). It takes two steps to walk. It takes two beats for the heart to pump blood. It takes breathing in and breathing out to live. The issue for the lost person is, "What must I do to be saved?" The issue for the saved person is, "What must I do to be Your disciple?" Believe in Jesus. Believe Jesus. Trust and obey. This is the answer to the Lord's prayer for you in John 17:17; "Sanctify them in Your truth. Your word is truth." In Mark's record of the story of the rich young ruler (10:21) Jesus' answer to the question, what do I lack, is universal in its application. "One thing you lack… take up the cross and follow Me."

WEEK FOUR   *HYMNS and POEMS*   **DAY 7**

Be Ye Holy

by Barney E. Warren (1867-1951)

What so great, so grand, and lovely,
Can our aspirations claim,
As the glory in this scripture,
"Be ye holy" through His name?

'Tis a perfect consecration,
That will save us from all sin;
Hear the sounding proclamation,
Be ye, therefore, pure within.

Through the great omnific Savior,
All-sufficient grace, we know,
Will sustain us all forever,
Keeping whiter than the snow.

In that holy land of blessing,
We're exalted by our King,
Ever loving and confessing
Him, whose grateful praise we bring.

https://library.timelesstruths.org/music/Be_Ye_Holy/

Record your insights, revelations, and meditations from this week. DATE:

_____

_____

_____

_____

_____

_____

_____

_____

_____

_____

_____

_____

_____

_____

_____

WEEK FIVE   *HYMNS and POEMS*   **DAY 1**

When All Thy Mercies

by Joseph Addison (1672-1719)

When all Thy mercies, O my God,
　My rising soul surveys,
Transported with the view, I'm lost
　In wonder, love and praise.

O, how shall words with equal warmth
　The gratitude declare,
That glows within my ravished heart!
　But Thou canst read it there.

Thy providence my life sustained,
　And all my wants redressed,
While in the silent womb I lay,
　And hung upon the breast.

To all my weak complaints and cries
　Thy mercy lent an ear,
Ere yet my feeble thoughts had learned
　To form themselves in prayer.

Unnumbered comforts to my soul
　Thy tender care bestowed,
Before my infant heart conceived
　From whom those comforts flowed.

When in the slippery paths of youth
　With heedless steps I ran,
Thine arm unseen conveyed me safe,
　And led me up to man.

Through hidden dangers, toils, and death,
　It gently cleared my way;
And through the pleasing snares of vice,
　More to be feared than they.

When worn with sickness, oft hast Thou
　With health renewed my face;
And when in sins and sorrows sunk,
　Revived my soul with grace.

Ten thousand, thousand precious gifts
　My daily thanks employ;
Nor is the least a cheerful heart
　That tastes those gifts with joy.

Through every period of my life
　Thy goodness I'll pursue
And after death, in distant worlds,
　The glorious theme renew.

When nature fails, and day and night
　Divide Thy works no more,
My ever grateful heart, O Lord,
　Thy mercy shall adore.

Through all eternity to Thee
　A joyful song I'll raise;
For, oh, eternity's too short
　To utter all Thy praise!

http://www.hymntime.com/tch/htm/w/h/e/n/a/whenallt.htm

INSIGHT and ENCOURAGEMENT

How Can I Please My Master?

by Andrew Murray (1828-1917)

We find the Christian life so difficult because we seek for God's blessing while we live in our own will. We would be glad to live the Christian life according to our own liking. We make our own plans and choose our own work, and then we ask the Lord Jesus to come in and take care that sin shall not conquer us too much, and that we shall not go too far wrong; we ask him to come in and give us so much of his blessing. But our relation to Jesus ought to be such that we are entirely at his disposal, and everyday come to him humbly and straightforwardly, and say: "Lord, is there anything in me that is not according to Thy will, that has not been ordered by Thee, or that is not entirely given up to Thee?" Oh, if we would wait and wait patiently, there would spring up a relationship between us and Christ so close and so tender that we should afterwards be amazed how far distant are intercourse with Him had previously been.

I know there are a great many difficulties about this question of holiness; I know that all do not think exactly the same with regard to it. But that would be to me a matter of comparative indifference if I could see that all are honestly longing to be free from every sin. But I am afraid that unconsciously there are in hearts often compromises with the idea: "We cannot be without sin; we must sin a little every day – we cannot help but." Oh, that people would actually cry to God: "Lord, do keep me from sin!" Give yourself utterly to Jesus and ask Him to do His very utmost for you in keeping you from sin.

Let me gather up all in one word. Christ Jesus said: "I am the vine, ye are the branches." In other words: "I, the living One who have so completely given Myself to you, am the Vine. You cannot trust me too much. I am the Almighty Worker, full of a divine life and power." Christians, you are the branches of the Lord Jesus Christ. If there is in your heart the consciousness: "I am not a strong, healthy, fruit-bearing branch, I am not closely linked with Jesus, I'm not living in Him as I should be" – then listen to Him saying: "I am the Vine, I will receive you, I will draw all you to Myself, I will bless you, I will strengthen you, I will fill you with My Spirit. I, the Vine, have taken you to be My branches; I have given Myself utterly to you; children, give yourselves utterly to me. I have surrendered Myself as God absolutely to you; I became Man and died for you that I might be entirely yours. Come and surrender yourselves entirely to be Mine."

Excerpted from *Divine Healing.* Fort Washington: Christian Literature Crusade, 1971. p. 110-111.

MONTH TWO

On my shelf is a copy of the King James Bible. I'm not sure when it was printed but on the dedication page there is an inscription to me. My parents gave me this Bible on the occasion of my conversion and baptism into the faith. I made a profession of faith on January 16, 1966 and was baptized the next week on January 23, 1966. I remember both of those events quite vividly.

The next event of note I recall in my Christian walk was at the age of 12 when I surrendered to the ministry. My family was pastoring in Massachusetts at the time. I don't remember much about that time in my life. I know on some Sunday I went forward during the invitation at the end of the service and told my father that I believed God was calling me to the ministry. If I recall, he asked me if I knew what that meant. I said I did but, of course, I did not. Nevertheless, he was delighted with my decision and announced it to the church.

Not long after that, I began my ministry career by serving as the song leader for our congregation. I had a minor talent in music and played several instruments in school, so music ministry was a natural transition for me. Besides, there was no one else to do it.

By the time I was 16, we had moved to Florida and it was there I preached my first sermon. I continued in the music ministry in my father's churches until my second year in college. I then transferred to a Baptist college in Texas and changed my focus to ministry fulltime. I served as the music minister in another small church while in college and as an interim pastor a couple of times. I preached as often as I could and as well as I could.

After graduation came marriage and after marriage came hardship. We struggled financially, which is not unusual for young couples, but our relationship suffered because of the choices I made as well. I continued to pursue ministry hopes even though my initial plans to pastor and perhaps teach on a college level came to an end when I was unable to complete my doctoral studies. While I became a police officer, which has been my vocation these past 35 years, I continued to have as a desire to minister. That desire often conflicted with the needs of my family, my wife in particular. I put ministry ahead of my family.

I was finally able to finagle the part time job with our church as the minister of prayer. It was a joy to me, and I believe a blessing to some others, but it was a hardship on the family. I treated the ministry as a fulltime job. Our pastor at the time realized what I was doing, trying to have a ministry at the expense of my family, and when the time came to renew to the position, he gave it to someone else. I was devastated – so much so that we left the church.

In the intervening years, as I have continued my walk with the Lord through various ups and downs and not a few colossal failures, the Lord has shown me part of the problem was I "surrendered to the ministry" but not to Him. I suspect the whole concept of surrendering to the ministry has caused many people much difficulty because they misplace their focus just like I did. We can only surrender to one thing, to one

Person, if we hope to live the victorious Christian life on every level. That has been a major motivation for me in writing this book: helping others learn how to absolutely surrender everything to the Lord.

WEEK FIVE   *HYMNS and POEMS*   **DAY 3**

In Full and Glad Surrender

by Frances Ridley Havergal (1836-1879)

In full and glad surrender,
I give myself to Thee,
Thine utterly and only
And evermore to be.

O Son of God, who lov'st me,
I will be Thine alone;
And all I have and am, Lord,
Shall henceforth be Thine own!

Reign over me, Lord Jesus;
Oh, make my heart Thy throne;
It shall be Thine, dear Savior,
It shall be Thine alone.

Oh, come and reign, Lord Jesus,
Rule over everything!
And keep me always loyal,
And true to Thee, my King.

https://www.hymnal.net/en/hymn/h/443

WEEK FIVE   **Confession about Faithfulness**   **DAY 4**

Psalm 119:137-144

Lord, you are righteous and good. The laws and commandments and principles you have revealed in your word are also righteous and good. I will trust your word completely. Sometimes my enthusiasm and devotion wear me out because no one else seems interested in paying any attention to what you say. But that will not stop me. I have put your promises to the test, and you have always been faithful to your word. I love the promises you give us. They too are righteous and good. Your goodness will never end, and your word is totally and completely and eternally true. I have been in distress before when trouble has come my way, but I have always trusted and continue to trust in your word. I love to come and feast on your delightful word. Even when your word convicts me of what I have done or am doing wrong, I will continue to confess that your word and your way are right and good. I believe that following your way and obeying your word is the only way to live abundantly. As you give me understanding to know you and to hear your word and see your way, I will gladly follow and obey.

Why the Flesh Must Die

by Major W. Ian Thomas (1914-2007)

That which is born of God in you is Jesus Christ, and it is He who does not commit sin, nor can He, for He is God! This is what the apostle John means when he writes, "Whoever has been born of God does not sin, for His seed remains in him; and he cannot sin, because he has been born of God" (1 John 3:9). The divine seed within us is the very nature of God Himself, and the nature He wants to share with you through his Son. Share the nature of Christ and you share His victory. You do not *achieve* it; you receive it, for Christ Himself "became for us wisdom from God – and righteousness and sanctification and redemption" (1 Corinthians 1:30). To be dominated by the "flesh" is to be dominated by the devil; and to be dominated by the Holy Spirit is to be dominated by God.

What really is this "flesh" of which the Bible speaks? The flesh is that perverted principle in human beings which perpetuates Satan's proud hostility and enmity against God. In our fallen condition, every person's soul is dominated by the flesh and destitute of the Holy Spirit. You and I were born in this unregenerate condition.

The Holy Spirit and the flesh are inveterate foes: "For the flesh lusts against the Spirit, and the Spirit against the flesh; and these are contrary to one another, so that you do not do the things that you wish" (Galatians 5:17). This is why any steps God takes to reestablish His law in our hearts are resisted tooth and nail. Being already entrenched within the human soul by nature, the flesh is in a commanding position to entice the mind, the emotions, and the will of unregenerate persons (and of carnal Christians) to defy God and resist His grace.

The Holy Spirit always exposes the flesh for what it is, and there is nothing more infuriating to the carnally minded Christian than when those who are spiritually discerning remain unimpressed with him in spite of so much self-advertisement. The crucified, risen, and living Lord Jesus alone can put the noose around the neck of your flesh and keep your flesh where it belongs, and this He does by His Holy Spirit. You cannot carry out the execution, but to you and to you alone belongs the moral responsibility of confirming the sentence of death.

This is the decision God is waiting for you to make, for in His sovereignty God limits Himself by that simple law of faith which gives to you the moral capacity to know Him and to love Him for yourself. Consent, therefore, to die to all that you are which does not derive from all that Christ is, and thank Him for His willingness to make it real in your experience.

Excerpted from *The Indwelling Life of Christ*. Colorado Springs: Multnomah Publishers, 2006. p. 39-41.

WEEK FIVE   *INSIGHT and ENCOURAGEMENT*   **DAY 6**

Crucify the Flesh

by Johann Arndt (1555-1621)

When God revealed his will in his Word, he never designed that the latter should be a dead letter, but that it should grow up in us to a new and inward man; otherwise the Word is of no benefit to us. These truths may be explained more clearly by a reference to some example, as that of Cain and Abel. The nature, manners, and actions of these two persons, as they are recorded in Scripture, clearly explain the motions and workings of the old and the new man in the breast of the believer. Cain perpetually endeavors to oppress and destroy Abel. What else is this but the daily strife of the flesh and spirit, and the enmity subsisting between the serpent and the seed of the woman? With Abraham, the Christian is required to quit his own country, leaving all that he possesses, even life itself, in order that he may walk before God with a perfect heart [Gen 17:1], obtain the victory, and enter into the land of promise and kingdom of heaven.

Such is the meaning of the Lord's words: "If any man come to me, and hate not his father, and mother, and wife, and children, and brethren, and sisters, yea, and his own life also, he cannot be my disciple;" that is, he must renounce all these rather than renounce Christ (Luke 14:26). Hither are all the wars and battles of Israel against the heathen and infidel nations to be referred; for what is represented under this history but the continual strife between the flesh and the spirit? Whatsoever is recorded of the Mosaical priesthood, the tabernacle, the ark of the covenant, or the mercy-seat, with the sacrifices, etc., — all has relation to the Christian believer. For unto him it appertains to pray in spirit and in truth; to burn spiritual incense; and to slay the sin-offering by presenting his body, through mortification, as a reasonable service and sacrifice, so that Christ may truly dwell in him by faith.

And if we advert to the New Testament itself, what is this but an outward expression of those truths, which are to be inwardly fulfilled by faith, in the experience of the believer? If I become a new creature in Christ, it is incumbent on me to live and walk in him; in him and with him, to flee into exile, and to be a stranger upon the earth. The virtues that resided in him I ought to practice; humility, contempt of the world, meekness, and patience; and I am bound to be fervent in acts of benignity, charity, and loving kindness. In and with Christ I should exercise mercy, and pardon and love my enemies, and, with him, do the Father's will. I must be tempted by Satan with him; and, with him, I must obtain the victory. I am to be derided, despised and vilified for the sake of the truth that is in me; and, if called to it, I ought to die for and with him, after the example of the saints, and in testimony that he, by faith, hath lived in me, and I in him. This is to be conformed to the image of Christ; this is to be born with and in Christ; to put on Christ; to grow up and be strong in Christ; to live with Christ in banishment; to be baptized with his baptism; to be scoffed and crucified with him; to die with him; to be buried with him; to rise with him from the dead; and to reign with him to all eternity. If ever thou desirest to live in a constant union and conformity with thy

Head and Savior, thou art in this manner to die daily with him, and to crucify the flesh. Should this divine harmony not exist, and another way be devised more consonant to thy fancy, then Christ will not be *within* but *without* thee.

Excerpted from, *True Christianity*. Philadelphia: Smith, English, & Co., (unk). p. 106-109.

WEEK FIVE   *HYMNS and POEMS*   **DAY 7**

Lord, When I All Things Would Possess
by Thomas Hornblower Gill (1819-1906)

Lord, when I all things would possess,
I crave but to be Thine;
O lowly is the loftiness
Of these desires divine.

Each gift but helps my soul to learn
How boundless is Thy store;
I go from strength to strength, and yearn
For Thee, my Helper, more.

How can my soul divinely soar,
How keep the shining way,
And not more tremblingly adore,
And not more humbly pray?

The more I triumph in Thy gifts,
The more I wait on Thee;
The grace that mightily uplifts
Most sweetly humbleth me.

The heaven where I would stand complete
My lowly love shall see,
And stronger grow the yearning sweet,
O Holy One! for Thee.

Written in 1850, it was published in Gill's *Golden Chain* in 1869, according to http://www.hymntime.com/

Record your insights, revelations, and meditations from this week. DATE:

_____

_____

_____

_____

_____

_____

_____

_____

_____

_____

_____

WEEK SIX   *HYMNS and POEMS*   **DAY 1**

Jesus Lives, and So Shall I

by Christian F. Gellert (1715-1769)

Jesus lives, and so shall I.
Death! thy sting is gone forever:
He, who deigned for me to die,
Lives, the bands of death to sever.
He shall raise me with the just:
Jesus is my Hope and Trust.

Jesus lives and reigns supreme;
And, His kingdom still remaining,
I shall also be with Him,
Ever living, ever reigning.
God has promised; be it must:
Jesus is my Hope and Trust.

Jesus lives, and God extends
Grace to each returning sinner;
Rebels He receives as friends,
And exalts to highest honor.
God is True as He is Just;
Jesus is my Hope and Trust.

Jesus lives, and by His grace,
Victory o'er my passions giving,
I will cleanse my heart and ways,
Ever to His glory living.
The weak He raises from the dust:
Jesus is my Hope and Trust.

Jesus lives, and I am sure
Naught shall e'er from Jesus sever,
Satan's wiles, and Satan's power,
Pain or pleasure ye shall never!
Christian armor cannot rust:
Jesus is my Hope and Trust.

Jesus lives, and death is now
But my entrance into glory.
Courage! then, my soul, for thou
Hast a crown of life before thee;
Thou shalt find thy hopes were just
Jesus is the Christian's Trust.

Tozer, A. W. *The Christian Book of Mystical Verse: A Collection of Poems, Hymns, and Prayers for Devotional Reading*. Chicago: Moody Publishers, 2016. p. 204-205.

WEEK SIX　　　　　**Confession about God's Faithfulness**　　　　　**DAY 2**

Read Psalm 119:145-152

When I cry out to You for help with my whole heart, Lord, you answer me. And I will keep your statutes. When I call you to rescue me, Lord, you save me. And I will observe our commandments. When I get up early in the morning and cry for help, Lord, you come to my aid. And I will put my trust in your word. Sometimes I cannot sleep because of the challenges I'm facing, so I recount and meditate on your promises. According to your just and never-failing love, you hear my voice and preserve my life. I am surrounded by people who are constantly thinking of ways to do evil and violate your righteous laws. But I will not worry about that because you are closer, and I know the commandments in your word are true. I know from experience having studied your word and learned your truths and been obedient to your commands that your promises are everlasting and will never ever fail.

WEEK SIX　　　　　*INSIGHT and ENCOURAGEMENT*　　　　　**DAY 3**

A Living Sacrifice

by Alexander MacLaren (1826-1910)

'I beseech you therefore, brethren, by the mercies of God, that you present your bodies a living sacrifice, holy, acceptable to God, which is your reasonable service.' Romans 12:1

A tacit contrast is drawn here between the sacrificial ritual, which was familiar to Romans as well as Jews, and the true Christian sacrifice and service. In the former a large portion of the sacrifices consisted of animals which were slain. Ours is to be 'a living sacrifice.' In the former the offering was presented to the Deity, and became His property. In the Christian service, the gift passes, in like manner, from the possession of the worshipper, and is set apart for the uses of God, for that is the proper meaning of the word 'holy.' The outward sacrifice gave an odor of a sweet smell, which, by a strong metaphor, was declared to be fragrant in the nostrils of Deity. In like manner, the Christian sacrifice is 'acceptable unto God.' These other sacrifices were purely outward, and derived no efficacy from the disposition of the worshipper. Our sacrifice, though the material of the offering be corporeal, is the act of the inner man, and so is called 'rational' rather than 'reasonable,' as our Version has it, or as in other parts of Scripture, 'spiritual.' And the last word of my text, 'service,' retains the sacerdotal [priestly] allusion, because it does not mean the service of a slave or domestic, but that of a priest.

And so the sum of the whole is that the master-word for the outward life of the Christian is sacrifice. That, again, includes two things – self-surrender and surrender to God.

Now, Paul was not such a superficial moralist as to begin at the wrong end, and talk about the surrender of the outward life, unless as the result of the prior surrender of the inward, and that priority of the consecration of the man to his offering of the body is contained in the very metaphor. For a priest needs to be consecrated before he can offer, and we in our innermost wills, in the depths of our nature, must be surrendered and set apart to God before any of our outward activities can be laid up on His altar. The Apostle, then, does not make the mistake of substituting external for internal surrender, but he presupposes that the latter has preceded. He puts the sequence more fully in the parallel passage in this very letter: 'Yield yourselves unto God, and your bodies as instruments of righteousness unto Him.' So, then, first of all, we must be priests by our inward consecration, and then, since a priest must have somewhat to offer, we must bring the downward life and lay it upon His altar.

So, dear friends, sacrifice is the keynote – meaning thereby surrender, control, and stimulus of the corporeal frame, surrender to God, in regard to the impressions which we allowed to be made upon our senses, to the indulgence which we grant to our appetites, and the satisfaction which we seek for our needs, and to the activities which we engage in by means of this wondrous instrument with which God has trusted us. The body is a good servant; it is a bad master.

Excerpted from, *Expositions of Holy Scripture. Vol. 13*. Grace-eBooks.com., (unk). p. 194-198.

WEEK SIX   **Confession about the Lord's Compassion**   **DAY 4**

Psalm 119:153-160

Lord, your compassion is great. When I am suffering for whatever reason, you will deliver me because I have not forgotten your laws. When I am in conflict, you will rescue me and uphold my life according to your promises. Salvation is never far from me because I seek after you decrees. Lord, your compassion is great. You will protect me according to your laws. Even during times of persecution, I will not turn from your word. I hate the idea of being faithless and disobedient to your word. On the contrary, I love your word and it's my heart's desire to live and walk daily in obedience to your word and your will. You will sustain me according to your love. All our words are true and completely trustworthy. Your word is right and good and will never fail and never end. Lord, your compassion is so very great.

WEEK SIX   *HYMNS and POEMS*   **DAY 5**

Thou Hidden Source of Calm Repose

by Charles Wesley (1707-1788)

Thou hidden Source of calm repose,
Thou all-sufficient Love Divine,
My help and refuge from my foes,
Secure I am, if Thou art mine;
And lo! from sin, and grief, and shame,
I hide me, Jesus, in Thy Name.

Thy mighty Name salvation is,
And keeps my happy soul above;
Comfort it brings, and power, and peace,
And joy, and everlasting love;
To me, with Thy dear Name, are given
Pardon, and holiness, and heaven.

Jesus, my all in all Thou art;
My rest in toil, my ease in pain,
The medicine of my broken heart;
In war my peace, in loss my gain,
My smile beneath the tyrant's frown,
In shame my glory and my crown:

In want my plentiful supply,
In weakness my almighty power;
In bonds my perfect liberty,
My light in Satan's darkest hour;
My joy in grief, my shield in strife,
In death my everlasting life.

Tozer, A. W. *The Christian Book of Mystical Verse: A Collection of Poems, Hymns, and Prayers for Devotional Reading*. Chicago: Moody Publishers, 2016. p. 178.

WEEK SIX   *INSIGHT and ENCOURAGEMENT*   **DAY 6**

Circumcision of the Heart

by John Wesley (1703-1791)

I am, First, to inquire, wherein that circumcision of the heart consists, which will receive the praise of God. In general we may observe, it is that habitual disposition of soul which, in the sacred writings, is termed holiness; and which directly implies, the being cleansed from sin, "from all filthiness both of flesh and spirit;" and, by consequence, the being endued with those virtues which were also in Christ Jesus; the being so "renewed in the spirit of our mind," as to be "perfect as our Father in heaven is perfect."

To be more particular: Circumcision of heart implies humility, faith, hope, and charity. Humility, a right judgment of ourselves, cleanses our minds from those high conceits of our own perfection, from that undue opinion of our own abilities and attainments, which are the genuine fruit of a corrupted nature. This entirely cuts off that vain thought, "I am rich, and wise, and have need of nothing;" and convinces us that we are by nature wretched, and poor, and miserable, and blind, and naked.

At the same time we are convinced, that we are not sufficient of ourselves to help ourselves; that, without the Spirit of God, we can do nothing but add sin to sin; that it is He alone who worketh in us by his almighty power, either to will or do that which is good; it being as impossible for us even to think a good thought, without the supernatural assistance of his Spirit.

A sure effect of our having formed this right judgment of the sinfulness and helplessness of our nature, is a disregard of that "honor which cometh of man," which is usually paid to some supposed excellency in us. He who knows himself, neither desires nor values the applause which he knows he deserves not. It is therefore "a very small thing with him, to be judged by man's judgment." This is that lowliness of mind, which they have learned of Christ, who follow his example and tread in his steps. And this knowledge of their disease, pride and vanity, disposes them to embrace, with a willing mind, the second thing implied in circumcision of the heart, —that faith which alone is able to make them whole.

The best guide of the blind, the surest light of them that are in darkness, the most perfect instructor of the foolish, is faith. But it must be such a faith as is "mighty through God, to the pulling down of strong-holds,"—to the overturning all the prejudices of corrupt reason, all evil customs and habits, all that "wisdom of the world which is foolishness with God;" as "casteth down imaginations, and every high thing that exalteth itself against the knowledge of God, and bringeth into captivity every thought to the obedience of Christ." Such a faith as this cannot fail to show evidently the power of Him that inspires it, by delivering his children from the yoke of sin, and "purging their consciences from dead works;" by strengthening them so, that they are no longer constrained to obey sin in the desires there of; but instead of yielding their members unto it, as instruments of unrighteousness," they now "yield themselves" entirely "unto God, as those that are alive from the dead."

Sermons on Several Occasions, Vol. 1. Digireads.com Publications, 2012. p. 263-268.

WEEK SIX   *INSIGHT and ENCOURAGEMENT*   **DAY 7**

Few Bearers of His Cross

by Thomas à Kempis (1380-1471)

Jesus has now many lovers of the heavenly kingdom, but few bearers of His cross. He has many desirous of consolation, but few of tribulation. He finds many companions of His table, but few of His abstinence. All desire to rejoice with Him, few are willing to endure anything for Him, or with Him. Many follow Jesus unto the breaking of bread, but few to the drinking of the cup of His passion. Many reverence His miracles, few follow the ignominy of His cross. Many love Jesus so long as no adversities befall then, many praise and bless Him so long as they receive any consolations from Him; but if Jesus hide Himself and leave them but a little while, they fall either into complaining or into too much dejection of mind.

But they who love Jesus for the sake of Jesus, and not for some special comfort of their own, bless Him in all tribulations and anguish of heart as well as in the state of highest comfort. Yes, although He should never be willing to give them comfort, they notwithstanding would ever praise Him, and wish to be always giving thanks.

O how powerful is the pure love of Jesus, which is mixed with no self-interest or self-love! Are not all those to be called mercenary who are ever seeking consolations? Do they not show themselves to be rather lovers of themselves than of Christ, who are always thinking of their own profit and advantage? Where shall one be found who is willing to serve God for nothing?

If you bear the cross cheerfully, it will bear you, and lead you to the desired end, namely, where there shall be an end of suffering, though here there shall not be. If you bear it unwillingly, you make for yourself a burden and increase your load, and yet notwithstanding you must bear it. If you cast away one cross, without doubt you shall find another, and that perhaps a more heavy one.

Baillie, John. *A Diary of Readings*. New York: Macmillan Publishing Co., 1955. p. 190.

Record your insights, revelations, and meditations from this week. DATE:

_____

_____

_____

_____

_____

_____

_____

_____

_____

_____

_____

_____

_____

_____

_____

_____

_____

WEEK SEVEN   *HYMNS and POEMS*   **DAY 1**

My Sins, My Savior!

by John S. B. Monsell (1811-1875)

My sins, my sins, my Savior!
They take such hold on me,
I am not able to look up,
Save only Christ to Thee;
In Thee is all forgiveness,
In Thee abundant grace,
My shadow and my sunshine
The brightness of Thy face.

My sins, my sins, my Savior!
How sad on Thee they fall;
Seen through Thy gentle patience,
I ten-fold feel them all;
I know they are forgiven,
But still, their pain to me
Is all the grief and anguish
They laid, my Lord, on Thee.

My sins, my sins, my Savior!
Their guilt I never knew
Till with Thee in the desert
I near Thy passion drew;
Till with Thee in the garden
I heard Thy pleading prayer,
And saw the sweat-drops bloody
That told Thy sorrow there.

Therefore my songs, my Savior,
E'en in this time of woe,
Shall tell of all Thy goodness
To suffering man below;
Thy goodness and Thy favor,
Whose presence from above
Rejoice those hearts my Savior,
That live in Thee alone.

Tozer, A. W. *The Christian Book of Mystical Verse: A Collection of Poems, Hymns, and Prayers for Devotional Reading*. Chicago: Moody Publishers, 2016. p. 69.

The Test of the Life

by Oswald Chambers (1874-1917)

The test of the life 'hid with Christ in God' is not the experience of salvation or sanctification, but the relationship into which those experiences have led us. Love is the sovereign preference of my person for another person, and Jesus says that other Person must be Himself. To love God with all my heart means to be weaned from the dominance of earthly things as a guide; there is only one dominant passion in the deepest centre of the personality, and that is the love of God.

'For whoever would save his life will lose it, but whoever loses his life for my sake will find it.'
Matthew 16:25

The only way to love God with all our soul is to give up our lives for His sake, not give our lives to God, that is an essential point, but when that has been done, after our lives have been given to God, we ought to lay them down for God. Jesus Christ has laid down His holy life for His Father's purposes, then if we are God's children we have to lay down our lives for His sake, not for the sake of the truth, not for the sake of devotion to a doctrine, but for Jesus Christ's sake – the personal relationship all through.

'Blessed are you when people hate you and when they exclude you and revile you and spurn your name as evil, on account of the Son of Man! Rejoice in that day, and leap for joy, for behold, your reward is great in heaven; for so their fathers did to the prophets.' Luke 6:22-23

Have I ever realized the glorious opportunity I have of laying down my life for Jesus? It does not mean that we lay down our lives in the crisis of death; what God wants is the sacrifice *through* death, which enabled us to do what Jesus did – He sacrificed his life; His death comes in as a totally new revelation. Every morning we wake, and every moment of the day, we have this glorious privilege of sacrificing our holy selves to and for Jesus Christ.

'I appeal to you therefore, brothers, by the mercies of God, to present your bodies as a living sacrifice, holy and acceptable to God, which is your spiritual worship.' Romans 12:1

Beware of the subtle danger that gets hold of our spiritual life when we trust in our experience. Experience is absolutely nothing if it is not the gateway only to a relationship. The experience of sanctification is not the slightest atom of use unless it has enabled me to realize that that experience means a totally new relationship. Sanctification may take a few minutes of realized transaction, but all the rest of the life goes to prove what that transaction means.

If Thou Wilt Be Perfect. Fort Washington, PA: Christian Literature Crusade, 1941. p. 83-85.

WEEK SEVEN   **Confession about Fearlessness**   **DAY 3**

Read Psalm 119:161-168

Those who love your law enjoy great peace and nothing can make them stumble. The government can come after me, important and powerful people can oppose me, but I will fear nothing but God and his word. Your promises make me so happy, it's as if I have found a great hidden treasure or received an unexpected inheritance. I can't stand it when people lie or say things that are patently false, but I love the truth even when it hurts. Your word, Lord, is truth. Those who know and love the truth have great peace. So, I will follow your commands and wait for your deliverance to come. I will obey what you tell me because I love your word with my whole heart. I will heed your guidance and follow your direction and practice your principles because you know everything about me. You know everything I do, everywhere I go, every thought I think and every word I say. Therefore, I will trust that your word is right and good and true. Those who love your law have great peace, and I am one.

WEEK SEVEN   *INSIGHT and ENCOURAGEMENT*   **DAY 4**

Progressive Sanctification

by J. Edwin Orr (1912-1987)

Once a student asked an evangelist if he had ups and downs in his Christian life before the crisis of surrender; the answer was yes. Then the student asked if he still had ups and downs; the answer again was yes. So, the student asked, "Then what is the difference?" The difference, he explained, was that the ups and downs of a carnal Christian are variations of a very low level of living, whereas the ups and downs of a spiritual Christian are variations of experience on a higher plateau of consecration. The victorious life has its ups and downs, but at an elevation far removed from the depressing ups and downs of the carnal life.

Just as positional Sanctification is incomplete without the full surrender of the critical experience, so the crisis is incomplete without the process following. Progressive Sanctification is the experience of the believer once he has reached the higher plane.

It is not denied that a new convert grows in grace during his first love, and that an ordinary Christian makes progress in many areas of his life. But if practical Sanctification be regarded as deliverance from the power of known sin, it is apparent that only progressive Sanctification can carry on the work, so that the obedient Christian continues to walk in the light. It is the experience of Christians surrendering their lives to the Master that as soon as the light of the Spirit's operation falls upon one area, which is then cleansed, further light is given upon another area of the Christian life. The moment a believer disobeys the leading of the Spirit, he is in darkness in that respect. He does not lose his Sanctification in every area, but only in the area of disobedience, although it is too often true that the area of disobedience spreads and the believer stumbles into darkness.

Thus it is necessary to seek to live a life of progressive Sanctification. But progressive Sanctification is difficult until the surrender of critical Sanctification has been made. Some advocates of automatic progressive Sanctification are willing to accept the crisis experience as a possible but not necessary experience, saying that there are many crises of the progressive experience. It should be pointed out that, in relation to given light or known darkness, a believer is either surrendered or not surrendered. A boy of eight can fully surrender his life and enjoy the blessings of being wholly sanctified. At eighteen, sex begins to play a part in his life unknown at eight, and he must surrender that area also, which would mean another crisis. At twenty-eight, in business, his developing acquisitiveness poses him with the problem of love of money, hitherto unknown, and he must surrender that area to the Lord as well. But he cannot surrender more than 100 per cent of his life in relation to given light or known darkness. The subsequent crises at eighteen and twenty-eight do not exceed the earlier experience at eight in so far as being wholly surrendered is concerned. The lives of saints seem to show that there was a first time when they consciously yielded their all to God, and that that yieldedness was renewed from time to time.

Adapted from *Full Surrender*. London: Marshall, Morgan & Scott, 1951. p. 41-42.

WEEK SEVEN　　　　　　　*HYMNS and POEMS*　　　　　　　**DAY 5**

My Heart Says Amen

by Charles W. Naylor (1874-1950)

I have yielded myself to Thy service,
And Thy presence my bosom doth fill;
O my Savior, I haste to obey Thee,
And my heart says amen to Thy will.

Refrain:
Yes, my heart says amen to Thy will, Lord,
And I know that Thou lovest me still,
While I bow low in humble submission,
And my heart says amen to Thy will.

All the pleasures of earth may be sundered,
So that I may Thy purpose fulfill;
Help me gladly submit and not murmur,
Ever saying amen to Thy will.

Tho' my plans and my hopes may seem blighted,
I will love Thee and trust in Thee still,

For I know all is well that Thou doest,
And my heart says amen to Thy will.

When I pass to that heavenly country,
And my soul with its glory doth thrill,
This forever shall be my rejoicing,
That my heart says amen to Thy will.

Written in 1904, according to http://www.hymntime.com/

WEEK SEVEN   **Confession about Confidence**   **DAY 6**

Read Philippians 1

This is what I am absolutely confident of: that the God who started a good work in me will carry it on to completion until the day I see Jesus Christ face to face. The more knowledge and insight I gain as I walk with you, the more my love for you and for others overflows. The more I grow in wisdom and understanding, the better I am able to discern your will and make good judgments and decisions. For the rest of my life, my goal and desire is to see Jesus Christ live out his pure and blameless life in me so that I can bear all kinds of good and righteous fruit that brings glory and praise to God. To that end, I strive to speak the word of God more courageously and fearlessly to comfort the hurting, convict the lost, and confound the enemy. I believe that through the prayers of the faithful and the Spirit of Jesus Christ living in me, I will be delivered from trouble whatever may come. In Christ, I will have the strength and courage I need to live a life I do not have to be ashamed of, one that brings Christ praise whether I live or die. Paul's motto will be my motto: Christ my life, death my gain. My lifestyle will be worthy of the gospel. I will stand firm with the believers, one in mind and spirit, striving together for the faith of the gospel without wavering and without fear.

WEEK SEVEN   *INSIGHT and ENCOURAGEMENT*   **DAY 7**

Our Surrender to Jesus

by Andrew Murray (1828-1917)

The chief element of what Jesus has done for me – always does for me – lies in His surrender of Himself for me. I have the main element of what He would have me do in my surrender to Him. For young Christians who have given themselves to Jesus, it is of great importance to always hold fast – to confirm and renew this surrender. This is the special life of faith which says again every day, "I have given myself to Him. I will follow and serve Him. He has taken me. I am His and entirely at His service."

Young Christian, hold firm your surrender and continue to make it firmer. When a stumbling or sin recurs after you have surrendered yourself, do not think that the surrender was insincere. No, the surrender to Jesus does not make us perfect at once. You have sinned because you were not thoroughly or firmly enough in His arms. Adhere to this, even though it is with shame, "Lord, I know I have given myself to you, and I'm yours." Confirm this surrender again. Say to Him that you now begin to see better how complete the surrender to Him must be. Every day, renew the voluntary, entire, and undivided offering up of yourselves to Him.

The longer we continue as Christians, the deeper our insight into God's word will lead us to surrender to Jesus. We will see more clearly that we do not yet fully understand or contemplate it. The surrender must become more undivided and trustful. The language which Ahab once used must be ours, "My lord, O king, according to thy saying, I am thine, and all that I have" (1 Kings 20:4). This is the language of undivided dedication – I am thine, and all that I have. Keep nothing back. Keep back no single sin that you do not confess and turn from. Without conversion there can be no surrender. Lay upon the altar all of your thoughts, your utterances, your feelings, your labors, your time, your influence, and your property. Jesus has a right to all – He demands the whole. Give yourself, with all that you have, to be guided and used and kept, undivided and blessed. "My Lord, O King, according to Thy saying, I am thine, and all that I have."

This is the language of trustful dedication. It is on the Word of the Lord – which calls upon you to surrender yourself – that you have done this. That word is your guarantee that He will take and guide and keep you. As surely as you give yourself does He take you. And what He takes He keeps. Only we must not take it out of His hand again. Let it remain fixed with you, that your surrender is in the highest degree pleasing to Him. Be assured of it, your offering is a sweet smelling savor. Not on what you are or what you experience or discover in yourselves do you say this, but on His Word. According to His Word you are able to stand on this – what you give He will take, and what He takes He will keep. Surrender yourselves continually to Jesus.

Excerpted from *Living the New Life*. Springdale, PA: Whitaker House, 1982. p. 47-49.

Record your insights, revelations, and meditations from this week. DATE:

_____

_____

_____

_____

_____

_____

_____

_____

_____

_____

_____

WEEK EIGHT   *INSIGHT and ENCOURAGEMENT*   **DAY 1**

Conditions of Discipleship (Part 1)

by J. Oswald Sanders (1917-1992)

"Anyone who does not carry his cross and follow me cannot be my disciple." (Luke 14:27)

As usual, Jesus was surrounded by the thronging crowds, who were listening to His every word. *"Large crowds were traveling with Jesus"* (Luke 14:25), fascinated by the novelty, winsomeness, and challenge of this new teaching, for it was still in the days of His popularity.

The situation presented Him with a unique opportunity to capitalize on their feverish interest. The whole nation was looking for a charismatic leader who would help them throw off the galling Roman yoke—and here was someone superbly qualified for the task. All He needed to do was to perform a few spectacular miracles and then lead them in a great insurrection.

Did He flatter them, offer some inducement, perform some miracle to win their allegiance? It seemed as though He were intent on alienating their interest and actually discouraging them from following Him. He began to thin their ranks by stating in the starkest of terms the exacting conditions of discipleship.

The line Jesus took with the impressionable crowd was the exact opposite of much evangelism today. Instead of majoring in the benefits and blessings, the thrills and excitement, the adventure and advantages of being His disciples, He spoke more of the difficulties and dangers they would meet and the sacrifices that would be involved. He placed the cost of being His disciple very high. He never concealed the cross.

It is a well-proved fact that dynamic leaders in all ages have always met with the best response when they confronted people with the difficult challenge rather than the soft option. The appeal to self-interest inevitably draws the wrong kind of follower.

In the early stages of World War II, when the highly mechanized German armies were sweeping forward almost unchecked. Great Britain was left alone with its "contemptible army" on foreign soil to face alone the German colossus. I well remember a speech by Prime Minister Winston Churchill at that critical juncture. It outlined in starkest terms the ominous situation in which the nation was placed, with inadequate weapons, weak defenses, and the possibility of an invasion imminent. He uttered no soft words of comfort but challenged the whole nation to rise to the occasion. *We will fight them on the streets; We will fight them on the beaches ... All I offer you is blood and sweat and tears.* Instead of depressing them, his words galvanized the nation into a super-human war effort that turned the tide and won the day.

WEEK EIGHT   *INSIGHT and ENCOURAGEMENT*   **DAY 2**

Conditions of Discipleship (Part 2)

by J. Oswald Sanders (1917-1992)

Why did Jesus impose such stringent terms? Had He been prepared to soften His conditions of discipleship the crowds would have swept along behind Him, but that was not His way. He was looking for men and women of quality; mere quantity did not interest Him.

In His message to the crowds concerning the conditions on which they could be His disciples, Jesus employed two illustrations: *Suppose one of you wants to build a tower. Will he not first sit down and estimate the cost to see if he has enough money to complete it? ... Or suppose a king is about to go to war against another king. Will he not first sit down and consider whether he is able with ten thousand men to oppose the one coming against him with twenty thousand?* (Luke 14:28, 31)

Jesus employed these illustrations to demonstrate His disapproval of impulsive and ill-considered discipleship. Like the builder, He too is engaged in a building program— *"On this rock I will build my church"* (Matthew 16:18). Like the king, He too is engaged in a desperate battle against the devil and the powers of darkness.

In this building and battling, Jesus desires to have associated with Him disciples who are men and women of quality—those who will not turn back when the fighting grows fierce. Are we disciples of this caliber?

The message Jesus proclaimed was a call to discipleship—not to faith alone but to faith and obedience. Jesus gave a solemn warning: "*Not everyone who says to me, 'Lord, Lord,' will enter the kingdom of heaven*" (Matthew 7:21). Obedience is evidence of the reality of our repentance and faith. Our obedience does not achieve salvation, but it is evidence of it. Present-day preaching finds little place for repentance, yet without repentance there can be no regeneration. Many have been encouraged to believe that because they have come forward to an appeal or signed a decision card, or prayed to receive Christ, they are saved—whether or not there is any subsequent change in their lives. It needs to be reiterated, as John MacArthur wrote, that "saving faith is more than just understanding the facts [of the gospel] and mentally acquiescing. It is inseparable from repentance, submission, and a supernatural eagerness to obey. The biblical concept of saving faith includes all those elements."

It is sad but true that whenever the way of the cross and its implications are preached, superficial believers, whose conversion experiences have been shallow, fall away. There are three indispensable conditions for true discipleship: ***unrivaled love, un-ceasing cross-bearing, and unreserved surrender.***

WEEK EIGHT   *INSIGHT and ENCOURAGEMENT*   **DAY 3**

Conditions of Discipleship (Part 3)

by J. Oswald Sanders (1917-1992)

AN UNRIVALED LOVE: The first condition of discipleship is an unrivaled love for Christ. In the realm of the disciple's affections He will allow no rival. The reader will have noticed that in Luke 14:25–33 one statement is repeated three times: "he cannot be my disciple." Each occurrence of the clause is preceded by a condition to which there is no exception. *If anyone comes to me and does not hate his father and mother, his wife and children, his brothers and sisters – yes, even his own life **he cannot be my disciple*** (v. 26; emphasis added). *Anyone who loves his father or mother more than me is not worthy of me.* (Matthew 10:37)

The use of the word *hate* here has been the cause of considerable misunderstanding. The word Christ used is far removed from the normal connotation of the word in today's usage. He does not tell us in one breath to love and honor our parents and then in the next to hate them. Jesus was using the language of exaggerated contrast. *Hate* here means simply "to love less." So the disciple is a follower of Christ whose love for Him transcends all earthly loves.

But note that because we love Christ supremely does not mean we will love our relatives less than we love them now. Indeed, the very reverse can be the case; for when Christ holds first place in our affections, our capacity to love will be greatly expanded. Romans 5:5 will then have a fuller meaning for us: "*God has poured out his love into our hearts by the Holy Spirit, whom he has given us.*"

Sometimes a clash of loyalties arises at this point, and the disciple must choose which love will prevail. When the China Inland Mission (now Overseas Missionary Fellowship) had to withdraw from China, one of the countries to which they transferred operations was Thailand. In one town, the first to be converted was a high school girl named Si Muang. Her heart opened to the gospel as a flower opens to the sun. She soon realized that she had to confess her faith in Christ to her parents, who were ardent Buddhists. She was under no illusions as to the possible outcome.

Overcoming her fears, she confessed her faith to her mother. Her mother was furious and told Si Muang that she must either renounce this new religion or leave home. The conflict was fierce. Would she give Christ an unrivaled love and "hate" her father and mother, brothers and sisters? That is what she did, and she was turned out of her home. The Lord did not desert her, and some months later she was received back.

There was yet another area that came under this condition of discipleship: "Yes, even his own life." The disciple's love for Christ is to be supreme over self-love. We are not to hold even our own lives dear. Love of self is soul-destroying, but love of Christ is soul-enriching. If the disciple is not prepared to comply with this condition: "He cannot be my disciple" (Luke 14:26).

WEEK EIGHT   *INSIGHT and ENCOURAGEMENT*   **DAY 4**

Conditions of Discipleship (Part 4)

by J. Oswald Sanders (1917-1992)

*"Anyone who does not carry his cross and follow me **cannot be my disciple.**"* Luke14:27 (Emphasis added)

*"Anyone who does not take his cross and follow me is **not worthy of me.**"* Matthew 10:38 (Emphasis added)

AN UNCEASING CROSS-BEARING: To understand what Jesus meant by His command to carry the cross, we must think what that expression would have meant to the people of that day.

What is the cross of which Jesus spoke? Those words were said before He went to the cross. In common parlance people speak of some physical infirmity, some temperamental weakness, some family problem, as their cross. One woman referred to her bad temper as her cross. "Oh, no!" was the reply. "That is the cross of the unfortunate people who have to live with you."

Those are not the circumstances the Jews would have associated with a cross—they are just the common lot of man. Crucifixion was an all too familiar sight to them. They would have thought of the cross as an instrument of agonizing suffering and eventual death.

What did the cross mean to Jesus? It was something He took up voluntarily, not something that was imposed on Him; it involved sacrifice and suffering; it involved Him in costly renunciations; it was symbolic of rejection by the world.

And it is to cross-bearing of this nature that the disciple is always called. It involves a willingness to accept ostracism and unpopularity with the world for His sake. We can evade carrying the cross simply by conforming our lives to the world's standards.

Contrary to expectation, taking our cross and following Christ is not a joyless experience, as the saintly Samuel Rutherford knew: "He who looks at the white side of Christ's cross, and takes it up handsomely, will find it just such a burden as wings are to a bird." If the disciple is unwilling to fulfill this condition, Jesus said, "He cannot be my disciple."

WEEK EIGHT   *INSIGHT and ENCOURAGEMENT*   **DAY 5**

Conditions of Discipleship (Part 5)

by J. Oswald Sanders (1917-1992)

"Any of you who does not give up everything he has cannot be my disciple." (Luke 14:33)

AN UNRESERVED SURRENDER: The first condition had to do with the heart's affections; the second with life's conduct; the third with personal possessions. Of the three, the third condition is probably the most unwelcome of all in our covetous and materialistic age. Did Jesus mean what He said to be taken literally? Everything?

What was the Lord really asking for? I do not think He meant that we are to sell all that we have and give it to the church, but He was claiming the right of disposal of our possessions. He has given them to us only as trustees, not as owners.

This was the test Jesus put to the young man who came inquiring about eternal life: "Jesus answered, '*If you want to be perfect, go, sell your possessions and give to the poor, and you will have treasure in heaven.* **Then come**, *follow me*' (Matthew 19:21; emphasis added). He had to choose between Christ and his many possessions. He flunked the test, and because he was unwilling to forsake all, he disqualified himself from being a disciple of Christ. Christ must be given preeminence over all earthly possessions.

There are two ways in which we can hold our possessions. We can hold them in our clenched fist and say, "These are mine to do with as I like." Or we can hold them with our hand inverted, the fingers lightly touching, and say, "Thank You, Lord, for loaning me these possessions. I realize I am only a trustee, not an owner. If You want any of them back again, tell me, and I will let them go." The latter is the attitude of the disciple.

Our attitude toward our possessions is a clue to the reality of our discipleship. When we are thinking of our stewardship of money, what is our attitude? Is it, "How much of my money will I give to God?" Or is it, "How much of God's money will I keep for myself?"

In view of the stringency of those conditions, it may be asked, "Has the Lord the right to demand them as conditions of discipleship?" The answer is that He is asking nothing that He has not first done Himself. Did He not love His Father supremely, more than He loved mother, brothers, sisters, and His own life also? Did He not carry and die on a literal, agonizing cross to secure our salvation? Did He not renounce all that He had as heir of all things? When He died, His personal estate consisted of the loincloth that the soldiers left Him after gambling away His outer garments.

WEEK EIGHT   *INSIGHT and ENCOURAGEMENT*   **DAY 6**

Conditions of Discipleship (Part 6)

by J. Oswald Sanders (1917-1992)

(Sanders quotes a verse from this hymn at the end of his chapter on the Conditions of Discipleship. Read the entire hymn below and see what insight Lyte can add to Sanders' lessons.)

Jesus, I My Cross Have Taken

by Henry Francis Lyte (1793-1847)

Jesus, I my cross have taken, all to leave and follow Thee;
Destitute, despised, forsaken, Thou from hence my all shall be.
Perish every fond ambition, all I've sought or hoped or known;
Yet how rich is my condition! God and heav'n are still mine own.

Let the world despise and leave me, they have left my Savior, too;
Human hearts and looks deceive me; Thou art not, like them, untrue.
And while Thou shalt smile upon me, God of wisdom, love and might,
Foes may hate and friends disown me, show Thy face and all is bright.

Go, then, earthly fame and treasure! Come, disaster, scorn and pain!
In Thy service pain is pleasure; with Thy favor, loss is gain.
I have called Thee, "Abba, Father"; I have set my heart on Thee:
Storms may howl, and clouds may gather, all must work for good to me.

Man may trouble and distress me, 'twill but drive me to Thy breast;
Life with trials hard may press me; heav'n will bring me sweeter rest.
Oh, 'tis not in grief to harm me, while Thy love is left to me;
Oh, 'twere not in joy to charm me, were that joy unmixed with Thee.

Take, my soul, thy full salvation; rise o'er sin, and fear, and care;
Joy to find in every station something still to do or bear:
Think what Spirit dwells within thee; what a Father's smile is thine;
What a Savior died to win thee, child of heav'n, shouldst thou repine?

Haste then on from grace to glory, armed by faith, and winged by prayer,
Heav'n's eternal day's before thee, God's own hand shall guide thee there.
Soon shall close thy earthly mission, swift shall pass thy pilgrim days;
Hope soon change to glad fruition, faith to sight, and prayer to praise.

(https://library.timelesstruths.org/music/Jesus_I_My_Cross_Have_Taken/)

Spiritual Discipleship: principles of following Christ for every believer. Chicago: Moody Publishers, 1994. p. 20-28.

WEEK EIGHT   *INSIGHT and ENCOURAGEMENT*   **DAY 7**

Conditions of Discipleship (Final)

by J. Oswald Sanders (1917-1992)

The term "disciple" means "learner." But implicit in the word is the idea of one who learns with the purpose of translating the lessons into action. A Christian disciple is a volunteer learner in the school of Christ. Jesus first invites, "Come unto me," and then follows it with "Come after me." But not all who come to Him for salvation are willing to come after Him in sacrificial service. Though they ought to be, "disciple" and "believer" are not in practice synonymous terms.

Why did our Lord make His terms of discipleship so exacting, when the inevitable result would be the loss of popular support? Because He was concerned more with *quality* than with *quantity*.
He desired a band of picked men and women, a Gideon's band, on whose unwavering devotion He could count in days of crisis. He wanted trustworthy disciples on whom He could rely when building His church or battling with the powers of evil (Luke 14:29, 31). Once the disciple is convinced of the majesty and the glory of the Christ he follows and of the cause in which he is enlisted, he will be willing for any sacrifice.

Christianity truly interpreted has never been popular. (Luke 6:26) On the contrary, the Christian is truly blessed when men revile him and say all manner of evil against him falsely for Christ's sake (Matthew 5:11). We are invited to share not His popularity but His unpopularity (Hebrews 13:13). We are to expect that "all who will live Godly shall suffer persecution," not enjoy popular favor. We are invited to share "the fellowship of His sufferings" rather than to bask in His reflected glory. If we experience little of the "offense of the cross," it is because we, like Peter, are following Christ "afar off."

With utter sincerity Jesus affirmed, "Strait is the gate, and narrow is the way, which leadeth unto life, and few there be that find it," so we need not be surprised if the way of full discipleship is not crowded. Teaching such as this soon thins the crowd and eliminates the superficial. "As long as the church wore scars," said Vance Havner, "they made headway. When they began to wear medals, the cause languished. It was a greater day for the church when Christians were fed to the lions than when they bought season tickets and sat in the grandstand."

In His discourse, our Lord spoke of "counting the cost." There are two interpretations of this reference. One is that would-be disciples should carefully count the cost before they embark on the exacting road of discipleship. This is of course true and is emphasized in these three irreducible claims of Christ. But there is a strong body of opinion that the only way in which the passage reads logically and coherently is that it is Christ who is the tower builder, Christ who is the campaigning King. It is He who is doing the calculating and counting the cost. Can He afford to use as His builders and soldiers those whose commitment to Him is merely nominal and not sacrificial? The issues involved are so stupendous that He can afford to number me among His disciples only if I comply with His conditions, only if I am willing to follow Him to the death.

Excerpted from, *Spiritual Maturity*. Chicago: Moody Publishers, 1994. p. 142-152.

Record your insights, revelations, and meditations from this week. DATE:

_____

_____

_____

_____

_____

_____

_____

_____

_____

_____

_____

_____

_____

WEEK NINE   *HYMNS and POEMS*   **DAY 1**

Jesus, I Am Resting, Resting

by Jean Sophia Pigott (1845-1882)

Jesus, I am resting, resting
In the joy of what Thou art,
I am finding out the greatness
Of Thy loving heart.

Here I gaze and gaze upon Thee,
As Thy beauty fills my soul,
For by Thy transforming power,
Thou hast made me whole.

O how great Thy loving-kindness,
Vaster, broader than the sea;
O how marvellous Thy goodness
Lavished all on me.

Yes, I rest in Thee, Beloved,
Know what wealth of grace is Thine,
Know Thy certainty of promise
And have made it mine.

Simply trusting Thee, Lord Jesus,
I behold Thee as Thou art,
And Thy love, so pure, so changeless,
Satisfies my heart,

Satisfies its deepest longing,
Meets, supplies my every need,
Compasseth me round with blessings:
Thine is love indeed.

Ever lift Thy face upon me	Brightness of my Father's glory,
As I work and wait for Thee;	Sunshine of my Father's face,
Resting 'neath Thy smile, Lord Jesus,	Let Thy glory e'er shine on me,
Earth's dark shadows flee.	Fill me with Thy grace.

Tozer, A. W. *The Christian Book of Mystical Verse: A Collection of Poems, Hymns, and Prayers for Devotional Reading*. Chicago: Moody Publishers, 2016. p. 129.

WEEK NINE *INSIGHT and ENCOURAGEMENT* **DAY 2**

True Practical Holiness

by J. C. Ryle (1816-1900)

1. Holiness is the habit of being of one mind with God, according as we find His mind described in Scripture. It is the habit of agreeing in God's judgment, hating with He hates, loving what He loves, and measuring everything in this world by the standard of His Word.

2. A holy man will endeavor to shun ever known sin, and to keep every known commandment. He will have a decided bent of mind towards God, a hearty desire to do His will, a greater fear of displeasing Him than of displeasing the world, and a love to all His ways.

3. A holy man will strive to be like our Lord Jesus Christ. He will not only live the life of faith in Him and draw from Him all his daily peace and strength, but he will also labor to have the mind that was in Him, and to be conformed to His image (Rom 8:29). It will be his aim to bear with and forgive others, even as Christ forgave us; to be unselfish, even as Christ pleased not Himself; to walk in love, even as Christ loved us; to be lowly-minded and humble, even as Christ made Himself of no reputation and humbled Himself.

4. A holy man will follow after meekness, patience, gentleness, kind tempers, and government of his tongue. He will bear much, forbear much, overlook much and be slow to talk of standing on his rights. We see a bright example of this in the behavior of David when Shimei cursed him, and Moses when Aaron and Miriam spoke against him (2 Sam 16:10; Num 12:3).

5. A holy man will follow after temperance and self-denial. He will labor to mortify the desires of the body, to crucify the flesh with its affections and lusts, to curb his passions, to restrain his carnal inclinations lest at any time they break loose.

6. A holy man will follow after love and brotherly kindness. He will endeavor to observe the "golden rule" of *doing* as he would have men do to him and *speaking* as he would have men speak to him. He will be full of affection towards his brethren, towards their bodies, their property, their characters, their feelings, their souls.

7. A holy man will follow after a spirit of mercy and benevolence towards others. He will not stand idle all the day. He will not be content with doing no harm; he will try to do good. He will strive to be useful in his day and generation, and to lessen the spiritual needs and misery around him as far as he can.

8. A holy man will follow after purity of heart. He will dread all immorality, and impurity of spirit, and seek to avoid all things that might draw him into it. He knows his own heart is like tinder and will diligently keep clear of the sparks of temptation.

9. A holy man will follow after the fear of God. I do not mean the fear of a slave who only works because he is afraid of punishment and would be idle if he did not dread discovery. I mean rather the fear of a child who wishes to live and move as if he was always before his father's face, because he loves him.

10. A holy man will follow after humility. He will desire, in lowliness of mind, to esteem all others better than himself. He will see more evil in his own heart than in any other in the world. He will understand something of Abraham's feeling, when he says, "I am dust and ashes!" And Jacob's feeling, when he says, "I am unworthy of the least of all Your all mercies!" And Job's feeling, when he says, "Behold! I am vile!" And Paul's feeling, when he says, "I am the chief of sinners!"

11. A holy man will follow after faithfulness in all the duties and relations in life. He will try, not merely to fill his place as well as others who take no thought for their souls, but even better, because he has higher motives and more help than they. Those words of Paul should never be forgotten: "Whatever you do, do it heartily as to the Lord" (Col 3:23). "Not slothful in business; fervent in spirit; serving the Lord" (Rom 12:11).

12. Last but not least, a holy man will follow after spiritual-mindedness. He will endeavor to set his *affections* on things above. And to hold things on earth with a very loose hand. He will not neglect the business of the present life; but the first place in his mind and thoughts will be given to eternal realities. He will aim to live like one whose treasure is in Heaven, and to pass through this world like a stranger and pilgrim traveling home.

Tim Tremaine

Excerpted from *Holiness*. Dublin, CA: FirstLove Publication, 2017. p. 77-82.

WEEK NINE   **Confession about Glorifying God**   **DAY 3**

Read Luke 1:46-55, Psalm 145

My soul will glorify the Lord. My thoughts, my affections, and my decisions will result in glory to God. My spirit rejoices in the presence of my Redeemer and my God. You have not forgotten me, your humble servant. My children and my children's children will know that you have blessed me because they will hear about the great things the Almighty God has done for me. They will see the things you do in and for and through me. They will hear about the glory you have given me to offer back to you. That glory will cause them to confess that the name of the Lord is holy, the word of God is holy, God Almighty is three times holy and you call them to be holy as well. Your mercy will extend to the generations who continue to walk in obedience to your word. They will see you perform mighty deeds to lift up the humble, fill up the hungry, protect the helpless, and shelter the homeless. One generation will commend your works to another. They will tell each other about your mighty acts. I will meditate on your wonderful works and proclaim the greatness of all your deeds. We all will speak of your glory and the power of your awesome works. We will celebrate your abundant goodness and righteousness with joyful singing.

WEEK NINE   *INSIGHT and ENCOURAGEMENT*   **DAY 4**

Holiness: Yes, But How?

by J. Sidlow Baxter (1903-1999)

No teaching of holiness can be strictly true to the New Testament which excludes *human effort*. Although the most strenuous human effort is totally powerless to *effect* inward holiness; and although the Holy Spirit alone can renew our moral nature; yet the Holy Spirit never sanctifies the mind and heart in suchwise as to render human cooperation superfluous. Furthermore, although human effort is equally powerless in itself to *maintain* inwrought holiness after the Holy Spirit has wrought the lovely miracle within us, yet human cooperation is all the while necessary in resisting encroachments of evil upon the sanctified territory, in cultivating prayerful responsiveness to the Holy Spirit, and in carefully culturing those *conditions* which are required for a continuous experience of holiness. The Holy Spirit never restores holiness to the human mind in the way that we repair the inner mechanism of a machine. The mind never is (it never can be) made holy in a way which "fixes it" to *remain* so.

One of the subtler blunders in much holiness teaching has been to play off faith and works as mutually antagonistic. Many have preached that sanctification is exclusively "by faith". Others, in dogged disapproval, have insisted that it is "by works." Both are right or wrong according to aspect. In every spiritual transaction there is an interplay of the divine and the human. Inasmuch as, on the divine side, sanctification is a work which God alone can effect, it must be appropriated "by faith." On the human side there must be self-separation from all controllable wrong in the life; complete self-yielding to Christ; obedience to the written Word of God; and a prayerful determination to live only to His glory. Sanctification is not real unless it expresses itself in obedience to the divine law – and obedience means "works."

Throughout the sanctified life, faith and works must go hand in hand. It is another case where we must distinguish between sanctification as a work of God in the soul, and as a life of obedience in the believer. The two must ever be distinguished but can never be separated.

Even in the promised land (which was possessed by "faith") Israel found that faith must express itself in works. There were enemies in plenty – though victory was assured to the "obedience of faith." God fought with them – but never *instead* of them. Israel must *do* as well as trust. So, there is a place for "works" on the human side – not to *enter* the goodly land, but to *remain* there; even as we read in 2 Corinthians 7:1, "Having therefore these promises [i.e. to faith] beloved, let us cleanse ourselves from all defilement of the flesh and spirit, completing holiness in the fear of God." (Emphasis his.)

A New Call to Holiness. Grand Rapids: Zondervan, 1973. p. 142-143.

MONTH THREE

In 1980, I was living in Abilene, Texas attending college. That summer I travelled back to Florida to see some old school friends and people from the churches I attended when we lived there. Apparently not too many people remember Arthur McDuffie. He was the George Floyd of 1980. McDuffie was a salesman and ex-Marine. He committed a minor traffic violation and apparently tried to elude police, which led to a beat down by four Miami-Dade police officers. I don't remember all the details, but McDuffie died a few days later. Even though the officers attempted to cover up the incident, eight arrests were made, and a trial was held for five of the officers. Five months after his death, an all-white jury acquitted the officers and all hell broke loose in the Overtown, Liberty City, and Coconut Grove areas of Miami.

I remember the Watts riots in 1965, the Chicago riots in 1968, and the Rodney King riots in 1992, but I did not see any of those personally. All my memories are from TV reports. Even though I was on the force in 1992, we did not have much trouble locally. But, in 1980, I was right in the middle of Miami. I can remember driving north on I-95 watching the columns of smoke rise from multiple locations west of the interstate. It is unfortunate that McDuffie's death did not result in the changes we needed to prevent everything that has happened since.

But that was not my first riot (if I may use that term loosely). The first large crowd experience I was a part of, which the police thought was a riot, was caused by my dad. In 1972, Worcester, Massachusetts was the drug capital of New England. The center of drug activity in Worcester was Kilby Street. Every summer, a group of "summer missionaries" would come up from somewhere in the Bible belt. Most were Southern Baptist college students on a 4-8 week mission trip. We were having an outdoor week-long revival in the back parking lot but were not drawing a crowd. My dad decided to move the event to the front of the church which faced a major street, blocks away from Kilby Street. Still no crowd. Dad discovered that there had been a murder on Kilby Street. People were hunkered down fearing retaliation and a gang war. Dad attended the victim's wake then decided to move the revival to where the people were – Kilby Street.

We loaded up the sound system and frightened college students, then set up shop on Kilby Street. The electric keyboard was plugged in through a tenement (apartment) window in the alley. The water used to clean the blood from the crime scene was still in the gutters. When the music started, people flooded the streets and were hanging out every tenement window. The choir sang hymns and choruses in Spanish – bad Spanish. It was nighttime and the cops were called because of the ruckus. Squad cars, motorcycles, and patty wagons screamed to the location, fearing the worst. Once they figured out what was going on, someone heard one of the officers on the police radio say, "It's only Pastor Tremaine having a sing-along."

When you're committed to the work of the Kingdom and the voice of the King, you sometimes have to go places and do things you would not normally go or do. But many were saved, and more violence was averted because the Church took the Light into the darkness and let it shine.

WEEK NINE   **Confession about Hope**   **DAY 5**

Read Psalm 25

Lord, to you I lift up my soul and put my trust in you. I know I will not be ashamed or destroyed by the enemy because no one who puts their hope in you is put to shame. You will show me your ways and teach me in your right paths and guide me with truth because you are my savior and my hope forever. You don't think of me in anger because of my sinful and rebellious past, but you remember your great love and mercy for me. In your goodness and righteousness, you teach your ways to sinners like me and guide the humble in what is right. All your ways, Lord, are loving and faithful for those who keep the demands of your covenant. For your own name's sake, you forgive all my sin. Because of your instruction, I will enjoy success as long as I am obedient, and my children will inherit a legacy of success and blessings. You take into your confidence those who obey you and reveal your will to them. Therefore, my eyes are focused on you for you are my only salvation. Even when lonely and afflicted, you will be gracious to me and relieve my anguish. You will guard my life and rescue me because I have totally surrendered myself and put all my hope in you. Your integrity and righteousness will protect me.

WEEK NINE   *HYMNS and POEMS*   **DAY 6**

Twice

by Christina Rossetti (1830-1894)

I took my heart in my hand,
   (O my love, 0 my love),
I said: let me fall or stand,
   Let me live or die,
But this once hear me speak
   (O my love, 0 my love) –
Yet a woman's words are weak;
   You should speak, not I.

You took my heart in your hand
   With a friendly smile,
With a critical eye you scann'd,
   Then set it down,
And said: "It is still unripe,
   Better wait awhile;
Wait while the skylarks pipe,
   Till the corn grows brown."

As you set it down it broke –
   Broke, but I did not wince;
I smiled at the speech you spoke,
   At your judgment I heard:
But I have not often smiled
   Since then, nor question'd since,
Nor cared for cornflowers wild,
   Nor sung with the singing bird.

I take my heart in my hand,
   O my God, O my God,
My broken heart in my hand:
   Thou hast seen, judge Thou.
My hope was written on sand,
   O my God, O my God:
Now left Thy judgments stand –
   Yea, judge me now.

This contemn'd of a man,
   This marr'd one heedless day,
This heart take Thou to scan
   Both within and without:
Refine with fire its gold,
   Purge Thou its dross away –
Yea, hold it in Thy whole,
   Whence none can pluck it out.

I take my heart in my hand –
   I shall not die, but live –
Before thy face I stand;
   I, for thou callest such:
All that I have I bring,
   All that I am I give,
Smile Thou and I shall sing,
   But shall not question much.

Eitel, Lorraine, ed. *The Treasury of Christian Poetry*. Old Tappan, NJ: Revell, 1982. p. 130.

How Serious is Sin?

by Henry Blackaby (1935-present)

'For if we sin willfully after we have received the knowledge of the truth, there no longer remains a sacrifice for sins, but a certain fearful expectation of judgment, and fiery indignation which will devour the adversaries. Anyone who has rejected Moses' law dies without mercy on the testimony of two or three witnesses. Of how much worse punishment, do you suppose, will he be thought worthy who has trampled the Son of God underfoot, counted the blood of the covenant by which he was sanctified a common thing, and insulted the Spirit of grace? For we know Him who said, "Vengeance is Mine, I will repay," says the Lord. And again, "The Lord will judge His people." It is a fearful thing to fall into the hands of the living God.' Hebrews 10:26-31

Sin is failing to do what the Spirit of God tells us we must do; failing to walk by faith when He is trying to get us to trust Him and demonstrate His greatness to His children, rebelling against the commands of God by simply not even trying to know what they are, or justifying ourselves to God. It is far more serious for a Christian to sin than an unbeliever, because for us to sin, we have to do it against the knowledge of the Truth. For us to continue in our sin means that we have to tread underfoot the Son of God, and we have to treat as common the blood of the covenant that set us apart as belonging to God. We also have to insult the Spirit of Grace, who has been telling us that it is sin and that we need to be careful. The passage above concludes by saying, "It is a fearful thing to fall into the hands of the living God." God is talking about us. Do you see your sin from God's perspective?

How serious is it? Second Chronicles 7:14 is still true: "If My people who are called by My name will humble themselves, and pray and seek My face, and turn from their wicked ways, then I will hear from heaven, and will forgive their sin and heal their land." God's people must say, "Oh, God, it is me. God, I have sinned." They must pray and seek His face and cry out as David did in Psalm 51 and immediately turn from their wicked ways. God wants to see his people acknowledging that their sin is as serious as He says it is. He wants to hear that we are determined that sin will not reign in us. God wants to see us on our knees crying out to Him for repentance and forgiveness.

The scripture says that if we will respond, then God will hear from heaven and will forgive our sin. And then, do you know what will happen next? Then the great healing of our country will begin to take place. When God's people return, then the presence filling the people of God will be so powerful in the hand of God that multitudes will come under the conviction of their sin – because they see God's people serious about their sin. Then they will say, "If judgment is beginning of the house of God, what chance do we have?

Excerpted from, *Holiness*. Nashville: Thomas Nelson, 2003. p. 52-57.

Record your insights, revelations, and meditations from this week. DATE:

_____

_____

_____

_____

_____

_____

_____

_____

_____

_____

_____

_____

_____

_____

_____

WEEK TEN　　　　　　　*HYMNS and POEMS*　　　　　　　**DAY 1**

God is Present Everywhere

by Oliver Holden (1765-1844)

They who seek the throne of grace Find that throne in every place; If we live a life of prayer, God is present everywhere.	When our earthly comforts fail, When the woes of life prevail, 'Tis the time for earnest prayer; God is present everywhere.
In our sickness and our health, In our want, or in our wealth, If we look to God in prayer, God is present everywhere.	Then, my soul, in every strait, To thy Father come, and wait; He will answer every prayer: God is present everywhere.

Tozer, A. W. *The Christian Book of Mystical Verse: A Collection of Poems, Hymns, and Prayers for Devotional Reading*. Chicago: Moody Publishers, 2016. p. 104.

WEEK TEN　　　　　*INSIGHT and ENCOURAGEMENT*　　　　　**DAY 2**

God's Glorious Plan

by Andrew Murray (1828-1917)

When Paul spoke of God in Christ reconciling the world to Himself, he immediately adds, "And hath committed unto us the word of reconciliation" (2 Corinthians 5:19). The responsibility of making reconciliation known was entrusted to the Church. The power that reconciliation works in the world depends on the faithfulness or failure of God's people. These thoughts suggest the glorious ministry of the Spirit, the terrible failure on the part of the Church, and the great need of restoration.

God's great purpose was that men should be saved by the witness of the men in whom He lived. The gift of the Spirit made this possible for everyone who yielded himself to God. Absolute dependence on the Spirit secures the continual presence and working of God in a Christian's life. Long prayers are offered for the power of the Holy Spirit, but few are ready to yield to His control. They do not know the secret of coming under His full power – the faith that dies to self and counts on God to do His perfect work.

The Spirit has been poured out. He is yearning over us, and He is ready and able to take possession of His Church. Let us be ready to confess honestly the current state of the Church and the share we have in it. Let all who believe in the love and almighty power of God proclaim that God is longing to fill His redeemed people with the power of the Spirit. God will manifest Himself to all who are longing to be temples of the Holy Spirit, filled with His power, and ready for the service of the living God.

What is the connection between the indwelling Spirit and the devotion of daily life? Our aim in our secret devotions must be to cast aside the ordinary standard of religion and make God's standard our unceasing desire. The Spirit has been given to us to reveal Christ and His life in us. No true progress can be made until we choose to live in unceasing dependence on the power of the Spirit in every area of our lives.

We must avoid the great hindrances along the way. We need to realize God's right to have absolute control of our lives. Our faith in His gracious and tender love will accomplish His work of power in our hearts. Ignorance of the power of the world as the great enemy of the blessed Spirit is dangerous. Unwillingness to take up the cross of Christ and follow Him can only be overcome be the Spirit. We must maintain that deep conviction of what a holy and almighty work it is for the Holy Spirit to take possession of our life and carry out His one desire – to make Christ live within us.

Excerpted from *Living to Please God.* Pittsburgh, PA: Whitaker House, 1984. p. 16-19.

WEEK TEN **Confession about Dependence** **DAY 3**

Read Psalm 86

I acknowledge my total dependence on you, O Lord. I daily rely on you for protection, mercy, joy, instruction, grace, and strength. I am completely devoted to you. I call on you and pay attention to you all day long. I bring all of my needs and desires to you. I experience your forgiveness and goodness because you overflow with love for those who call on your name. You answer my prayers and respond to my cries for help. There is none like you. Nothing compares to you. All people will come and worship you and glorify your name. You are great and do great things. You alone are God. As you teach me your way, I will walk in your truth. Give me an undivided heart that I may always be obedient to you. I will forever praise and glorify your name with all my being. Your love for me is so great. I confess and believe that you, O Lord, are a compassionate and gracious God. You are slow to anger. Your love and faithfulness are inexhaustible. I know I can trust and rely on your mercy. I can depend on you to give me the strength I need for the service you have called me to perform. Your glorious provisions will be an ongoing sign to me and those around me of your amazing goodness.

WEEK TEN *INSIGHT and ENCOURAGEMENT* **DAY 4**

The Circumcision of the Heart Recalled

by John Wesley (1703-1791)

On January 1, 1733, I preached before the University in St. Mary's Church, on "The Circumcision of the Heart"; an account of which I gave in these words: "It is that habitual disposition of soul which, in the sacred writings, is termed holiness; and which directly implies, the being cleansed from sin; 'from all filthiness both of flesh and spirit'; and, by consequence, the being endued with those virtues which were in Christ Jesus; the being so 'renewed in the image of our mind,' as to be 'perfect as our Father in heaven is perfect.'"

In the same sermon I observed, "'Love is the fulfilling of the law, the end of the commandment.' It is not only 'the first and great' command, but all the commandments in one. 'Whatsoever things are just, whatsoever things are pure, if there be any virtue, if there be any praise,' they are all comprised in this one word, *love*. In this is perfection, and glory, and happiness. The royal law of heaven and earth is this, 'You shall love the Lord your God with all your heart, and with all your soul, and with all your mind, and with all your strength.' The one perfect good shall be your one ultimate end. One thing shall you desire for its own sake—the fruition of him who is all in all. One happiness shall you propose to your souls, even an union with him that made them, the having 'fellowship with the Father and the Son,' the being 'joined to the Lord in one spirit.' One design you are to pursue to the end of time—the enjoyment of God in time and in eternity. Desire other things so far as they tend to this; love the creature, as it leads to the Creator. But in every step you take, be this the glorious point that terminates your view. Let every affection, and thought and word, and action, be subordinate to this. Whatever you desire or fear, whatever you seek or shun, whatever you think speak, or do, be it in order to your happiness in God, the sole end, as well as source, of your being."

I concluded in these words: "Here is the sum of the perfect law, the circumcision of the heart. Let the spirit return to God that gave it, with the whole train of its affections. Other sacrifices from us he would not, but the living sacrifice of the heart has he chosen. Let it be continually offered up to God through Christ, in flames of holy love. And let no creature be suffered to share with him; for he is a jealous God. His throne will he not divide with another; he will reign without a rival. Be no design, no desire admitted there, but what has him for its ultimate object. This is the way wherein those children of God once walked, who being dead, still speak to us: 'Desire not to live but to praise his name; let all your thoughts, words, and works tend to his glory. Let your soul be filled with so entire a love to him that you may love nothing but for his sake. Have a pure intention of heart, a steadfast regard to his glory in all your actions.' For then, and not till then, is that 'mind in us, which was also in Christ Jesus,' when in every motion of our heart, in every word of our tongue, in every work of our hands, we 'pursue nothing but in relation to him, and in subordination to his pleasure'; when we, too, neither think, nor speak, nor act, to fulfil 'our own will, but the will of him that sent us'; when, 'whether we eat or drink, or whatever we do,' we do it all 'to the glory of God.'"

Christian Perfection. Franklin, TN: Seedbed Publishing, 2014. p. 20-22.

WEEK TEN   **Confession about Dedication**   **DAY 5**

Read Psalm 26

I see in your word instructions for living a blameless life. With the presence and the power of the Holy Spirit, I desire to live that life to please, honor, and glorify you. I will live a life founded on faith and trust you without wavering. I will embrace testing and invite you to examine my heart and mind and reveal anything that should not be there. I will live according to your word and walk continually in truth. I will avoid guilt by association and refuse to participate in deceitful or hypocritical ways. I will not condone evil or sin in or around my life or dwell in wickedness. When I do sin, I will confess it and repent of it and receive your forgiveness so that I can continue to worship you in spirit and in truth. I will be a radical worshipper, proclaiming out loud praise to your name. I will be a witness to your glory and grace telling everyone about your wonderful deeds. I will be a lover of God and always desire to be in your presence. I will be conscious of your abiding presence with me always so that I can continually experience your grace and glory in my life, to the praise of your wonderful name.

WEEK TEN   *HYMNS and POEMS*   **DAY 6**

The Fervor of Holy Desire
by Jeanne Marie De La Motte-Guyon (1648-1717)

Still, still, without ceasing,
I feel it increasing,
This fervor of holy desire;
And often exclaim,
Let me die in the flame
Of a love that can never expire!

Had I words to explain,
What she must sustain,
Who dies to the world and its ways;
How joy and affright,
Distress and delight,
Alternately checker her days;

Thou, sweetly severe!
I would make thee appear,
In all thou art pleas'd to award,
Not more in the sweet,
Than the bitter I meet,
My tender and merciful Lord.

This Faith, in the dark
Pursuing its mark,
Through many sharp trials of Love,
Is the sorrowful waste,
That is to be pass'd,
In the way to the Canaan above.

Tozer, A. W. *The Christian Book of Mystical Verse: A Collection of Poems, Hymns, and Prayers for Devotional Reading*. Chicago: Moody Publishers, 2016. p. 96.

WEEK TEN   *INSIGHT and ENCOURAGEMENT*   **DAY 7**

A Deeper Death to Self
by George D. Watson (1845-1923)

There is not only a death to sin, but in a great many things there is a deeper death to self – crucifixion in detail, and in the minutia of life – after the soul has been sanctified. This deeper crucifixion to self in the unfolding and application of all the principles of self-renunciation which the soul agreed to in its full consecration. Job was a perfect man and dead to all sin; but in his great sufferings, he died to his own religious life; died to his domestic affections; died to his theology; all his views of God's providence; he died to a great many things which in themselves were not sin, but which hindered his largest union with God.

Peter, after being sanctified and filled with the Spirit, needed a special vision from heaven to kill him to his traditional theology and Jewish high churchism. The very largest degrees of self-renunciation, crucifixion, and abandonment to God, take place after the work of heart purity. There are a multitude of things which are not sinful; nevertheless our attachment to them prevents our greatest fulness of the Holy Spirit and our amplest co-operation with God. Infinite wisdom takes us in hand, and arranges to lead us through deep, interior crucifixion to our fine parts, our lofty reason, our brightest hopes, our cherished affections, our religious views, our dearest friendships, our pious zeal, our spiritual impetuosity, our narrow culture, our creeds and churchism, our success, our religious experiences, our spiritual comforts; the crucifixion goes on until we are dead and detached from all creatures, all saints, all thoughts, all hopes, all plans, all tender heart yearnings, all preferences; dead to all troubles, all sorrows, all disappointments; equally dead to all praise or blame, success or failure, comforts or annoyances,; dead to all climates and nationalities; dead to all desires but for Himself, There are innumerable degrees of interior crucifixion in these various lines. Perhaps not one sanctified person in ten thousand ever reaches that degree of death to self that Paul and Madame Guyon and similar saints have reached.

In contradistinction to heart cleansing, this finer crucifixion of self is gradual; it extends through months and years; the interior spirit is mortified over and over on the same points, till it reaches a state of divine indifference to it. A great host of believers have obtained heart purity, and yet for a long time have gone through all sorts of "dying daily" to self, before they found that calm, fixed union with the Holy Ghost which is the deep longing of the child of God. Again in contradistinction to heat cleansing, which is be faith, this deeper death to self is by suffering. This is abundantly taught in Scripture, and confirmed by the furnace experiences of thousands.

Joseph was a sanctified man before being cast into prison; but there the iron entered into his soul (Ps 105:116-19), and by suffering he reached the highest death of self. There are literally scores of Scripture passages like Ps 71:19-21, teaching that the upper ranges of the sanctified state are wrought out through suffering. Perhaps the most remarkable passage of the Word on the subject is in Romans, fifth chapter; the first verse teaches that justification by faith, the second teaches full salvation by faith, and verses three to five teach a deeper death and fuller Holy Ghost life by tribulation.

When the soul undergoes this deeper death to self, it enters into a great wideness of spiritual comprehension and love; a state of almost uninterrupted prayer, of boundless charity for all people; of unutterable tenderness and broadness of sympathy; of deep, quiet thoughtfulness; of extreme simplicity of life and manners; and of deep visions into God and coming ages. In this state of utter death to self, suffering, sorrow, pain and mortification of all kinds are looked upon with a calm, sweet indifference. Such a soul looks back over its heartbreaking trials, its scalding tears, its mysterious tribulations, with gentle subduedness, without regret, for it now sees God in every step of the way. Into such a soul the Holy Spirit pours the ocean current of His own life; its great work henceforth is to watch the monitions (warnings) and movements of the Spirit within it, and to yield prompt, loving, unquestioning cooperation with Him. Such a soul has at last, in deed and in truth, reached the place where there is "none of self and all of Thee."

Excerpted from *Soul Food, Being Chapters on the Interior Life*. Cincinnati, OH: M. W. Knapp, 1896. p. 11-14.

Record your insights, revelations, and meditations from this week. DATE:

_____

_____

_____

_____

_____

_____

_____

_____

_____

_____

_____

_____

_____

_____

_____

WEEK ELEVEN   *HYMNS and POEMS*   **DAY 1**

Jesus, Thy Boundless Love to Me

by Paul Gerhardt (1607-1676)

Jesus, Thy boundless love to me
No thought can reach, no tongue declare;
O knit my thankful heart to Thee,
And reign without a rival there:
Thine wholly, Thine alone I am:
Be Thou alone my constant flame.

O grant that nothing in my soul
May dwell, but Thy pure love alone;
O may Thy love possess me whole,
My joy, my treasure, and my crown:
Strange fires far from my soul remove;
May every act, word, thought, be love.

O Love, how cheering is Thy ray;
All pain before Thy presence flies;
Care, anguish, sorrow, melt away,
Where'er Thy healing beams arise;
O Jesus, nothing may I see,
Nothing desire, or seek, but Thee.

In suffering, be Thy love my peace;
In weakness, be Thy love my power;
And, when the storms of life shall cease,
Jesus, in that important hour,
In death, as life, be Thou my guide,
And save me, who for me hast died.

Tozer, A. W. *The Christian Book of Mystical Verse: A Collection of Poems, Hymns, and Prayers for Devotional Reading.* Chicago: Moody Publishers, 2016. p. 116.

Consecration and Its Result

by James Smith (1802-1862)

Exodus 40:33-38   The tabernacle is a type of the body of Christ (Heb 9:11), the sacrifices prefigure his shed blood. In that it was the habitation of God, it is also a figure of our body which is the temple of the Holy Ghost (I Cor 6:19). In these verses we have a golden chain of holy connections.

I. **There was the Yielding up of all to God**. "They reared up…and set up. So, Moses finished the work" (v. 33). Everything made and prepared for the tabernacle was now set in its place. Putting every vessel and hanging in their places just meant the giving up of all to God. Many things had been in their own hands for preparation. Now all was handed over as belonging to the Lord. This is the first step to a consecrated life. Yield to Him what is His own. "*Yourselves*, ye are not your own." "Present yourselves" (Romans 12:1).

II. **The claiming of all by God**. "The cloud *covered* the tent" (v. 34). This cloud was the symbol of Jehovah's presence. When it covered or rested on the tents it was the assurance to Israel that what had been offered was now accepted and sealed for His use. God demands our all – for what have way that we have not received? – and when our all is sealed to Him our all is accepted by Him, and the seal of the Spirit's presence is as surely given, although we may not yet be conscious of it. "He is able to *keep* that which I have committed to Him," and also able to *use* it (Romans 6:13).

III. **The Filling**. "The glory of the Lord filled the tabernacle" (v.34). The order is perfect: *surrender, acceptance, possession*. The disciples were completely surrendered to the will of God when they waited in the upper room, and they were all *filled* with the Holy Ghost. The tabernacle was filled before it was used. The *filling* of the tent with the glory was the *consecration* of it on the divine side. We can give – or yield – God alone can consecrate by the filling. To be filled with the Holy Ghost is to be consecrated in the truest and fullest sense. "Be filled with the Spirit" (Ephesians 5:18).

IV. **The result which followed the filling**. 1. The Exclusion of Man. "Moses was not able to enter because the glory of the Lord filled the tabernacle" (v. 35). Man's place is outside when God comes in. Self must stand back when the Holy Spirit fills. There is no room or place for the energy of the flesh when the power of the Holy Spirit possesses us. When Christ is enthroned within, then it is "not I, but Christ" (Gal 2:20). 2. The Divine Leading. The cloud which filled the house became their guide. "When the cloud was taken up, then they went onward" (v. 36). The same Spirit who fills our souls is to guide us in all the ways and will of God. 3. Witness- Bearing. "The cloud of the Lord was…in the sight of all the house of Israel" (v. 38). The tent was called "the tabernacle of witness." It was a witness to the presence, power, and holiness of God. But we, like the tabernacle, are no witness till we are *filled*. (Emphasis his.)

Excerpted from *Handfuls on Purpose II*. London: Pickering & Inglis, 1923. p. 123-125.

WEEK ELEVEN   **Confession about Trust**   **DAY 3**

Read Psalm 27

Lord, you illuminate my way with your word and your Spirit. You are my salvation, my hiding place, and my stronghold of protection. Whom shall I fear? What is there to dread? I will not live in fear but in confident faith and trust. I will pursue one thing: to live in intimacy with you every day. Come what may, you will keep me safe, you will shelter me in the place of worship, and you will establish a firm foundation for me that cannot be shaken. I won't be smothered or overwhelmed by troubles. I will lift up my head and shout for joy. I will sing and make music to the Lord. When I call, you mercifully hear my prayer and answer me. You invite me to seek you and get to know you more and I will seek you with all my heart. I trust that you will not hide from me or turn away in anger or reject me or forsake me because you are my God and my savior. Everyone else may forsake me, but you won't. I will learn your ways and conduct myself accordingly. I will not despair because I am confident that I will see the goodness of the Lord in this life. I'm waiting with expectation for you, Lord. Your Spirit will give me the strength and courage to continue to wait, with confidence, upon the Lord.

WEEK ELEVEN   *INSIGHT and ENCOURAGEMENT*   **DAY 4**

Follow After Sanctification

by Andrew Murray (1828-1917)

Follow after sanctification, literally "holy-making." We know this word. Holiness is the highest glory of God, and so holy-making is the being taken up into His fellowship, and being made partakers of His holiness. It is receiving into our nature and character the spirit of that heavenliness and holiness in which He dwells. **Follow holy-making, without which no man shall see the Lord.** Holy-making is the spiritual preparation, the inner capacity for meeting the Lord, and being at home with Him. The passage in the epistle, in which we have already had the word, will be our best instruction as to the way in which we are to follow after holiness.

Both He that sanctifieth, and they who are sanctified, are all of one (Heb 2:11). It is Jesus who makes holy. *Of God are ye in him, who is made of God unto us sanctification.* It is the living Christ who is our sanctification; the more deeply we enter into His life on earth, His obedience, His doing God's will, His giving Himself up to God alone, the more we have His life abiding in us, the holier shall we be. Holiness is the losing of self and being closed upon with the spirit and likeness of Jesus.

Jesus spake: **I come to do Thy will, O God. In which will we have been sanctified. By one offering He hath perfected forever them that are sanctified** (Heb 10:4, 10, 14). The more deeply I entered into the truth, or rather the truth enters into my life, that the sacrifice of Jesus is the crowning act of his perfect surrender to God's will in giving up everything to be one with it, and that it is in His doing of that will, that *I have been sanctified* – the clearer will my insight grow that holiness is the actual living in the will of God with my will, having the will of God the moving power of my life.

Jesus doing the will of God, and sanctifying me in it, has taken me up into it, and planted me forever in it. As I live in the living union with it, doing it and rejoicing in it, that holy will be comes my holiness. It was in the doing of God's will, and glorifying God thereby, that He was prepared for the glory; the heavenly life, which He sends down by His Spirit into my heart, is a life in which God's will is always been perfectly done; to live in God's will is the true following after sanctification. (Emphasis his.)

The Holiest of All. Old Tappan, NJ: Fleming H. Revell Co, 1978. p. 498-499 (reprint of 1894).

WEEK ELEVEN   **Confession about Happy Songs**   **DAY 5**

Read Isaiah 12

My Lord and my God, I give you all the thanks and all the praise. When I have done things that displease you, things that are not according to your will and your word, things that you have a right to be angry with me about, you have not dealt with me out of anger. I take great comfort in the fact that you are my salvation, your great mercy and grace and love have rescued and redeemed me. I will place all my faith and all my trust in you. I am not afraid to totally rely on you and completely surrender my all to you. You are *THE* Lord and *MY* Lord, and the source of all my strength. You are the music of my life and the song I sing every day. I have accepted you as my one and only savior. I will give thanks to your name always. Daily, moment by moment, I will call on your name. I will be a testimony of the great things you have done. I will proclaim that your name should be lifted up above all names. I will sing happy songs about the glorious things you are doing so that everyone will know how great you are. I will sing and shout for joy because you make me so happy and I will encourage others to share in that joy with me. The people of God should acknowledge that you are indeed the Holy God and are great and marvelous in our midst.

WEEK ELEVEN   *HYMNS and POEMS*   **DAY 6**

God Moves in A Mysterious Way

by William Cowper (1731-1800)

God moves in a mysterious way
His wonders to perform;
He plants His footsteps in the sea
And rides upon the storm.

Deep in unfathomable mines
Of never failing skill
He treasures up His bright designs
And works His sov'reign will.

Ye fearful saints, fresh courage take;
The clouds ye so much dread
Are big with mercy and shall break
In blessings on your head.

Judge not the Lord by feeble sense,
But trust Him for His grace;
Behind a frowning providence
He hides a smiling face.

His purposes will ripen fast,
Unfolding every hour;
The bud may have a bitter taste,
But sweet will be the flow'r.

Blind unbelief is sure to err
And scan His work in vain;
God is His own interpreter,
And He will make it plain.

https://ighymns.herokuapp.com/hymns/god-moves-in-a-mysterious-way

WEEK ELEVEN   *INSIGHT and ENCOURAGEMENT*   **DAY 7**

Entire Consecration

by George D. Watson (1845-1923)

Entire consecration is misunderstood by many who place it at one of two extremes. Some put it down with repentance and make it an element in repentance, or taking place at the same time. Others placed it up with sanctification and identify it with the work of cleansing. That true zone of entire consecration lies between these two extremes. Entire consecration viewed Scripturally and experimentally comes after repentance and can be for performed only by a living subject of grace, and on the other hand it precedes the work of purification, and prepares the way for the experience. Let us notice wherein consecration differs from repentance. Repentance has reference to our relation to sin and punishment; entire consecration has reference to our relation to the will and service of God. Repentance is the renunciation of all our sins, evil associations, ungodly alliances, unholy pursuits and business.

Entire consecration is just the opposite of this, it is that cordial yielding up of all our good things, our affections, our loved ones, our possessions, our reputation, our legitimate plans, purposes and prospects, are free will, our very life and destiny to the perfect will of God, subject to His disposal at all times. The first is giving up the bad things, the second is giving up the good things. If I may so speak, in repentance we let Satan take what belongs to him, and in consecration we let God take what belongs to him. Again, the motive to repentance is to escape punishment, to flee from the wrath to come; the motive that prompts entire consecration is a longing for a better experience, the desire to be like Jesus. Consecration is of the nature of making a will, of giving ourselves up a free-will offering to God, of making a quitclaim deed of ourselves and all our efforts. But in order to execute such a will or deed, we must be citizens of the heavenly kingdom. Under our civil laws, a man who is under the sentence of death, be he ever so rich, cannot make a will, or deed away a piece of property, for in the eye of the law he is dead. In like manner all impenitent sinners are condemned already, they are under the death sentence, and only awaiting the execution. Hence, they cannot make a free-will offering of themselves to God, or deed themselves away to Christ in the true sense of Scriptural consecration, until they are pardoned and restored to heavenly citizenship. So the Scriptures speak of offering ourselves "a living sacrifice," and of "yielding ourselves unto God as those which are alive from the dead." The same thought is illustrated by joining the army. A soldier in joining the army virtually offers himself up to die, he is a living sacrifice on the altar of his country, but it is only an uncondemned citizen who can thus offer himself.

No foreigner or unnaturalized person can join the army [this was in 1894]. Citizenship must precede soldiership. Such is true in grace, we must first be adopted and become citizens of the kingdom of grace before we can enter the true soldier covenant, and offer ourselves up to die for the King.

The Secret of Spiritual Power. Boston: The McDonald & Gill Co., 1894. p. 60-62.

Record your insights, revelations, and meditations from this week. DATE:

_____

_____

_____

_____

_____

_____

_____

_____

_____

_____

_____

_____

_____

_____

_____

_____

_____

WEEK TWELVE   *HYMNS and POEMS*   **DAY 1**

All Must Be Well

by Mary Bowley Peters (1813-1856)

Through the love of God our Savior,
All will be well;
Free and changeless is His favor,
All, all is well;

Precious is the blood that heal'd us,
Perfect is the grace that seal'd us,
Strong the hand stretch'd out to shield us,
All must be well.

Though we pass through tribulation,
All will be well;
Ours is such a full salvation,
All, all is well;

Happy, still in God confiding,
Fruitful, if in Christ abiding
Holy, through the Spirit's guiding,
All must be well.

We expect a bright tomorrow,
All will be well;
Faith can sing, through days of sorrow,
All, all is well;

On our Father's love relying,
Jesus ev'ry need supplying,
For in living or in dying,
All must be well.

Tozer, A. W. *The Christian Book of Mystical Verse: A Collection of Poems, Hymns, and Prayers for Devotional Reading*. Chicago: Moody Publishers, 2016. p. 124.

WEEK TWELVE   Five Keys to Living the Christian Life (part 1)   **DAY 2**
                                1.   FEAR GOD

The first key is to learn how to live in the fear of the Lord. This has been God's heart for His people from the beginning. "Oh that they had such a heart as this always, to fear me and to keep all my commandments, that it might go well with them and with their descendants forever!" (Deut 5:29). Read Deut 10:12-13. But the phrase "fear of the Lord" means more than just being afraid of God. Let's examine all the aspects of the meaning of this phrase in God's Word.

The fear of the Lord is, first of all, REVERENCE. "Let all the earth fear the Lord; let all the inhabitants of the world stand in awe of him!" (Ps 33:8). This is what most people think of when they consider the concept of the fear of God. To revere or stand in awe and amazement of all God is and does. (Read Heb 12:28-29). But there is more.
The fear of the Lord is also REJECTION OF EVIL. Both Testaments have much to say about this. 'The fear of the Lord is hatred of evil' (Pro 8:13). 'Hate the evil, and love the good, and establish justice in the gate' (Amos 5:15). 'Let love be genuine. Abhor what is evil; hold fast to what is good' (Rom 12:9). 'Abstain from every form of evil' (1 Thes 5:22).

Fear of the Lord is REVELATION. 'The fear of the Lord is the beginning of knowledge' (Pro 1:7). ...the beginning of wisdom (Ps 111:10). Ps 25:14 says, 'The Lord confides in those who fear him; he makes his covenant known to them.' Pro 3:32 says, God 'takes the upright into His confidence.' Read Isaiah 33:5-6. The fear of the Lord can be learned (Ps 34:11).

The fear of the Lord is clearly REWARDED in Scripture. 'As a father has compassion on his children, so the Lord has compassion on those who fear Him' (Ps 103:13). 'The fear of the Lord leads to life and whoever has it rests satisfied; he will not be visited by harm' (Pro 19:23). (See also Pro 22:4, Ps 34:9 and 145:19).

Fear of the Lord is RIGHTEOUSNESS. This is hinted at in many of the verses above. Pro 14:2, 16, 27. Pro 1:29 '...choose to fear the Lord.' 'The end of the matter; all has been heard. Fear God and keep his commandments, for this is the whole duty of man' (Eccl 12:13). This is not just an Old Testament concept: see Eph 5:21 and I Pet 2:17. 'Then the churches throughout all Judea, Galilee, and Samaria had peace and were edified. And walking in the fear of the Lord and in the comfort of the Holy Spirit, they were multiplied' (Acts 9:31). *The fear of the Lord is often synonymous with **obedience**.* If there is no obedience, there is no fear of the Lord. Obedience implies changing from what you are doing to what God wants you to do. The important thing is not to resist change. "Because they do not change, therefore they do not fear God." Ps 55:19.

WEEK TWELVE   Five Keys to Living the Christian Life (part 2)   **DAY 3**

2.   PLEASE GOD

The second key is to learn how to live a life that is totally pleasing to God. Pleasing God should be our GOAL. "…we make it our aim to please him" (2 Cor 5:9). "Whoever claims to live in him must live as Jesus did" (1 John 2:6) and Jesus lived a life well pleasing to God (Mark 1:11).

Pleasing God is NOT AUTOMATIC. We have two choices. We can either live in the flesh, which is hostile to God and cannot please Him, or we can live in the Spirit (Gal 6:8; Rom 8:7-8). Now that we have been transferred from the kingdom of darkness into the Kingdom of light, we must make it our chief concern to discern what is pleasing to God and pursue that (Eph 5:8-10).

Pleasing God must be COMPLETE. Paul encourages us that we should "…live a life worthy of the Lord and please him in every way…" (Col 1:9-10). "Now may the God of peace… make you complete in every good work to do His will, working in you what is well pleasing in His sight, through Jesus Christ…" (Heb 13:20-21).

Pleasing God will INCREASE. Again, Paul "(teaches)…how you ought to walk and to please God, just as you (*He acknowledges they are doing it*) are doing, that you (*but then he urges them to*) do so more and more" (1 Thes 4:1).

Pleasing God results in BLESSING. Answers to pray are partly conditional upon our pleasing God. "Beloved, if our heart does not condemn us, we have confidence before God; and whatever we ask we receive from him, because we keep his commandments and do what pleases him" (1 John 3:21-22). "We know that God does not listen to sinners, but if anyone is a worshiper of God and does his will (*This is the definition of pleasing God*), God listens to him." (John 9:1).

One secret to living a life totally pleasing to God is knowing that the desire and ability to do so come from God. "…for it is God who works in you, both to will and to work for his good pleasure" (Phil 2:12-13). Another secret to living a life totally pleasing to God is understanding the true nature of the Kingdom of God. "For the kingdom of God is not a matter of eating and drinking, but of righteousness, peace and joy in the Holy Spirit, because anyone who serves Christ in this way is pleasing to God and receives human approval" (Rom 14:17-18). A final secret to living a life totally pleasing to God is knowing that His goal is to reveal His Son in you. "But when <u>it pleased God</u>, ..., <u>to reveal His Son in me</u>, that I might preach Him among the Gentiles, I did not immediately confer with flesh and blood," (Gal 1:15-16). The more Christ lives His life through your surrendered life, the more pleased God is with you.

WEEK TWELVE Five Keys to Living the Christian Life (part 3) **DAY 4**

3. FOLLOW GOD

The third key is learning how to follow God. We follow God by living according to the will of God. Doing the will of God is:

REQUIRED for the Christian life. Matthew 7:21 "Not everyone who says to me, 'Lord, Lord,' will enter the kingdom of heaven, but the one who does the will of my Father who is in heaven."

EXPECTED of the Christian life. Hebrews 10:36 "For you have need of endurance, so that when you have done the will of God you may receive what is promised."

POSSIBLE for the Christian life. The writer of Hebrews prays that "the God of peace ... (will) equip you with everything good that you may do his will... Hebrews 13:20-21

Specifically EXPRESSED in God's word. 1 Thessalonians 4:3 "For this is the will of God, your sanctification: that you abstain from sexual immorality." In Biblical commands like Colossians 3:17, 'And whatever you do, in word or deed, do everything in the name of the Lord Jesus, giving thanks to God the Father through him.' Not every action possible is covered in Scripture but if you live by the principle stated in this verse, you will succeed in following God.

Specifically REVEALED by the Holy Spirit. John 7:17 'If anyone's will (desire) is to do God's will, he will know whether the teaching is from God or whether I am speaking on my own authority.' Romans 12:1-2 specifically says that if we surrender to God and do not conform to the world but have our minds transformed and renewed, we can prove what is the perfect will of God. People often ask God for specifics regarding the decisions of life. If you are walking in absolute surrender to God, the details will fall into line.

Romans 10:17 says "So faith comes from hearing, and hearing through the <u>word of Christ</u>." It does not say, "Faith comes from the Word of God." Many people know what the Bible says, but they do not have faith. The Bible refers to this as the Rhema (living, breathing) word of God. Logos is the living Word of God – Christ, and the written Word of God – the Bible.

Korean pastor Dr. Cho explains that the difference between "logos" and "rhema" is the difference between rice, and cooked rice. When Holy Spirit "cooks" the logos word of God for you and makes it personal, practical, and real in your life, it is much more nutritious, beneficial, and satisfying. Through prayer and learning to hear the voice of the Holy Spirit, He can turn the logos word of your personal Bible study into the rhema word for following God's will.

WEEK TWELVE Five Keys to Living the Christian Life (part 4) **DAY 5**

4. TRUST GOD

by Manley Beasley (1932-1990)

The fourth key is learning what it means to trust God. What does it mean to 'walk by faith not by sight'? (2 Cor 5:7). Hebrews 11:6 says, "without faith it is impossible to please him, for whoever would draw near to God must believe that he exists and that he rewards those who seek him." Faith is not just belief. The Bible says demons believe. It is not just what you believe, it's that you believe. It is not just believing in God, it's believing God.

What is faith? Hebrews 11:1 "Now faith is the assurance of things hoped for, the conviction of things not seen." Faith is not just hope, not guessing, not just wanting. The KJV translates this verse; "Now faith is the <u>substance</u> of things hoped for, the <u>evidence</u> of things not seen." Holman says; "Now faith is the <u>reality</u> of what is hoped for, the <u>proof</u> of what is not seen."

Faith is intellectual having to do with what we believe. Faith is also emotional having to do with what we desire, or better what God desires. But that is not enough because faith must also be volitional. Faith involves action.

'But someone will say, "You have faith and I have works." Show me your faith apart from your works, and I will show you my faith by my works. You believe that God is one; you do well. Even the demons believe—and shudder!' (James 2:18-19).

- Faith is calling those things which are not as though they are.
- Faith is dependency upon God, and this God-dependency begins only when self-dependency ends.
- Faith is the confidence and active trust which enables the believer to understand the invisible and spiritual things of God.
- Faith enables the believer to treat the future as present and the invisible as visible.
- Faith enables the believer to attack the impossible with just one thing, the Word of God.

The full definition of Biblical faith is "believing (acting) that it is so, when it is not so, in order for it to be so, because God said so." This is demonstrated in the life of Abraham as explained in Romans 4:18 (NIV). "In hope he believed (*believing it is so*) against hope (*when it is not so*), that he should become the father of many nations (*in order for it to be so*), as he had been told, 'So shall your offspring be'" (*because God said so*). [I was fortunate to hear Manley give this lesson in person. I never forgot it. His original faith definition was, "Believing it is so, when it is not so, in order for it to be so." In the years since, as I have studied this verse, I added the fourth phrase, *because God said so.* I think it is in line with Manley's teachings and clearly reflected in this verse as Paul's example from Abraham.]

How do we know this is true? Look at the previous verse: "…he believed in God, who gives life to the dead and calls things into existence that do not exist" Romans 4:17 (Holman).

WHAT IS TRUTH?   Truth is based upon the revealed word of God, not what we perceive with our senses or understand with our reason. Through the scriptures God can speak to us just as definitely as he spoke to the men and women of the Bible. Here is a principle that is foundational to the life of victory: *you must come to the absolute conviction that the word of God is truth regardless of what the sense-world might say.*

Faith is an act of man on the revealed truth of God that converts the doctrines of the scripture into reality in your life. This principle holds true when the lost person comes to Christ for salvation. When God speaks to you, you realize that you are a sinner and on the road to hell. You also realize that Jesus became a substitute and took your sins upon himself and fully paid the penalty for your sin. All you have to do as a lost sinner is to act on that truth. By a simple act of your will you can ask Jesus Christ to forgive your sin and invite Jesus Christ to come in and fill your life. You accept the truth of God regardless of what your reason or your senses tell you and by an act of faith, convert that truth into reality.

When we choose to stand by faith upon the truth of God regardless of what our sense-world faculties tell us, we will experience Kingdom of God realities in our daily life. There is only one permanent experience in the Christian life, and that is redemption. The rest of the Christian life is conditional, and that condition is the presence or absence of a constant and active faith.

So, what is the key to activating faith that moves mountains? It is moving from viewing the Word of God as JUST fact or doctrine, to viewing the Word of God as covenant, as a binding agreement. Nehemiah calls it, "the covenant of love." It is the difference between believing in God and believing God; between reading about what God did and reading about what God does. That is the key. Faith steps out on God's word and acts like the thing is so when it is not so in order for it to be so. Faith says, "God's word is my reality." An example of that is the ten lepers in Luke 17. They were healed as they went.

<u>Steps of Faith:</u>

Need for faith	Phil 4:19	Act of faith	Hebrews 11:1
Word of faith	Rom 10:17	Fight of faith	Ex 17; Lk 18
Prayer of faith	Mark 11:24	Rest of faith	1 John 3:21-22
Confession of faith	Rom 10:10	Reward of faith	Heb 11:6; 6:11-12

How do you start? Read the Psalms until God puts His finger on a verse and says, "This is for you." Believe it, obey, go get another one. Don't despise little victories. See Heb 10:36-38.

Adapted from *Adventures in Faith*. Kindle Edition, 2013. (Originally a self-published workbook.)

WEEK TWELVE   Five Keys to Living the Christian Life (part 5)   **DAY 6**
Surrender to God

What does it mean to surrender to God? We see an Old Testament example or picture of what surrender looks like in 1 Kings 20:1-4 when Ahab, king of Israel, sends a message to Ben-Hadad, king of Syria, in an effort to prevent war "I am yours, and all that I have."

Romans 12:1-2 "Therefore, I urge you, brothers and sisters, in view of God's mercy, to offer your bodies as a living sacrifice, holy and pleasing to God—this is your true and proper worship. Do not conform to the pattern of this world but be transformed by the renewing of your mind. Then you will be able to test and approve what God's will is—his good, pleasing and perfect will."

Principle: ***The way you started the Christian life is the way you continue in the Christian life.***
You are saved by grace through faith. You must continue to live by grace through faith. (See Gal 3:1-3) "Therefore, as you received Christ Jesus the Lord, so walk in him" (Colossians 2:6).

The chief characteristics of what the New Testament calls the "life hidden with Christ in God" are, a life of <u>entire surrender</u> to the Lord and a <u>perfect trust</u> in Him. This is how victorious Christian living differs from the normal Christian experience. These are the two steps in order to have this blessed life of rest and victory, <u>absolute surrender and complete faith</u>. (See John 15:5)

Believe that God COMMANDS surrender of you.	Romans 12:1-2
Believe that God WORKS surrender for you.	Philippians 2:12-13
Believe that God ACCEPTS surrender from you.	Mark 9:23-24
Believe that God MAINTAINS surrender in you.	2 Corinthians 3:18
Believe that God BLESSES surrender to you.	2 Peter 1:3-4

Be willing to be made willing and you will become willing to yield yourself in absolute surrender to God. "The Lord takes pleasure in those who fear (obey) Him, in those who hope (faith, trust) in His steadfast love" (Ps 147:11). "I tell you the truth, unless a grain of wheat falls into the earth and dies, it remains alone; but if it dies, it bears much fruit. Whoever loves his life loses it, and whoever hates his life in this world will keep it for eternal life. *If anyone serves me, he must follow me*; and where I am, there will my servant be also. If anyone serves me, the Father will honor him" (John 12:24-26). How do you serve AND follow? Fear Him, Please Him, Follow Him, Trust Him, and Surrender to Him.

Adapted from Murray, Andrew. *Absolute Surrender*. Chicago, Moody Press. Chapter one.

WEEK TWELVE   **Confession about Suffering**   **DAY 7**

Read 1 Peter 4:1-11

I know that You suffered in Your body for me. Therefore, I will have the same attitude toward suffering that You did. Suffering is not something to be avoided or resisted or complained about but to be thought of as a doorway to blessing, as a pathway to becoming more like You. Giving up a sinful habit or changing a sinful mindset or letting go of an inappropriate desire can be painful. Enduring the harassment and ridicule of old friends who don't understand or like the fact that I won't participate with them anymore in sinful activities is not pleasant. But I realize that getting to the place where I am living according to the will of God may involve temporary suffering, but the reward far outweighs the difficulty. By Your grace, I will learn how to be self-controlled and not be dominated by the passions and urges of the flesh. I will think clearly about what I'm doing and how I'm behaving so that my conversation with You is not hindered. I will be loving and gracious and generous to everyone without complaint because that's what forgiveness looks like. I will serve with whatever abilities I have as Your grace enables me to serve. When I speak, let it be as though You are speaking words of encouragement and blessing through me, so that in all things You receive the glory and all the credit through Jesus Christ, my Lord.

Record your insights, revelations, and meditations from this week. DATE:

_____

_____

_____

_____

_____

_____

_____

_____

_____

_____

_____

_____

_____

WEEK THIRTEEN   **Confession about God's Pursuit of Me**   **DAY 1**

Read Isaiah 64-65

You sought me when I was not seeking you. You stood before me with outstretched arms and I looked the other way. I lived in ways that were not good and chased after whatever I could imagine. I openly rebelled against you. I put my faith in things and people that did not deserve it. I followed after ideas that were completely worthless. I looked for advice and guidance in all the wrong places, listening to voices that were totally false. I defiled myself by partaking in things that I should never have been involved with. And all the while, I convinced myself that I was completely right and justified in what I was doing. No one could tell me otherwise. I became like an unclean person. Even the good things I thought I was doing turned out to be as good as dirty rags. I embraced worldly wealth and toasted the destiny that fortune would bring. I didn't answer you when you called. I didn't listen to you when you spoke. I did things that were evil in your sight, things that were all about pleasing myself instead of pleasing you. Instead of calling on your name and passionately following after you, my life wasted away like snow melts in your hand. But thanks be to God, you are still my Father and you were not angry forever. You have made a way of salvation for me. Because of your lovingkindness and forgiveness, you remember my sins no more. I can walk in the way of joy and blessing because of you. Glory to your name.

WEEK THIRTEEN   *HYMNS and POEMS*   **DAY 2**

First-Day Thoughts
by John Greenleaf Whittier (1807-1892)

In calm and cool and silence, once again
    I find my old accustomed place among
    My brethren, where, perchance, no human time
    Shall utter words; where never hymn is sung
    Nor deep-toned organ blown, nor sensor swung,
Nor dim light falling through the pictured pane!
There, syllabled in silence, let me hear
The still small voice which reached the prophets ear;
Read in my heart a still diviner law
Than Israel's leader on his tables saw!
There let me strive with each besetting sin
    Recall my wandering fancies, and restrain
    The sore disquiet of a restless brain;
    And, as the path of duty is made plain,
May grace be given that I may walk therein,
    Not like the hireling, for his selfish gain,
With backward glances, and reluctant tread,
Making a merit of his coward dread,
    But, cheerful, in the light around me thrown,
    Walking as one to pleasant service led;
    Doing God's will as if it were my own,
Yet trusting not in mine, but in his strength alone!

Eitel, Lorraine, ed. *The Treasury of Christian Poetry*. Old Tappan, NJ: Revell, 1982. p. 119.

WEEK THIRTEEN   *INSIGHT and ENCOURAGEMENT*   **DAY 3**

Difficulties Concerning Consecration
by Hannah Whithall Smith (1832-1911)

I suppose that you have trusted the Lord Jesus for the forgiveness of your sins, and know something of what it is to belong to the family of God, and to be made an heir of God through faith in Christ. And now you feel springing up in your heart the longing to be conformed to the image of your Lord. There must be an entire surrender of yourself to Him, that He may work in you all the good pleasure of His will; and you have tried over and over to do it, but hitherto without any apparent success. What you must do now is to come once more to Him, in a surrender of your whole self to His will, as complete as you know how to make it. You must ask Him to reveal to you, by His Spirit, any hidden rebellion; and if He reveals nothing, then you must believe that there is nothing, and that the surrender is complete. This must, then, be considered a settled matter; you have wholly yielded yourself to the Lord, and from henceforth you do not in any sense belong to yourself; you must never even so much as listen to a suggestion to the contrary. If the temptation comes to wonder whether you really have completely surrendered yourself, meet it with an assertion that you have. You meant it then, you mean it now, you have really done it. Your emotions may clamor against the surrender, but your will must hold firm. It is your purpose God looks at, not your feelings about that purpose; and your purpose, or will, is therefore the only thing you need to attend to.

The surrender, having been made, never to be questioned or recalled, the next point is to believe that God takes that which you have surrendered, and to reckon that it His. Not that it will be at some future time, but that it is now; and that He has begun to work in you to will and to do of His good pleasure. And here you must rest. There is nothing more for you to do except to be henceforth an obedient child; for you are the Lord's now, absolutely and entirely in His hands. But you must hold steadily here. If you question your surrender, or God's acceptance of it, then your wavering faith will produce a wavering experience, and He cannot work in you to do His will. But while you trust, He works; and the result of His working always is to change you into the image of Christ, from glory to glory, by His mighty Spirit.

Do you, then, now at this moment, surrender yourself wholly to Him? Yes? Then begin at once to reckon that you are His, that He has taken you, and that He is working in you. You will find it a great help to put your reckoning into words, and say it over and over to yourself and to your God, "Lord, I am yours; I do yield myself up entirely to you, and I believe that you take me. I leave myself with you. Work in me all the good pleasure of your will, and I will only lie still in your hands and trust you." Make this a daily, definite act of your will, as being your continual attitude before the Lord. Confess it to yourself, and to your God, and to your friends.

Adapted from *The Christian's Secret of a Happy Life*. Grand Rapids: Revell, 1952. p. 65-67.

WEEK THIRTEEN *INSIGHT and ENCOURAGEMENT* **DAY 4**

The Purpose of Adversity

by Paul Billheimer (1897-1984)

Most of us feel that as soon as we give ourselves to God in full consecration, things ought to run smoothly, but God cannot make us until he first "breaks" us. He cannot mold us until he melts us. He cannot melt us except by fire. God has indeed promised to supply all of our needs, but the very man who wrote this scripture, "My God shall supply all your needs," also said in 1 Cor. 4:11,12, "to this very hour we both hunger and thirst, we are ill-clad and knocked about. We work hard for our living" (Phillips). I do not know how Paul would reconcile that statement with his wonderful promise in Phil. 4:19, "My God shall supply all your needs, according to His riches in glory by Christ Jesus." There is never any lack in any life because of the short supply in heaven's storehouse or because of God's indifference. *The reason is always on the human side.* Paul evidently recognized that if God was to keep alive in his life that heroic spirit of self-sacrifice, He must occasionally permit him to experience need.

In the 4th chapter of Philippians, before Paul wrote this wonderful promise, he said, "How grateful I am and how I praise the Lord that you are helping me again. I know you have always been anxious to send what you could, but for a while you didn't have the chance. Not that I was ever in need, for I have learned how to get along happily whether I have much or little. I know how to live on almost nothing or with everything. I have learned the secret of contentment in every situation, whether it be a full stomach or hunger, plenty or want; for I can do everything God asks me to with the help of Christ who gives me the strength and the power" (Living Bible).

It is no great accomplishment to be victorious in prosperity. The real problem is how to live triumphantly in privations. Paul had them and most of us have them. *Until you have learned to face, overcome and utilize adversity, you are dangerously vulnerable,* because Paul tells us in Acts 14:22 that "we must through much tribulation enter into the kingdom of God." We cannot avoid tribulation, adversity, and affliction, but if we understand that these things may be good, *that nothing intrinsically evil can come to a child of God, that only a wrong reaction can injure him; if he learns how to utilize his problems for spiritual growth, then he has it made. If God's blessings are our good and if Satan's assaults are transformed into blessings by our reaction, we have nothing to fear because everything is working for our good.*

It is a comfort to know that if God is God, the universe he has made is the best one possible. This does not mean that there is no evil in God's universe. *It does mean that God is using that evil for his purpose. His purpose is to obtain and train an eternal companion for His Son who is to rule and reign with Him in the ages to come.* If this universe were not the best universe possible, then God would not be God, that is, He would not be supreme. (Emphasis his)

Excerpted from *Adventure in Adversity*. Wheaton: Tyndale House, 1984. p. 31-33.

WEEK THIRTEEN   *HYMNS and POEMS*   **DAY 5**

Hymn #1   *"He who was manifested in the flesh."* 1 TIM. 3:16.

by Ann Griffiths (1776-1805)

THY Pavilion's One Foundation,
Fortress for the fugitive,
In Thy Blood we see salvation,
Jesu, through Thy Death we live.
At Thy footstool humbly bending
Only can we be forgiven,
On Thy Righteousness depending
Only have we hope of Heaven.

O the fulness of Salvation!
Merciful, mysterious plan!
When the God of all creation
Dignified the dust of man,
To redeem us yearning, sighing,
Pleading, bleeding on the tree,
And in dying verifying
Promise, type and prophecy.

Prior to this earth's creation
Man's redemption was ordained, —
By Thy predetermination
Long lost Eden was regained.
Undeserved regeneration,
Blissful immortality,
Pardon, peace, purification, —
All are offered, Lord, by Thee.

Lowly born to be The Brother
Of the powerless and poor,
To unite us to each other
And invite us to be pure,
With one touch The Famed Physician
Healed the blotch of leprosy,
For His voluntary mission
Was to free humanity.

Victim of the foul deceiver,
Faint at heart and travel stained,
Recognise in Thy Redeemer
More than Paradise regained.
Faithfulness is what the golden
Girdle of Thy God displays,
This memento should embolden
Every penitent who prays.

Ark of Refuge, Rock Eternal,
Balm beside the dying bed,
Tree of Life forever vernal,
Fountain to revive the dead,
One with us, our pardon pleading,
One with God, He grants the plea,
While His Spirit interceding
Certifies His victory.

The Hymns of Ann Griffiths. Translated by George R. G. Pughe. Blackburn: Geo. H. Durham, Exchange Works, 1900. p. 5-6.

WEEK THIRTEEN   *HYMNS and POEMS*   **DAY 6**

As Pants the Heart (Psalm 42 Paraphrase)
by Nahum Tate (1652-1715) and Nicolaus Brady (1659-1726)

As pants the hart for cooling streams,
When heated in the chase;
So longs my soul, O God, for Thee,
And Thy refreshing grace.

For Thee, my God, the living God,
My thirsty soul doth pine;
Oh, when shall I behold Thy face,
Thou Majesty divine?

Why restless, why cast down, my soul?
Trust God; who will employ
His aid for thee, and change these sighs
To thankful hymns of joy.

God of my strength, how long shall I,
Like one forgotten, mourn;
Forlorn, forsaken, and exposed
To my oppressor's scorn?

I sigh to think of happier days,
When Thou, O Lord! wast nigh;
When every heart was tuned to praise,
And none more blessed than I.

Why restless, why cast down, my soul?
Hope still; and thou shalt sing
The praise of Him who is Thy God,
Thy health's eternal spring.

Tozer, A. W. *The Christian Book of Mystical Verse: A Collection of Poems, Hymns, and Prayers for Devotional Reading.* Chicago: Moody Publishers, 2016. p. 91.

WEEK THIRTEEN   *INSIGHT and ENCOURAGEMENT*   **DAY 7**

Long-suffering – Speedily

by Andrew Murray (1828-1917)

To enable us, when the answer to our prayer does not come at once, two combine quiet patience and joyful confidence in our persevering prayer, we must specially try to understand the two words in which our Lord sets forth the character and conduct, not of the unjust judge, but that of our God and Father, towards those whom He allows to cry day and night to Him: "He is *long-suffering* over them; he will avenge them *speedily*." (Luke 18:1-8)

The insight into this truth leads the believer to cultivate the corresponding dispositions: patience and faith, waiting and hasting, by the secret of his perseverance. By faith in the promise of God we know that we have the petitions we have asked of Him. Faith takes and holds the answer in the promise, as an unseen spiritual possession, rejoices in it, and praises for it. But there is a difference between the faith that thus holds the word and knows it has an answer, and that clearer, fuller, riper faith that obtains the promise as a present experience. It is in persevering, not unbelieving, but confident and praising prayer, that the soul grows up into that full union with its Lord in which it can enter upon the possession of the blessings in Him. There may be in God's government, things that have to be put right through our prayer, ere the answer can fully come: the faith that has, according to the commandment, believed that it has received, can allow God to take His time. In quiet, persistent, and determined perseverance it continues in prayer and thanksgiving until the blessing come. And so we see combined what at first sight appears so contradictory; the faith that rejoices in the answer of the unseen God as a present possession, with the patience that cries day and night until it be revealed. The *speedily* of God's *long-suffering* is met by the triumphant but patient faith of his waiting child.

Our great danger in this school of the answer delayed is the temptation to think that, after all, it may not be God's will to give us what we asked. If our prayer be according to God's word, and under the leading of the Spirit, let us not give way to these fears. If we only give Him time, that is, time in the daily fellowship with Himself, for Him to exercise the full influence of His presence on us, and time, day by day, in the course of our being kept waiting, for faith to prove its reality and to fill our whole being. He Himself will lead us from faith to vision; we shall see the glory of God. Let no delay shake our faith. Of faith it holds good: first the blade, then the ear, then the full corn of the ear. Each believing prayer brings a step nearer the final victory. Each believing prayer helps to ripen the fruit and bring us nearer to it; it fills up the measure of prayer and faith known to God alone; it conquers the hindrances in the unseen world; it hastens the end. Child of God! give the Father time. "Long-suffering – speedily," this is God's watchword as you enter the gates of prayer: be it yours too. **(Emphasis his.)**

With Christ in the School of Prayer. Old Tappan, NJ: Fleming H. Revell, Co., 1953. p. 88-91.

Record your insights, revelations, and meditations from this week. DATE:

_____

_____

_____

_____

_____

_____

_____

_____

_____

_____

_____

_____

_____

_____

_____

MONTH FOUR

Sometime in the early 1990s, I remember working a police call involving the death of an infant. The mother had left the months-old child asleep on the master bed. That was a tragic mistake because the bed had a thick comforter. The baby was strong enough to roll over onto her stomach but not to reverse the process. She rolled over and suffocated in the comforter.

I stood at the edge of the bed, with the mother's cries filling the air, as I thought, *I am a believer in Christ. I should be able to do something about this*. But I did not know how. I did not have the relationship with God I should have had, even as a part-time minister and preacher of the Gospel. I did not have any power of my own or understand the power available to me through the Holy Spirit. My point is not to comment on the present day ability to raise the dead but to simply describe the event that started my journey to find the deeper life in Christ that others seemed to have. I did not even have words of comfort for the bereaved parents.

I began to seek in earnest to understand what it meant to be filled with the Holy Spirit. My attitude in the past was staunchly opposed to the charismatic movement. Slowly, I began to read books and attend meetings that were led by men and women who were in that camp. I had seen and heard about the excesses and exaggerations of some in the Pentecostal/Charismatic movement, but I wanted to know if there was any truth in it because some seemed to have what I was looking for. In particular, I was interested in the gift of tongues. Many taught that tongues was an indication that you had been baptized in the Holy Spirit. I even read one guy who explained how he taught himself how to speak in tongues. I tried it. It didn't work.

This path also led me to a renewed interest in evangelism. My new associations led me to attend a meeting in Dallas around 1995 or early 1996. Dr. Ed Silvoso was explaining the principles from his book, *That None Should Perish*, about reaching cities for Christ through prayer evangelism. I immediately connected with his message, so much so that I attended the annual Harvest Evangelism International Conference (now Transform Our World) in Buenos Aires, Argentina. I went to learn more about prayer evangelism and see the great revival down there, but also to pursue my desire to have more of God. These people seemed to have what I wanted.

The conference was a blessing and a treasured memory, but two things happened there that had a lasting effect. I watched as the Lord touched many people. At one point I was on the top row of the stadium that seated 20,000, far away from the stage and other people. I began to get hot. Not temperature hot but hot in my chest. The presence of the Holy Spirit hit me in a way I can best describe as "Road to Emmaus" fire. Later I went forward and received prayer from that night's featured speaker. I lay on the stage in tears for 45 minutes. God healed many things. Later, on the flight to the second stage of the conference in La Plata, God let me sit next to another keynote speaker, Lawrence Khong, a pastor from Singapore. We talked and he answered many questions. Then he asked if I wanted him to pray for me to be filled with the Holy Spirit and receive the gift of tongues. I said yes. He did, and I did. God took me to Argentina to be prayed for by a pastor from Singapore. What an amazingly gracious God.

WEEK FOURTEEN   **Confession about Worship**   **DAY 1**

Read 1 Chronicles 16

Thank you, Lord. I will call on our name and tell everyone about the wonderful things you have done. I will sing praises to your holy name with a joyful heart. I will look to you and your strength and always seek your face. I won't forget the amazing things you have done. You are the Lord God. Your sovereignty is evident in all the earth. I will always remember your covenant and promises. I will worship you with songs of praise, proclaiming your salvation, declaring your glory, and recounting your marvelous works. Lord, you are great and worthy of all praise. You deserve respect, reverence, and obedience for there is no God but you. There is incredible beauty and strength and joy in your presence. I will give all the glory to your name. I offer myself in worship in the splendor of holiness. Everyone in all the earth should tremble in your presence. When all the people proclaim, "The Lord reigns!" it makes the heavens rejoice and the earth be glad. All of creation and everything in nature will sing for joy because you come as the righteous judge of all the earth. I give thanks to you Lord for you are good and your love endures forever. I will continually cry out with all the saints, "Save us, O God our savior." Deliver us from all our enemies so that we can give thanks to your holy name and glory in your praise. Praise the Lord forevermore.

WEEK FOURTEEN   *HYMNS and POEMS*   **DAY 2**

The Pain of Love

by Frederick William Faber (1814-1863)

Jesus! why dost Thou love me so?
What hast Thou seen in me
To make my happiness so great,
So dear a joy to Thee?

Wert Thou not God, I then might think
Thou hadst no eye to read
The badness of that selfish heart,
For which Thine own did bleed.

But Thou art God, and knowest all;
Dear Lord! Thou knowest me;
And yet Thy knowledge hinders not
Thy love's sweet liberty.

Ah, how Thy grace hath wooed my soul
With persevering wiles!
Now give me tears to weep; for tears
Are deeper joy than smiles.

Each proof renewed of Thy great love
Humbles me more and more,
And brings to light forgotten sins,
And lays them at my door.

The more I love Thee, Lord! the more
I hate my own cold heart;
The more Thou woundest me with love,
The more I feel the smart.

What shall I do, then, dearest Lord!
Say, shall I fly from Thee,
And hide my poor unloving self
Where Thou canst never see?

Or shall I pray that Thy dear love
To me might not be given?
Ah, no! love must be pain on earth,
If it be bliss in heaven.

Tozer, A. W. *The Christian Book of Mystical Verse: A Collection of Poems, Hymns, and Prayers for Devotional Reading*. Chicago: Moody Publishers, 2016. p. 176-177.

WEEK FOURTEEN   *INSIGHT and ENCOURAGEMENT*   **DAY 3**

The New Man

by Johann Arndt (1555-1621)

The way by which we are to arrive at true and substantial wisdom, and become friends of God, is to submit ourselves to the discipline of repentance, and to lead a life conformable to the Word of God. Such a life as this cannot fail to be attended with true illumination of the mind, and an increase of all divine graces; nay, with so close an alliance with God himself, as to make us "partakers of the divine nature, having escaped the corruption that is in the world through lust" (2 Peter 1:4). To such a holy life as this David aspired with the utmost fervor of spirit, proposing two means by which to obtain it: the first, *fervent prayer*; and the second, *a diligent practice of the word of God*. "I cried," says he, "with my whole heart; hear me,

O Lord: I will keep thy statutes. I cried unto thee; save me, and I shall keep thy testimonies" (Ps. 119:145, 146).

These words set forth the difficulties which he encounters who seeks to be a true Christian, and to keep the word of God in holiness of life. For flesh and blood naturally strive against the word of God, and that holiness of life which it requires: and are, besides, inconstant and weak, and prone to yield to the enticements of the world. The devil on all occasions hinders our progress, and opposes our endeavors on every side. This is followed by a multitude of evil examples, and the persecutions which wicked men raise in opposition to those souls that enter upon another course of life. Against obstinate evils, such as these, all the strength of the soul is to be opposed. This we learn from the example of David, who cried unto the Lord *with his whole heart*, in order that he might better digest the Word, and by leading such a life as that Word requires, continue in the favor of God. This ought also to be our main concern; the favor of God being infinitely preferable to all that the world affords. Whoever pleases God, and is His friend, most effectually secures himself thereby from the malice of all his enemies. Hence *serious and fervent prayer* is, as I said before, the first step to a holy life.

The second means to obtain a holy life, is expressed in the following words of the same Psalm: "I prevented [*preceded*] the dawning of the morning and cried: I hoped in thy word. Mine eyes prevent the night watches, that I might meditate in thy word" (Ps. 119:147, 148). Here the Psalmist declares the earnest study, love, and affection, which are due to the word of God; and the time best suited for meditating in it, namely, the morning. The faculties of the mind are then more vigorous than at other times; and are best disposed for searching into divine subjects.

This is that exercise of the cross, or school of affliction, in which all saints are most effectually trained for a happy eternity. Whoever is not inured to this sort of trials, can know but little of God and of his word. In this exercise, all the natural powers of soul and life consume away, that God alone may become our strength and support. By such inward trials as these, the carnal life is likewise more and more weakened, and the quickening power of God and of his word, perceived with the greater effect and experience. And truly, all our efforts ought to center in this, that the external hearing and reading of the divine word be practically applied to the mind, and improved into Christian experience.

Excerpted from, *True Christianity*. Philadelphia: Smith, English, & Co., (unk). p. 471-473.

WEEK FOURTEEN   **Confession of Devotion to the Word of God**   **DAY 4**

Read Psalm 1

I confess and believe that you bless the one who refused to accept the advice and counsel of ungodly people about how he should live, who decides not to take up the posture of evil men and determines not to be found in the company of the arrogant. Instead of listening to, contemplating, or adopting the ways of evildoers, I will make the law of the God my delight. I will enjoy meditating on the word of God day in and day out. I will give attention to your word in the daytime and in the nighttime. I will plant myself in the word and receive nourishment like the tree that's planted by a river and has a never-ending source of food and water. The word of the lord will produce results in my life at the proper time. As long as I stay rooted in the word, I will continually show signs of life and everything I do will prosper. I know what it's like to be blown around like a dead leaf. There is no future in that. But the Lord will watch over my righteous life and keep me from the way of the wicked which only leads to death.

WEEK FOURTEEN   *INSIGHT and ENCOURAGEMENT*   **DAY 5**

The Five Ingenious Ways of Christians

A. W. Tozer (1897-1963)

There seem to be five ways we have fallen into this strange ingenuity. The first is by seeking our own interests while pursuing spiritual interests under the guise of seeking God's interest. Being self-serving is where the strange ingenuity of Christians begins. Under the guise and pretense of seeking God's interest, we have a sly way of serving our own interests. We have become very clever in this endeavor. But we are only fooling ourselves into thinking that we are "about our Father's business" when we are actually doing our own business.

A second way is by talking about the cross and living in the shadow of the cross, but never actually surrendering to it. I do not find many people talking about to cross these days. But the few that do mention the cross seem only to live in the shadow of the teaching. They never actually fully surrender to the cross as an instrument of death to self. We want to die on the cross, but we always seem to find a way to rescue ourselves. Nothing is easier to talk about than dying on the cross and surrendering ourselves, but nothing is harder than actually doing it.

A third way is by begging for the Holy Spirit to fill us while at the same time rejecting Christ's work in us and keeping things well in our own hands. It would be difficult to find a Christian not interested in being filled with the Holy Spirit. The only problem is that when God begins to move upon them, they reject that move. They want God to take full control of their lives, but at the same time, they want to keep everything in their own control. However, the Holy Spirit works alone in my heart and needs no help from me, other than me simply surrendering absolutely to Him.

A fourth way that we fall into this strange ingenuity is by talking about the dark night of the soul but rejecting the darkness. The dark night of the soul is not something pleasant to go through and does not end with the fellowship supper after church on Sunday night. It is a grueling experience that requires an absolutely strict detachment from everything that you normally rely on so that you're left with only Christ. Darkness speaks of not knowing. We want God to do, but we want Him to do what He does within the scope of our comprehension.

The final way is by using religion to promote our personal interests and advancement. This is another strange ingenuity of the Christian. We want to be involved in the work of the Lord, but we want to also be known as that faithful servant of the Lord. We are perfectly willing to be as religious as possible as long as we can promote ourselves.

Excerpted from, *The Crucified Life: How to Live Out a Deeper Christian Experience*. Minneapolis: Bethany House, 2017. p. 140-143.

WEEK FOURTEEN　　　*HYMNS and POEMS*　　　**DAY 6**

Prayer for Purity
by Nicolaus Ludwig Von Zinzendorf (1700-1760)

O Thou, to whose all-searching sight
The darkness shineth as the light,
Search, prove my heart; it pants for Thee;
O burst these bonds, and set it free!

Wash out its stains, refine its dress,
Nail my affections to the Cross;
Hallow each thought; let all within
Be clean, as Thou, my Lord, art clean!

If in this darksome wild I stray,
Be Thou my Light, be Thou my Way;
No foes, no violence I fear,
No fraud, while Thou, my God, art near.

When rising floods my soul oerflow,
When sinks my heart in waves of woe,
Jesus, Thy timely aid impart,
And raise my head, and cheer my heart.

Savior, where'er Thy steps I see,
Dauntless, untired, I follow Thee;
O let Thy hand support me still,
And lead me to Thy holy hill!

If rough and thorny be the way,
My strength proportion to my day;
Till toil, and grief, and pain shall cease,
Where all is calm, and joy, and peace.

Tozer, A. W. *The Christian Book of Mystical Verse: A Collection of Poems, Hymns, and Prayers for Devotional Reading*. Chicago: Moody Publishers, 2016. p. 85.

WEEK FOURTEEN　　　*INSIGHT and ENCOURAGEMENT*　　　**DAY 7**

True Holiness
by Paul Billheimer (1897-1984)

Sanctification is something more than a blessing, it is a Person, a Person displacing your own ego. We do not wish to minimize the experience side of sanctification. I question the genuineness of any experience of sanctification which does not result in a mighty moving of the emotions, called the witness of the Spirit. But the ethical, not the emotional, content of any religious experience is primary. The real evidence of a sanctified state of grace is not emotional ecstasy or demonstration, but the decentralization of the ego. Self-will is the mother tincture of all sin. Living for self is the essence of all "unholiness." Lucifer became Satan through self-will. The essence of holiness is the "decentralization of the ego," the displacement of self by Christ. You may grow in your ability to demonstrate a certain kind of religious emotionalism without growing in grace. You are growing in grace only when you are growing in meekness, submission, yieldedness, brokenness, and selflessness.

Self-promotion is inconsistent with true holiness. Increasing holiness means increasing sensitiveness to sin, increasing tenderness of conscience, increasing repudiation of self-promotion and self-glorification. I say again that you are not growing in grace no matter how you appear to be; you are not deeply spiritual no matter how you claim to be, unless you are growing in meekness, in submission, in yieldedness, and obedience to the discipline of the circumstances and environment in which God has placed you.

Make no mistake about it, there is no real "decentralization of the ego," and therefore no real depth of holiness while we are seeking to manufacture our own circumstances instead of accepting them as from God. Refusal to accept the discipline of the circumstances in which God has placed us is evidence of the activity of our own ego. Any real depth of holiness puts an end to this, for it substitutes Christ for our personal self. If your religious emotion makes you sweeter, kinder, lest self-assertive, more meek and submissive, lest self-centered and more broken, then it is good. If it does not, it is probably largely an escape, something by which you avoid facing up to your real self and letting the cross deal with. In true holiness, there is a balance between experience and ethics.

Another thing behind which much carnal corruption can highlight is an exact theology, a theological traditionalist, which some people substitute for the real essence of holiness, which is meekness, submission, brokenness, defenselessness, and selflessness. It is possible to be correct, according to the generally accepted teaching of holiness, while tolerating in the life all the earmarks of unbroken self-will. No one can experience a real crisis of holiness until self-will has been broken. There is only one place of true holiness and that is on the cross.

Adapted from *Destined for The Cross*. Wheaton: Tyndale House Publishers, Inc. 1982. p. 34-36.

Record your insights, revelations, and meditations from this week. DATE:

_____

_____

_____

_____

_____

_____

_____

_____

_____

_____

_____

_____

WEEK FIFTEEN **Confession of a Sacrificed Life** **DAY 1**

Read Psalm 5

I believe that because you are my Lord, you will hear the groaning of my heart. Because I pray to you, my King and my God, you will hear my cry for help. In the morning, I will speak aloud all my requests, live a sacrifice laid out before you, and I will watch and wait with expectation. I know that you take no pleasure in evil. The wicked cannot live with you. The arrogant, boastful, and prideful person cannot stand in your presence. You hate evildoers, liars, and deceitful people. But, through your abundant love and mercy, I will come into your presence and bow before you in humble reverence and obedience. Lead me in your righteousness and make your way clear to me. I will take refuge and hide myself in you. In you I will rejoice and be glad and sing for joy the rest of my life. I will live under the protection you spread out over me. The love of your name, knowing and loving who you are, will bring me great joy and happiness. I confess without a doubt that you, my Lord, bless those who walk and live in righteousness before you. Because of your great love, I will live surrounded by your favor like a shield on every side.

WEEK FIFTEEN   *HYMNS and POEMS*   **DAY 2**

Olives That Have Known No Pressure

by Watchman Nee (1903-1972)

Olives that have known no pressure
No oil can bestow;
If the Grapes escape the winepress,
Cheering wine can never flow;

Spikenard only through the crushing,
Fragrance can diffuse.
Shall I then, Lord, shrink from suff'ring
Which Thy love for me would choose?

Refrain:
Each blow I suffer
It's true gain to me.
In the place of what Thou takest
Thou dost give thyself to me.

Do my heart-strings need Thy stretching,
Songs divine to prove?
Do I need for sweetest music
Cruel treatment of thy love?

Lord, I fear no deprivation
If it draws to Thee;
I would yield in full surrender
All Thy heart of love to see.

I'm ashamed, my Lord, for seeking
Self to guard alway;
Though Thy love has done its stripping,
Yet I've been compelled this way.

Lord, according to thy pleasure
Fully work on me;
Heeding not my human feelings,
Only do what pleases Thee.

If Thy mind and mine should differ,
Still pursue Thy way;
If Thy pleasure means my sorrow,
Still my heart shall answer, "Yea!"

'Tis my deep desire to please Thee,
Though I suffer loss,
E'en though thy delight and glory
Mean that I endure the cross.

Oh, I'll praise Thee, e'en if weeping
Mingle with my song.
Thine increasing sweetness calls forth
Grateful praises all day long.

Thou hast made Thyself more precious
Than all else to me:
Thou increase and I decrease, Lord –
This is now my only plea.

http://www.witness-lee-hymns.org/hymns/H0626.html

WEEK FIFTEEN   *INSIGHT and ENCOURAGEMENT*   **DAY 3**

My Laws in Their Hearts

by Watchman Nee (1903-1972)

Those whose eyes have been really opened to this world's true character find they must touch everything in it with fear and trembling, looking continually to the Lord. They know that at any moment they are liable to be caught in Satan's entanglements. Just as the drug which, in the first instance, is welcomed to relieve sickness may ultimately become itself the cause of sickness, so equally the things of the world which we can legitimately use under the Lord's authority may, if we are heedless, become a cause of our downfall. Only fools can be careless in circumstances like these.

No wonder we look with envy upon John the Baptist! How easy, we feel, if like him we could simply withdraw into a safe place apart! But we are *not* like him. Our Lord has sent us into the world in His own footsteps, "both eating and drinking." Since God so loved, His command to us is to go "into all the world" and proclaim His good news; and surely that "all" includes the folk with whom we must rub shoulders daily!

So a serious problem faces us here. As we have said, presumably there must be a limit. Presumably God has drawn somewhere a line of demarcation. Stay within the bounds of that line and we will be safe; cross it and grave danger threatens. But where does it lie? We have to eat and drink, to marry and bring up children, to trade and to toil. How do we do so and yet remain uncontaminated? How do we mingle freely with the men and women whom God so loved as to give His Son for them, and still keep ourselves unspotted from the world?

If the Lord had limited our buying and selling to so much a month, how simple that would be! The rules would be plain for any to follow. All who spent more than a certain amount per month would be worldly Christians, and all who spent less than that amount would be unworldly.

But since our Lord has stipulated no figure, we are cast on Him unceasingly. For what? I think the answer is very wonderful. Not to be tied by the rules, but that we may remain all the time within bounds of another kind: the bounds of His life. If our Lord had given us the set of rules and regulations to observe, then we could take great care to abide by these. In fact, however, our task is something far more simple and straightforward, namely, to abide in the Lord Himself. Then, we could keep the law. Now, **we need only keep in fellowship with Him**. (Emphasis mine) And the joy of it is that, provided we live in close touch with God, His Holy Spirit within our hearts will always tell us when we reach the limit!

Love Not the World. Philadelphia: Christian Literature Crusade, 1973. p. 74-75.

Wonderful Passion for God

by Watchman Nee (1903-1972)

The Gospel of salvation is necessary and vital in order to meet man's need. But if as God's servants we are only laboring for others we are missing God's first aim in creation, which was to supply not merely man's need about His own. For as we have said already, the creation of man was to meet the need of God. Thus if today we are going to meet God's need, we must go a step further and deal with Satan himself. We must steal back from him his power, evict him from his territory, spoil him of his goods and set free his captives – for God. The question is not merely, Of what account are we in the winning of souls? Rather it is, Of what account are we in the realm of principalities and powers? And for that there is a price to pay.

It is often possible to move man when it is quite impossible to move Satan. The plain fact is that it costs much more to deal with Satan then to win souls. It demands an utterness of spirit Godward that in itself effectually deprives Satan of any moral ground in us he may claim to possess. This is the costly thing. God in His merciful love for the lost can often bypass and overlook in his servants what one might justly feel to be appalling weakness and even failure. But while He may do this for the sole-winner, when it comes to our dealing with the devil it is another matter.

Evil spirits can see right through the witness of man. They can tell when it is compromised by being half-hearted or insincere. They are aware when we are holding back a part of the price. Looking at us they are under no illusions as to whom they can safely defy or ignore; and conversely, they know perfectly well against whom they are powerless. "Jesus I know, and Paul I know; but who are ye?" (Acts 19:15). Because they believe, they know when to tremble. And let me say this: since our most important task is their overthrow, it is better always that we should have the witness of evil powers than the praise of man.

The price of this witness to the principalities and powers is, I repeat, an utterness of allegiance to God that is unqualified. To entertain our own opinions or desires, or to prefer our own variant and contrary choices, is simply to present the enemy with his advantage. It is, in short, to throw the game away. In any other sphere there may perhaps – I do not know – be room among our motives for something of self-interest, without appreciable loss. But never, and I repeat never, in this. Without such utterness for God nothing can be achieved, for without it we make even God powerless against his enemy. So I say it once again: the demand is very high. Are you and I here on earth, utterly committed, utterly given to God Himself? And because this is so, are we tasting even now the powers of that future glorious age? Are we reclaiming territory from the prince of this world for the One whose alone it rightly is?

Love Not the World. Philadelphia: Christian Literature Crusade, 1973. p. 85-87.

WEEK FIFTEEN   **Confession about Overcoming Temptation**   **DAY 5**

Read Proverbs 2:8-19

I know that the world, evil people, and even sometimes friends and family are going to entice me to leave the righteous path and do things that are not the will of God. I am determined not to give in to them, no matter the cost. They will invite me to join then in taking advantage of someone or some situation or some opportunity that offers profit or benefit in some way but that is not the will of God for my life. They will paint a beautiful picture of how we can all share in the profit, if only I will cast my lot with them and join in on their schemes. I am deciding now that I will not go that way. I will not be deceived by them to think that their ideas are any good at all. Their plans are as useless as setting out a trap while the animal is standing there watching. These plans always end up hurting people and they usually backfire on the ones that make the plans. Even if they get some kind of gain from it, it will end up ruining their lives. I will not give in to them. I will not go along with them. I will not set foot on the path to destruction.

WEEK FIFTEEN   *HYMNS and POEMS*   **DAY 6**

The Praises of God and the Blessing
by St. Francis of Assisi (c. 1182 – 1226)

You are the holy Lord God Who does wonderful things.
You are strong. You are great. You are the most high.
You are the almighty king. You holy Father,
King of heaven and earth.
You are three and one, the Lord God of gods;
You are the good, all good, the highest good,
Lord God living and true.

You are love, charity; You are wisdom, You are humility,
You are patience. You are beauty, You are meekness,
You are security, You are rest,
You are gladness and joy, You are our hope,
You are justice,
You are moderation, You are all our riches to sufficiency.

You are beauty, You are meekness,
You are the protector, You are our custodian and defender,
You are strength, You are refreshment, You are our hope,
You are our faith, You are our charity,
You are all our sweetness, You are our eternal life:
Great and wonderful Lord, Almighty God,
Merciful Savior.

The Prayers of St. Francis of Assisi. https://ofm.org/wp-content/uploads/2017/01/Prayers.pdf p.6.

WEEK FIFTEEN   *INSIGHT and ENCOURAGEMENT*   **DAY 7**

The Morning Watch

by Andrew Murray (1828-1917)

What a power the morning watch may be in the life of one who makes the determined resolve to meet God there; to renew the surrender to absolute obedience; humbly and patiently to wait on the Holy Spirit to be taught all God's will; and to receive the assurance that every promise given him in the Word will infallibly be made true! He that thus prays for himself, will become a true intercessor for others.

It is in the light of these thoughts I want now to say a few words on *what prayer is to be* in the morning watch. First of all, *see that you secure the presence of God.* Do not be content with anything less than seeing the face of God, having the assurance that He is looking on you in love, and listening and working in you.

If our daily life is to be full of God, how much more the morning hour, where the life of the day alone can have God's seal stamped upon it. In our religion we want nothing so much as more of God – His love, His will, His holiness, His spirit living in us, His power working in us for men. Under heaven there is no way of getting this but by close personal communion. And there is no time so good for securing and practicing it, as the morning watch.

The superficiality and feebleness of our religion and religious work all come from having so little real contact with God. If it be true that God alone is the fountain of all love and good and happiness, and that to have as much as possible of His presence and His fellowship, of His will and His service, is our truest and highest happiness, surely then to meet Himself alone in the morning watch ought to be **Our First Care**.

To have God appear to them, and speak to them, was with all the Old Testament saints the secret of their obedience and their strength. To give God time in secret so to reveal Himself, that your soul may call the name of the place Peniel (Gen 32:30), - 'for I have seen Him face to face.'

My next thought is: *let the renewal of your surrender to absolute obedience for that day be a chief part of your morning sacrifice.* Let any confession of sin be very definite – a plucking out and cutting off of everything that has been grieving to God. Let any prayer for grace for a holy walk be as definite – an asking and accepting in faith of the very grace and strength you are specially in need of. Let your outlook on the day you are entering on be a very determined resolve that obedience to God shall be **Its Controlling Principle**. (Emphasis his)

The School of Obedience. Chicago: Moody Press, no date. p. 60-62 (reprint from 1898).

Record your insights, revelations, and meditations from this week. DATE:

_____

_____

_____

_____

_____

_____

_____

_____

_____

_____

_____

_____

_____

_____

_____

_____

WEEK SIXTEEN   *HYMNS and POEMS*   **DAY 1**

First-Day Thoughts

by George Herbert (1593-1633)

A broken ALTAR, Lord, thy servant rears,
Made of a heart and cemented with tears;
Whose parts are as thy hand did frame;
No workman's tool hath touch'd the same.

A HEART alone
Is such a stone,
As nothing but
Thy pow'r doth cut.
Wherefore each part
Of my hard heart
Meets in this frame
To praise thy name.

That if I chance to hold my peace,
These stones to praise thee may not cease.
Oh, let thy blessed SACRIFICE be mine,
And sanctify this ALTAR to be thine.

https://www.poemhunter.com/poem/the-altar/ (The format of the poem is by design and is presented as found in the source.)

WEEK SIXTEEN   **Confession of Absolute Confidence**   **DAY 2**

Read Psalm 46

God, you are my safe place. You are the source of all my strength. You are always here to help me with whatever problem or situation I face. Because that is true, I will not be afraid even when it feels like the ground has fallen away beneath my feet. I will not fear when it feels like a ton of bricks has fallen on my head or when it seems like I've been caught in a flash flood with nothing to hold on to. I will be like a fortified city, refreshed by the river of the Holy Spirit, dwelling in the presence of the Most High God. Every day you will be my help right from the start. I know that the almighty God is with me. I will accept the Lord's invitation to come and see your mighty works in all the earth. If you can do amazing, fearful, wonderful things in the earth, if you can put an end to wars and defeat strong enemies that have powerful weapons, then surely, you can overcome the attacks launched against me and lead me to victory over the enemies I battle. I confess that the secret to this victorious life is stillness and quiet and trust and rest before you, Lord, and to know without a doubt that you are my almighty fortress. For this I will constantly give you praise.

WEEK SIXTEEN   *INSIGHT and ENCOURAGEMENT*   **DAY 3**

Divine Holiness Incarnated

by J. Sidlow Baxter (1903-1999)

What, then, is it that we seek in Jesus? He was often in secret prayer, but he is no mystic. He was fond of periodic solitude, but he was no monastic. He was abstemious, but he was no ascetic. He had nothing in common with the religious "Zealots" and their contentious violence; yet neither did he ever once visit the nonpartisan "Essenes" in their cloistered isolationism. There was moral apartness, yet no social aloofness. There was sanctity, but no frigidity. He abhorred hypocrisy, but was overflowingly sympathetic where there was contrition. He neither fawned on the rich nor despised the poor. He neither coveted wealth nor condoned poverty. He never compromised principle a hair's breadth, yet He was a congenial mixer with a keen aliveness toward people and things. He had boundless compassion, friendship, understanding, for boys and girls, for the aged, for the sick, for the suffering, for the bad who wanted to be different, and the good who wanted to be better. He sought God everywhere and in everything; and His master passion was to do the Father's will. He was utterly guileless in his self-abnegating outreach of heart to heal and mend and bless others. He was the sublimest embodiment of gracious otherism ever known: and, most significant of all, in revealing the one true Godhead, He revealed also the one ideal *manhood*. There is no mistaking Him, except by the blind: He is "God manifest in the flesh"; sinless in essence, stainless in conduct, guileless in motives, quenchless in love.

In Jesus the ideal and the actual are one. He is the superb *norm* of true humanhood, that is, humanhood as originally created and divinely intended. As Professor Henry Drummond said, with a permissible touch of refined colloquialism, "Jesus is the perfect gentleman" – the exquisite blend of "gentle" and "man," of tenderness and virile heroism; "meek and lowly in heart," but with an awesome flash of ire in His eyes before which the temple money traffickers cowered and slunk away.

Years ago, at a large gathering in Manchester, England, the minister prayed a prayer which has had a decided influence on my thinking ever since: "O God, make us *intensely spiritual*, but keep us *perfectly natural*, and always *thoroughly practical* – even as Jesus was." That prayer was finely photographic. It captured the dominant lineaments of our Lord's holy manhood: "intensely spiritual"; "perfectly natural"; "thoroughly practical"; the living expression of "God is *spirit*," "God is *light*," "God is *love*." Yes, that was Jesus; and that was the divine holiness incarnate. So then, holiness, which we have preliminarily described as moral likeness to God, may now be more concretely represented *as likeness in heart and life to Christ*. (Emphasis his.)

A New Call to Holiness. Grand Rapids: Zondervan, 1973. p. 112-113.

WEEK SIXTEEN   *HYMNS and POEMS*   **DAY 4**

Jesus, Master, Whose I Am

by Frances Ridley Havergal (1836-1879)

Jesus, Master, whose I am,
Purchased Thine alone to be,
By Thy blood, O spotless Lamb,
Shed so willingly for me,
Let my heart be all Thine own,
Let me live for Thee alone.

Other lords have long held sway;
Now Thy name alone to bear,
Thy dear voice alone obey,
Is my daily, hourly prayer;
Whom have I in Heaven but Thee?
Nothing else my joy can be.

Jesus, Master, I am Thine;
Keep me faithful, keep me near;
Let Thy presence in me shine

All my homeward way to cheer,
Jesus, at Thy feet I fall,
O be Thou my all in all.

Jesus, Master, whom I serve,
Though so feebly and so ill,
Strengthen hand and heart and nerve
All Thy bidding to fulfill;
Open Thou mine eyes to see
All the work Thou hast for me.

Lord, Thou needest not, I know,
Service such as I can bring,
Yet I long to prove and show
Full allegiance to my king.
Thou an honor art to me;
Let me be a praise to Thee.

123

Jesus, Master, wilt Thou use
One who owes Thee more than all?
As Thou wilt! I would not choose;

Only let me hear Thy call.
Jesus, let me always be
In Thy service glad and free.

Written in 1865 and published in her *Ministry of Song* in 1869, according to http://www.hymntime.com/.

WEEK SIXTEEN   *INSIGHT and ENCOURAGEMENT*   **DAY 5**

The Death of President William McKinley

by Gary Scott Smith

McKinley's response to being fatally wounded provided a vivid testimony to his faith, and his subsequent death evoked an outpouring of theological reflection, spiritual anguish, and praise for his Christian character and conviction. On Friday September 6, 1901 McKinley spoke at the Pan-American Exposition in Buffalo, New York. According to the Presbyterian Banner, he came to the exposition "at the height of his splendid fame. The strength and purity of his character and the solidity and success of his administration" had "won him the confidence and admiration of all parties and classes." He was "personally loved as few presidents" had been loved. While greeting people after the speech, McKinley was shot twice at point blank range by anarchist Leon Czolgosz. Worried about his wife who had recently suffered a life-threatening illness, the president urged his personal secretary George Cortelyou not to tell her what had happened. He then turned to the assassin who had been subdued by guards. Fearing that the crowd might beat him to death, McKinley raised his blood-stained hand and entreated, "Let no one hurt him; may God forgive him." Many Americans were later struck by the similarity with Christ's words on the cross. Like Jesus during his crucifixion and Stephen while being stoned, an Episcopal rector avowed, he prayed for his murderer. The assassin, McKinley added, was "some poor misguided fellow." Next the president apologized for having "been the cause of trouble to the exposition." As the Presbyterian Banner put it, after being shot, McKinley's "thoughts went out in tenderness to his wife, in forgiveness to his enemy, and in unselfish regard for the public interest."

Two bullets struck McKinley. One of them penetrated his stomach walls, shredding his kidneys. Surgeons quickly operated, but could not locate the bullet. From all quarters, the president's friends and associates flocked to Buffalo: Mark Hanna from Cleveland, Senator Charles Fairbanks from Indianapolis, Vice-President Theodore Roosevelt from Vermont, and many others. As Americans prayed and waited, the initial news was hopeful. Writing to Cortelyou, A. B. Farquhar of York, Pennsylvania, declared, "I would gladly give my life to save his, and everyone feels the same way." McKinley's patience, calmness, cheerfulness, and sense of peace impressed the nation. By Thursday the president seemed to be getting better. However, his condition changed dramatically the next morning. Realizing the end was near, the president called his surgeons to his bedside, prayed the Lord's Prayer, and murmured some of the words of his favorite hymn "Nearer, My God, to Thee." His last words, as reported by the 24 newspapers around the nation were, "Good-bye all, good-bye. It is God's way. His will, not ours, be done." Having regarded his whole life as under God's direction and control," Frederick Barton emphasized, "he even declared his dying at the hands of an assassin to be 'God's way.'" It was as though he bravely answered "the Master's call, which others could not hear," reported the Washington Post. The Baltimore Sun expressed thanks that McKinley lived long enough to experience "the outpouring of national love," the universal goodwill and esteem of all sections of the country, and the solace of prayers offered for his recuperation. Although "the Divine Healer did not answer . . . our prayers for his recovery," God gave him eternal life. Both fervent prayer and the best efforts of modern science, declared the Charleston News and Courier, were impotent and McKinley "surrendered to the inscrutable will of the Ruler of life and death."

One hundred thousand sermons, contended Henry C. McCook, "could not have taught us as much as these last words: 'It is God's way; His will, not ours, be done.'" All the sermons on the subject of Christian courage, patience, and hope in heaven for the last ten years, DeWitt Talmage argued, did "not make such an impression as [did] the magnificent demeanor of this dying chief magistrate." The way McKinley faced death encouraged those with tuberculosis, cancer, and other life-threatening illnesses to endure their suffering patiently. "No Christian virgin seeking the martyr's crown in Rome's empurpled amphitheater," declared the Rocky Mountain News, "faced death with courage more superb than William McKinley." During his last hours, McKinley's radiant faith in God and eternal life, maintained the New York Herald, eloquently reminded Americans of both Christ's death and resurrection. "Christian faith and trust," declared William Jennings Bryan, McKinley's opponent in both 1896 and 1900, was "never better exemplified than in his death." McKinley died "wonderfully as the Master died," another added, providing a marvelous Christian example. "From thy Calvary of pain, whereon thou died for the weal of all mankind, we lift and lay thy body down to sleep," wrote a man from Kansas City. Congressman Charles Grosvenor predicted that McKinley's death would be remembered as the most Christ-like the world had known since Calvary. Many praised his submission to God's will.

Numerous commentators struggled to find meaning in McKinley's assassination. The Presbyterian Interior of Chicago expressed hope that "through the flame of affliction God would lead the nation from its jaunty pride of prosperity to soberness and introspection." Through this tragedy God was summoning America to repent of its national sins—disrespect for law and toleration of corruption, oppression, and iniquity. His death challenged Americans to ask if they had been worshipping wealth and pleasure and ignoring the spiritual and eternal. This national ordeal had melted political and sectional differences and promoted unity and brotherhood. If the death of "our noble and beloved president . . . can make us more faithful to God, then indeed has he not died in vain and he is mightier and more beneficent in his death than in his life." Because of the way he died, argued W. B. Huntingdon, the rector of Grace Church in New York City, religion was stronger in America. Many Southerners praised McKinley's efforts to restore national unity. As one of them put it, "Where he found distrust, he left faith; where he found strife, he left peace; where he found bitterness, he left love; where he found an open wound, he poured his dissolving life as a precious ointment to soothe and heal." Some predicted that God would use McKinley's life and death as an instrument to convert many Americans. His sudden death challenged people to examine their own spiritual state. Ministers emphasized that McKinley was with God in paradise because he trusted in Jesus Christ as his redeemer and urged Americans to give their lives to God so they would someday experience heavenly life. Preaching at Metropolitan Methodist Church in Washington the Sunday after

McKinley's death, W. H. Chapman declared, "May we all imitate his virtues and at the last be counted worthy of a place with him in the Kingdom of Heaven."

"William McKinley: America as God's Instrument." *Religion in the Oval Office*. New York: Oxford University Press, 2015. Reprinted in www.visionandvalues.org. p. 23-24.

WEEK SIXTEEN *HYMNS and POEMS* **DAY 6**

Call to Consecration   (Col. 3:1-4; I Peter 1:13-16; II Cor. 5:14-15; Gal. 2:20; 6:14)

If ye (I) then be risen with Christ, (I will) seek those things which are above, where Christ sitteth on the right hand of God.

(I will) Set your (my) affections on things above, not on things on the earth.

For ye are (I am) dead, and your (my) life is hid with Christ in God.

When Christ, who is our (my) life, shall appear, then shall ye (I) also appear with him in glory.

Wherefore (I will) gird up the loins of your (my) mind, be sober, and hope to the end for the grace that is to be brought unto you (me) at the revelation of Jesus Christ:

As obedient children (an obedient child), not fashioning yourselves (myself) according to the former lusts in your (my) ignorance:

But as he which hath called you (me) is holy, so be ye (I will be) holy in all manner of conversation ["living"];

Because it is written, Be ye holy; for I am holy.

For the love of Christ constraineth us; because we thus judge, that if one died for all, then were all dead:

And that he died for all, that they which live should not henceforth live unto themselves, but unto him which died for them, and rose again.

I am crucified with Christ: nevertheless I live; yet not I, but Christ liveth in me: and the life which I now live in the flesh I live by the faith of the son of God who loved me, and gave himself for me.

God forbid that I should glory, save in the cross of our Lord Jesus Christ, by whom the world is crucified unto me, and I unto the world.

Sims, Walter H, ed. *Baptist Hymnal*. Convention Press, Nashville: 1956. Responsive Reading #73.

WEEK SIXTEEN   *INSIGHT and ENCOURAGEMENT*   **DAY 7**

The School of Disappointment

by John Newton (1725-1807)

It is indeed natural to us to wish and to plan, and it is merciful in the Lord to disappoint our plans, and to cross our wishes. For we cannot be safe, much less happy, but in proportion as we are weaned from our own wills, and made simply desirous of being directed by His guidance. This truth (when we are enlightened by His word) is sufficiently familiar to the judgment; but we seldom learn to reduce it into practice without being trained a while in the school of disappointment. The schemes we form look so plausible and convenient that when they are broken we are ready to say, What a pity! We try again, and with no better success; we are grieved, and perhaps angry, and plan another, and so on; at length, in the course of time, experience and observation began to convince us that we are not more able than we are worthy to choose aright for ourselves. Then the Lord's invitation to cast our cares upon Him, and His promise to take care of us, appear valuable; and when we have done planning, His plan in our favor gradually opens, and He does more and better for us then we could either ask or think. I can hardly recollect a single plan of mine, of which I have not since seen reason to be satisfied that, had it taken place in season and circumstance just as I proposed, it would, humanly speaking, have proved my ruin; or at least it would have deprived me of the greater good the Lord had designed for me. We judge of things by their present appearance, but the Lord sees them and their consequences; if we could do so likewise, we should be perfectly of His mind; but as we cannot, it is an unspeakable mercy that He will manage for us, whether we are pleased with His management or not; and it is spoken of as one of His heaviest judgments, when he gives any person or people up to the way of their own hearts, and to walk after their own counsels.

Baillie, John. *A Diary of Readings*. New York: Macmillan Publishing Co., 1955. p. 186.

Record your insights, revelations, and meditations from this week. DATE:

_____

_____

_____

_____

_____

WEEK SEVENTEEN   **Confession of the Truth of God's Word**   **DAY 1**

Read Psalm 19

All of creation declares the glory of God. Day and night, without words, their testimony goes out to the whole world. I cannot escape the witness creation brings of what God has done. Like the penetrating rays of the sun, I cannot escape the penetrating truth of God. I confess and believe the truth that so penetrates my heart and mind comes from the perfect law of the Lord. It comes from the trustworthy and sure testimony of the Lord. It comes from the precepts and statutes of the Lord which are always right. It comes from the commandments of the Lord which are radiant and pure. It comes through the purity of reverent obedience to the righteous decrees and judgments of the Lord. By God's penetrating truth, my soul is revived, my mind is instructed, my heart is filled with joy, and my understanding is enlightened. Your truth is more precious and desirable than anything of value or enjoyment found in this world. Your truth protects me and in obedience there is great reward. Forgive me when I sin against you in ignorance and teach me your ways. Strengthen me to stop committing known, willful sins that presume against your lovingkindness. Do not let them rule over me so that I can stand blameless in your presence. Let everything I say and everything I think be acceptable and pleasing in your sight, for you Lord, are my solid ground and my savior.

WEEK SEVENTEEN   *HYMNS and POEMS*   **DAY 2**

At Thy Feet I Fall
by Catherine Booth-Clibborn (Katie Booth) (1858-1955)

O Lamb of God! Thou wonderful sin-bearer,
Hard after Thee my soul doth follow on;
As pants the hart for streams in desert dreary,
So pants my soul for Thee, O Thou life-giving One.

Refrain:
At Thy feet I fall,
Yield Thee up my all,
To suffer, live, or die
For my Lord crucified.

I mourn, I mourn the sin that drove Thee from me,
And blackest darkness brought into my soul;
Now I renounce the cursed sin that hindered,
And come once more to Thee, to be made fully whole.

Descend the heav'ns, Thou whom my soul adoreth!
Oh, come just now, fill my poor longing breast;
For Thee, for Thee, I watch, as for the morning!
Apart from Thee, I find neither joy, peace, nor rest.

Come, Holy Ghost, Thy mighty aid bestowing,
Destroy the works of sin, the self, the pride;
Burn, burn in me, my idols overthrowing;
Prepare my heart for Him—for my Lord crucified.

https://library.timelesstruths.org/music/At_Thy_Feet_I_Fall/

WEEK SEVENTEEN   *INSIGHT and ENCOURAGEMENT*   **DAY 3**

Absolute Surrender vs. Absolute Control
by Francis Chan (1967-present)

You know, when most people talk about the American dream, it's about safety, security, I want to grow old with my kids, my grandkids, have all sorts of money, it's all about the here and now. It's antithetical to Scripture where Jesus says, "Deny yourself take up your cross and follow Me." He didn't invite the disciples into the American dream, He invited them into a life of suffering. In fact, the Scriptures teach that anyone who wants to live a Godly life in Christ Jesus will be persecuted.

So, we're kind of signing up for a war. The American dream versus this spiritual warfare that we're in and so anyone who has spent any time in the New Testament can see that following Christ isn't easy. In fact, the people that were begging Him to follow, saying "I want to follow You, Jesus," He says, you sure? "The foxes have holes and the birds have nests, but the Son of Man has nowhere to lay His head. If you follow me, we're homeless tonight." And so, you're really leaving things up in the air rather than controlling them, which is what the American dream is all about. I have control over my life, I have everything set up for the rest of my life, that's the dream. It's absolute control versus absolute surrender.

When Jesus called people to Himself, it was a call to follow Him. He just said, "Follow Me." It's implied in there clearly the sense of lordship. He's our Master, I go where He tells me to go. That's why He asks questions like, "Why do you call me Lord, Lord, when you don't do what I say?" This doesn't make sense. You're giving Me this lip-service and you're calling Me "Lord" yet you're not doing what I ask you to do.

I remember when I was younger, there was this big debate, I think it's died out by now, but back in the day it was like, well can you accept Him as Savior but not as Lord? Can you say, "I want You to save me, but I don't to follow You?" And I think back then there was actually the belief that, oh yeah sure, we can follow Him as Savior and then later on we can decide if we want Him as our Lord. I think most of that's died out and we see the foolishness of it. That doesn't make any sense. Where can we find any type of Biblical mandate or promise that all we have to do is have this intellectual assent and say, yeah I want Him to be my Savior but I have no desire to follow Him. How can anyone read the New Testament and get that? It was just something that we wanted. Can I still control my life and have the assurance that I'm not going to hell? That's basically what we were after.

What I love about this generation is that they are reading Scripture for themselves and seeing the obvious like, of course He is Lord, He is God. He is in control. We fear Him, we follow Him, we love Him. The whole idea of trusting Him is saying, I trust Your commands will actually lead to life. I actually trust that if I lose my life, I'm actually going to find it because that's what You told me. So let me let go, surrender, it's a little scary, because we're all about control. It's like, ok, "You're my new Master, I just surrendered myself to You." That's what it means. That's what baptism was. I'm dying to myself. That means I'm giving up control. Francis is no longer alive. Now it's Christ who lives in me. So, take me where You want me to go because I trust, this is going to be a better life for me. This is the way to fulfillment, the full abundant life that Christ talks about. Which doesn't mean it's always going to be easiest, in fact most of the time it's not. It doesn't mean it's the most fun all of the time, because it does include pain and suffering and sacrifice. But the conclusion will always be our blessing. Even the suffering is going to be more abundant than us holding onto our lives, controlling our own lives, and our destiny and saying, no "Jesus, I surrender to You."

Transcribed from an interview for www.ekballoproject.com.

WEEK SEVENTEEN   *HYMNS and POEMS*   **DAY 4**

Jesus, Thine All-victorious Love

by Charles Wesley (1707-1788)

Jesus, thine all-victorious love	Refining fire, go through my heart;
Shed in my heart abroad:	Illuminate my soul;
Then shall my feet no longer rove,	Scatter Thy life through every part,
Rooted and fix'd in God.	And sanctify the whole.
O that in me the sacred fire	My steadfast soul, from falling free,
Might now begin to glow;	Shall then no longer move;
Burn up the dress of base desire,	While Christ is all the world to me,
And make the mountains flow.	And all my heart is love.

O that it now from heaven might fall,
And all my sins consume:
Come, Holy Ghost, for Thee I call;
Spirit of burning, come.

Tozer, A. W. *The Christian Book of Mystical Verse: A Collection of Poems, Hymns, and Prayers for Devotional Reading*. Chicago: Moody Publishers, 2016. p. 87.

WEEK SEVENTEEN   *INSIGHT and ENCOURAGEMENT*   **DAY 5**

The Christian's Life of Faith

by Augustus Hermann Francke (1663-1727)

This is the confession of my faith, the truth which I have learned from the Word of God, and which the Holy Ghost has sealed up on my heart; this is the course in which I run the Christian race, and the path by continuing in which I shall be preserved from every false way, and obtain the prize of life. I have, by sinfulness, exposed myself to temporal and eternal death. But the Son of God has given himself for me, and reconciled me to the Father by his blood, so that God no more imputes my sins unto me, but reckons to me for justification, the righteousness of his Son, which I receive by faith. Through this faith, which is the operation of the Holy Ghost, I am truly justified, and in this justification have found peace with God. I do not, however, profess to be without faults, and infirmities.

On the contrary, I know that those which I have discovered in myself, are almost innumerable; and those which his eye alone beholds, are far more numerous. Yet since I am in Christ, God pardons, and overlooks them all, as a tender father the failings and misconduct of his child. But though I thus trust that I am not under condemnation, his grace does not render me careless, and secure; it rather excites me, daily, to be more and more renewed in the spirit of my mind. God has implanted within me a filial fear of him, which preserves me from sinning against his grace. I daily fight again sin, and crucify the flesh, with its affections and lusts; yet I cannot do this in my own strength; but through the Holy Spirit, which dwells in me. He purgeth me daily, as a branch of the vine, that I may bear more fruit. I am, in truth, cleansed through the word which Christ has spoken, and in which I have believed; and this is no vain imagination; for Christ has truly loved me, and washed me in his blood, so that my salvation is rendered sure, through Christ. My beginning, progress, and ending, is by faith in Jesus Christ.

When I feel my utter inability, and the knowledge that I can do nothing of myself, and cast myself alone upon his mercy, and look to the Lamb of God, who bore our sins, I feel a new power communicated to my soul. I do not seek to be justified in one way, and sanctified in another. I have but one way and that is Christ, who is the way, the truth, and the life. I rest on nothing but Christ, when I plead for the pardon of sin, so I cleave to him alone, in my efforts, to increase faith, and hope, and love. When I yield myself to his control, and do not oppose the workings of his Spirit, he then works in me, both to will and to do of his good pleasure.

While the soul acknowledges no merit in itself, but finds its all in Christ, we shall be filled with heavenly peace: but as soon as we become puffed up, we tread the path of error, strewed with anxiety and danger. Nevertheless, God has his appointed seasons for the trial and humiliation of his people; and although the believer may not depart from the right way, he must expect to pass through many tribulations, that the secret depravity of his heart may be revealed to him. How readily do we deviate from the straight and narrow way! How often does the believer suffer himself to be led away from Christ, and his trust in him, to attempt a mere legal obedience! How prone is he to forsake the gospel, for the law!

Memoirs of A. H. Francke. Philadelphia: American Sunday School Union, 1831. p. 35-38.

WEEK SEVENTEEN   **Confession of Trust in Victory**   **DAY 6**

Read Psalm 21

I am ecstatic with joy over the victory of your strength in salvation. You have heard the prayer of my heart and given me the answer I desired. You have gone before me with blessings of goodness and life. You have acknowledged, confirmed, and validated my victory. I have survived this battle and can bask in the glory of the victory you have won for me. You have heaped your blessings upon me, and I rejoice with gladness in your presence. I have trusted and will continue to trust in your strength and mighty love. Because of your mercy and unfailing love, I will never be moved or shaken up. I know your enemies cannot stay hidden from you. You will discover them all. When you show up on the battlefield, they will all be burned up, swallowed up and consumed in the fire of your wrath. Your victory over them and any that follow them will be complete. Even though they make evil plans and devise wicked schemes, they will not succeed. When you lower your weapons and take aim at their faces, to reveal who and what they really are, they will turn and run in a panic. I will forever sing the praises of your might and strength, O Lord my savior.

WEEK SEVENTEEN   *INSIGHT and ENCOURAGEMENT*   **DAY 7**

The Prayer of Faith Answered

by Augustus Hermann Francke (1663-1727)

It being almost impossible to have a full insight into the means whereby this building, and the charity schools were begun and carried on, except there be some instances given of the wonderful providence of the Lord, whereby he hath remarkably finalized his care and assistance in advancing this affair. I will here set down a number of such providential occurrences as seemed most conspicuous to me.

Before Easter, 1696, I found the provision for the poor very low, and so far exhausted, that I did not know where to get anything toward defraying the charges of the ensuing week (which happened before I had been used to such awakening trials) but God was pleased to relieve our wants in a very seasonable hour, by an unexpected help; he inclined to the heart of a person (who it was, where residing, or of what sex, the Lord knoweth) to pay down one thousand crowns for the relief of the poor, and this sum was delivered to me when our provision was brought to the last crumb. The Lord reward the benefactor a thousand fold. At another time all provision was gone, when the steward declared there was a necessity of buying some cattle to furnish the table; and providing 20 or 30 bushels of flour to be laid up; besides other necessities, as wool, wood, etc. if we would manage our business to the best advantage: these necessities being offered up to God as the true Father of the fatherless ones, an opportunity was presented to discover our straits to a person who was then with us, and who, in all likelihood, would readily have supplied our wants to the utmost of his power; but I thought it more convenient to give God the glory, and not to stir from before his door, he being able to assist us in such a way as both his providence might be thereby rendered the more conspicuous and his name more cheerfully extolled; and another reason why I was more shy in adventuring upon this person, was because the same had already shown some tokens of his charitable inclinations towards our poor.

In the midst of these pressing circumstances I found one comfort, which was a presence of mind in prayer, joined with a confident dependence upon the Lord who heareth the very cry of the young ravens. When prayer was over, and I was just sitting down at the table, I heard a knocking at the door, which when I opened, there was an acquaintance of mine holding in his hand a letter and a parcel of money wrapped up, which he presented to me; I found therein fifty crowns, being sent a great way, and this gift was soon followed by twenty crowns more. This proved a reasonable relief, and a suitable supply, to our then low condition, and a proof that the Lord had heard even before we cried unto him, whereby his Name was not a little magnified.

The Prayer of Faith Answered, or An Encouragement to Live by Faith, In the Promises and Faithfulness of God. Plymouth Dock: Printed by J. Heydon. 1705. P. 18-19.

Record your insights, revelations, and meditations from this week. DATE:

_____

_____

_____

_____

_____

_____

_____

_____

_____

_____

_____

_____

_____

_____

_____

_____

WEEK EIGHTEEN   **Confession about being Puzzled over wickedness**   **DAY 1**

Read Psalm 10

I have to confess I am puzzled when it seems like You stand far off and hide Yourself when times of trouble come. Especially when we are troubles by evil men. They are all the same. They take advantage of the poor and helpless. They brag about everything and boast of all the things they are going to have someday. They act like total atheists. They don't give God a single thought. Some go so far as to claim you don't even exist. And yet, everything they do succeeds. Everything they touch seems to turn to gold. It's like they are a law unto themselves. Anyone who opposes them are blown away. They think they are invincible. All you hear from them is cursing and lies. The atrocities they commit against the helpless are unbelievable. They don't think they are accountable to anyone. But that is not true. You do see, and you will not forget the afflicted. When I am in this position and am helpless to do anything, I will commit myself to you. I know in Your time You will destroy the power of the wicked, because You are King forever. I believe You hear the prayers of the afflicted and will give them courage until their deliverance comes. And it will come, and we will praise You.

Be Still, My Soul

by Katharina A. von Schlegel (1697-1768)

Be still, my soul: the Lord is on thy side.
Bear patiently the cross of grief or pain.
Leave to thy God to order and provide;
In every change, He faithful will remain.
Be still, my soul: thy best, thy heav'nly Friend
Through thorny ways leads to a joyful end.

Be still, my soul: thy God doth undertake
To guide the future, as He has the past.
Thy hope, thy confidence let nothing shake;
All now mysterious shall be bright at last.
Be still, my soul: the waves and winds still know
His voice Who ruled them while He dwelt below.

Be still, my soul: when dearest friends depart,
And all is darkened in the vale of tears,
Then shalt thou better know His love, His heart,
Who comes to soothe thy sorrow and thy fears.
Be still, my soul: thy Jesus can repay
From His own fullness all He takes away.

Be still, my soul: the hour is hast'ning on
When we shall be forever with the Lord.
When disappointment, grief, and fear are gone,
Sorrow forgot, love's purest joys restored.
Be still, my soul: when change and tears are past
All safe and blessed we shall meet at last.

Be still, my soul: begin the song of praise
On earth, believing, to Thy Lord on high;
Acknowledge Him in all thy words and ways,
So shall He view thee with a well-pleased eye.
Be still, my soul: the Sun of life divine
Through passing clouds shall but more brightly shine.

MONTH FIVE

In 1996, I was working patrol on evening shift and was dispatched to a domestic disturbance call right at shift change. All the other officers were already at the station and the midnight shift had not come out yet, so I responded alone. The call information said a woman had been injured by her husband. The Fire Department and EMS were staged down the street from the house. By the time I arrived, the wife had left the house and was in the ambulance being treated for a broken arm. While I was speaking with her, the husband drove up, got out of his car, and aggressively approached the ambulance.

The only thing I could do was try to stop him from getting to her. He was a big man (I'm not small but he was stocky) and about my age. I ordered him to stop, but it was apparent he was not seeing or hearing me. I followed our guidelines and deployed pepper spray. That turned him away, but it did not stop him. I followed him, trying to get him to yield so I could arrest him. I tried baton strikes, but that just made him mad. He turned and rushed me. He pushed me into a large tree. The next thing I remember is him sitting on top of me punching me in the face. I covered up and turned my head to the left. I saw three pairs of fire boots and an axe head pass by. The next thing I knew, the man was laying on the ground beside me. The only ones there to offer help were the firefighters and they stopped my attacker with the flat end of a fire axe.

Help soon arrived and the situation was contained. I spent a few hours in the hospital and had some pretty impressive bruises. That was the only fight I lost in 33 years of police work. But it led to an interesting discussion with the Lord, one the clearest times in that season of my life that I heard His voice. He said, "Drop the charges and forgive him." It was unheard of for a police officer to do that after being assaulted. But that was clearly what God said, so that is what I did. That process led to a meeting with the chief, a meeting with the district attorney's office, an article in the association newsletter, and a number of heated discussions with people who thought I was doing the wrong thing. Finally, the assistant district attorney said if I wrote him a letter asking for the charge to be dropped, he would take into consideration.

Here is the text of that letter:
To Whom It May Concern:

As the victim in the above case, I will not be opposed to the prosecution seeking a probated or deferred sentence with a counseling stipulation. I feel that, although the offense committed against me was serious, it would serve no useful purpose in terms of the defendant's recovery and rehabilitation to seek a sentence that included incarceration and/or fine.

It is not my intent to minimize the nature of the defendant's actions nor to imply that any misgivings exist on my part regarding my actions on the night in question. My intent is to try and respond to the defendant's total situation with a measure of compassion and understanding. I realize that his attack on me was not personal and was driven by numerous other negative events that preceded it. I sincerely hope that my decision to request leniency on the defendant's behalf will be of some help to him during this difficult period.

I was convinced that God could take something meant for evil and turn it into good. God gave me a number of scriptural confirmations during this time which I have included below. I still have my journal entry from those days as well:

6/14   Wednesday: lunch with Pastor; assault occurs.

6/15-19   Recuperating; Lord directs to forgive and drop charges and gives scriptural basis; testify to Sunday School class; questioned by attorneys in class.

6/19   Monday: receive scriptural confirmation (Prov 19:11; Rom 8:17; Heb 12:4-15; Matt 5:23-26; Matt 18:32-35; James 5:20; Gen 50:20; Luke 6:27-36; 2 Cor 5:14-21; Col 1:24)

6/20   Tuesday: notify DA of desire to drop charges.

6/21   Wednesday: return to work.

6/22   Thursday: go by the house to try and talk with the wife, no one home. DA calls and says he wants to meet in person about the situation next Wed. Talked with Jeff, he thinks I'm crazy.

6/23   Friday: counsel with Dad; 1. speak to the man in person to explain. 2. get legal counsel for protection. 3. stay under authority, notify supervisors. heard from DA: the charge was reduced.

I did not understand the issue of absolute surrender then like I do now, but that is what I committed to do in this instance. It was unheard of, it was inconvenient for me, and many people disagreed with my decision. I finally had an opportunity to meet with the man outside the courtroom sometime later. He listened to what I had to say. I gave him a Bible and shared that the reason I dropped the charges was because if God had forgiven me, how could I not forgive him. We had a wonderful conversation and hugged as we left.

I only shared this story one other time, that I can recall. It was not long after when I was trying to open a ministry relationship with local black church. They were somewhat skeptical of my intentions because they knew I was a police officer. But when the pastor heard I was the one involved in this incident, a story he already knew from someone else, it opened doors for me to have a relationship with him that exists to this day.

A couple of years later, I ran into the man at the mall. He had not reconciled with his wife and he was dealing with the consequences of the assault. He was at the mall with his grown daughter. They shared with me that the incident had come at a crucial time in the daughter's life and my decision, which basically kept him out of prison, had been instrumental in her being able to finish college and get on with her life. He was now a faithful church member. I lost track of him years ago, but I was grateful to the Lord for letting me get a glimpse of what being surrendered to His word, no matter what, could do.

The Prayer of Faith (Part 1)

by George Müller (1805-1898)

What is meant by the prayer of faith? is a question which is beginning to arrest, in an unusual degree, the attention of Christians. What is the significance of the passages both in the New Testament and the Old which refer to it? What is the limit within which they may be safely received as a ground of practical reliance? Were these promises limited to prophetical or apostolical times; or have they been left as a legacy to all believers until the end shall come?

Do not men believe that God means what he appears plainly to have asserted? or, if we believe that he means it, do we fear the charge of fanaticism if we openly avow that we take him at his word? The thoughtful Christian, when in his daily reading of the Scriptures he meets with any of those wonderful promises made to believing prayer, often pauses to ask himself, What can these words mean? Can it be that God has made such promises as these to me, and to such men as I am? Have I really permission to commit all my little affairs to a God of infinite wisdom, believing that he will take charge of them and direct them according to the promptings of boundless love and absolute omniscience? Is prayer really a power with God, or is it merely an expedient by which our own piety may be cultivated? Is it not merely a power (that is, a stated antecedent accompanied by the idea of causation), but is it a transcendent power, accomplishing what no other power can, over-ruling all other agencies, and rendering them subservient to its own wonderful efficiency? We ask them, but we do not often wait for an answer.

These promises seem to us to be addressed either to a past or to a coming age, but not to us, at the present day. Yet with such views as these the devout soul is not at all satisfied. If an invaluable treasure is here reserved for the believer, he asks, why should I not receive my portion of it? He cannot doubt that God has in a remarkable manner, at various times, answered his prayers; why should he not always answer them? and why should not the believer always draw near to God in full confidence that he will do as he has said? He may remember that the prayer which has been manifestly answered was the offspring of deep humility, of conscious unworthiness, of utter self-negation, and of simple and earnest reliance on the promises of God through the mediation of Christ. Why should not his prayers be always of the same character? With the apostles of old he pours out his soul in the petition, "Lord, increase our faith."

And yet it can scarcely be denied that the will of God has been distinctly revealed on this subject. The promises made to believing prayer are explicit, numerous, and diversified. If we take them in their simple and literal meaning, or if in fact we give to them any reasonable interpretation whatever, they seem to be easily understood. Our difficulty seems to be this: the promise is so "exceeding great" that we cannot conceive God really to mean what he clearly appears to have revealed. The blessing seems too vast for our comprehension; we "stagger at the promises, through unbelief," and thus fail to secure the treasure which was purchased for us by Christ Jesus.

Excerpted from the Introduction to *The Autobiography of George Müller*. Dallas: Gideon House Books, 2017.

WEEK EIGHTEEN   **Confession about Overcoming Depression**   **DAY 4**

Read Psalm 42-43

I am so thirsty for the presence and voice of the Lord. When will I hear your voice again? I'm sad all the time. People are questioning, where is God in this situation? I am reminding myself of the good times when I joyfully worshipped in Your presence. I will keep saying to myself, "Why are you feeling depressed and confused? Put your faith in God! He is your salvation." When I get depressed, I will remember you in this desolate place. When I'm overcome with despair, I will call to you from the depths of my soul. Your commandment to love and pray remains even though it feels like you have forgotten me, and I grieve over the oppressions of my enemies. These wounds constantly bring up the question, "Where is your God now?" But I will continue to say to myself, "Why are you feeling dejected and disturbed? Put your trust in God! He is your salvation." Vindicate me and deliver me from ruthless, deceitful people. You are my safe place even when I am sad and confused. Reveal the truth. Speak into my situation. Lead me back into your presence. I will joyfully surrender to you and worship you with a sacrifice of praise. I will keep on encouraging myself, "You do not have to feel downtrodden and troubled. Your faith and hope are in God. He is your God and your salvation."

WEEK EIGHTEEN   *INSIGHT and ENCOURAGEMENT*   **DAY 5**

The Prayer of Faith (Part 2)

by George Müller (1805-1898)

The conditions on which prayer will be heard are in various places specified, but particularly in John xv. 7: "If ye abide in me and my words abide in you, ye shall ask what ye will, and it shall be done unto you." That is, if I understand the passage, prevalence in prayer is conditioned by the conformity of our souls to the will of God; "if ye abide in me and my words abide in you." On this condition, and on this only, may we ask what we will, with the assurance that it will be done unto us. Faith, in its most simple meaning, is that temper of the mind in the creature which responds to every revealed perfection of the Creator. Just according to the degree in which this correspondence exists, is the promise made that we shall have whatsoever we ask. It is evident, from the eleventh of Hebrews, that the views of the (author) concerning faith were entirely in harmony with the passages recited above. He reviews the lives of the most eminent saints, for the express purpose of showing that the impressive events in their history, whether physical or moral, were controlled entirely by faith. He sums up the whole in Hebrews 11:32-35. We are, I think, taught by this passage that the (author) believed faith to be a power capable of transcending and modifying every other agency, by which changes became possible which to every other known power were impossible. We see that in this catalogue of the victories of faith he includes the subjection of almost every form of what we call natural laws. The whole passage seems an illustration of the meaning of our Lord, when he says, "If ye have faith as a grain of mustard seed, ye shall say to this sycamine tree, Be thou removed and planted in the midst of the sea, and it shall obey you." It seems then apparent that the doctrine of the peculiar and wonderful power of the prayer of faith is as clearly revealed in the Scriptures as any other doctrine. It would seem evident, at any rate, from the passages just quoted, that the (author) understood the teachings of our Savior to mean what they say. From the general tenor of the Scriptures I think we may learn two important truths: First, that there is a certain state of mind in a devout soul to which God has promised all that it asks, subject, however, as to the manner of the answer, to the dictates of his infinite wisdom and goodness; and, second, that in granting such petitions he does not always limit his action within the ordinary or acknowledged laws of matter or of mind. I do not perceive how we can interpret the passages above cited, as well as many others, without giving them a meaning at least as extensive as this. Why should we limit either the goodness or the power of God by our own knowledge of what we call the laws of nature? Why should we deny that there is a power in prayer to which we have not commonly attained? We interpret the gracious promises of our most loving Father in heaven by the rule of our own imperfect and unbelieving piety. We ask for light from without, while the light can only come from a more elevated piety within. We ask for examples of the effects of faith at the present day, corresponding to those spoken of in the sacred Scriptures. Thoughtful men acknowledge that there must be a meaning in these promises, which they have not yet understood, and they see plainly that the kingdom of God can never come with power until this prevalence in prayer shall have become a matter of universal attainment; and yet they dare hardly believe that God is as good as he has revealed himself to be.

Excerpted from the Introduction to *The Autobiography of George Müller*. Dallas: Gideon House Books, 2017.

WEEK EIGHTEEN   *HYMNS and POEMS*   **DAY 6**

The Quaker of the Olden Time!

by John Greenleaf Whittier (1807-1892)

THE Quaker of the olden time!
How calm and firm and true,
Unspotted by its wrong and crime,
He walked the dark earth through.
The lust of power, the love of gain,
The thousand lures of sin
Around him, had no power to stain
The purity within.
With that deep insight which detects
All great things in the small,

And knows how each man's life affects
The spiritual life of all,
He walked by faith and not by sight,
By love and not by law;
The presence of the wrong or right
He rather felt than saw.
He felt that wrong with wrong partakes,
That nothing stands alone,
That whoso gives the motive, makes
His brother's sin his own.

And, pausing not for doubtful choice
Of evils great or small,
He listened to that inward voice
Which called away from all.
O Spirit of that early day,
So pure and strong and true,

Be with us in the narrow way
Our faithful fathers knew.
Give strength the evil to forsake,
The cross of Truth to bear,
And love and reverent fear to make
Our daily lives a prayer!

[Despite some peculiarities, there were a number of smaller religious groups in our history that sought after a deeper experience of the spiritual life. The Quakers, Mennonites, and Moravians are in this group, just to name a few. Baron von Zinzendorf is referenced herein as an example.

Living the surrendered life will result in rejecting certain means and associations with the world as you bring your life more into line with Kingdom living, as the Holy Spirit directs, but it will not require total abstinence from all modern comforts, a monastic bunker mentality, or an overly ascetic lifestyle. These outward expressions of devotion cannot accomplish the needed inward reform. Inward reform worked by the Spirit in response to our surrender of self to the Lord will perfect devotion with an outward result. We don't spend hours worshipping and praying because we have to, to be accepted by God. We do that because we want to, in humble gratitude for His accepting our surrender and working His reform in our spirits.

Find a saintly old elder in your church or in your city and spend time with them. Let them speak into your heart from their experience and walk with the Lord. Listen as the Holy Spirit anoints that conversation with His presence and power and speaks truth to the point of your need to recognize and accomplish the next right thing to do.]

https://www.poemhunter.com/poem/the-quaker-of-the-olden-time/

WEEK EIGHTEEN   *INSIGHT and ENCOURAGEMENT*   **DAY 7**

Feeding Our Faith

by George D. Watson (1848-1923)

Inasmuch as faith is the condition of all the spiritual life, of the entrance into that life, and the steps to progress in that life, it behooves us to give it all the nourishment possible. Faith can be strengthened, and fed, and thus will grow; but the growth of faith is often very opposite to our notions concerning it. We often suppose that faith is made strong by receiving great encouragement, by having quick and abundant answers to prayer, by high stakes of joy, by lofty visions of divine things; but in reality these things do not strengthen our faith as much as we fancy. Our faith is to be nourished on the promises of God. Those promises are contained in his written word. They may be also promises communicated to the soul by the

Holy Spirit, or through other souls who are in close fellowship with God, and who may speak to us great promises of what God has told them concerning us. When God first called Abraham, he inundated his soul with a sea of promises; he spoke to him from the starry heavens, and from the soil of Canaan on which he walked, and by the visits of angels, and by the Holy Ghost in the deep of his nature. Abraham saw great fields of light – great possibilities of things for himself and his posterity. His soul drank in these promises, until his faith became wide and powerful, even before any of them were fulfilled. God deals with souls in a similar way; yet when he and calls anyone to great degrees of perfection or of usefulness, he begins by opening up to them the promises of his Word, and the possibilities which they may achieve, even before there are any outward symptoms of their fulfillment. The heart that anchors itself in the promises of God, until those promises become as real as God himself, will have strong faith.

Another nourishment of faith is the removing from the soul of natural and human props. Naturally we lean on a great many things in nature, and society, and the church, and friends, more than we are aware of. We think we depend on God alone, and never dream of how much we depend on other things, until they are taken from us, and if they are not removed, we should go along, self-deceived, thinking that we relied on God for all things. But God desires to concentrate our faith in him alone by removing all other foundations, and, one step after another, detaching us from all other supports. There are many souls which cannot endure this utter desolation of secondary supports, which would be more than they could bear, and they would react in open rebellion; so God allows them to have a junior faith, and to lean on other things more or less. But to those who are able to undergo the strain of faith, he allows all sorts of disappointments – the death of bright hopes, the removing of friendships or property, multiplied infirmities, misunderstanding, to compel the soul to house itself in God alone.

At the time the soul is having all secondary support removed, it does not perceive what is taking place within itself, but afterwards it finds that faith has been growing and expanding with every way that is beat against it. Faith grows when we least expect it; storms and difficulties, temptations and conflicts, are its field of operation; like the stormy petrel (*a long-winged bird that flies far from land*) upon the ocean, faith has a supernatural glee in the howling of the storm and the dash of the spray.

Faith not only is nourished by the removal of earthly props, but by the seeming removal of divine consolation. Our answer to prayer seem to long delayed, and faith is tested to its uttermost, when it seems as if the Lord has turned against us and all we can do is to continue holding on, with a pitiful cry of "Lord, help me!" Even then faith is expanding and growing beyond all we are aware of, by the very extension of the answer. The longer the Lord delayed in answering the prayer of the woman of Syrophenicia, the more her faith became purified and intense. Long delays serve to purify our faith, till everything that is spasmodic and ephemeral and whimsical is purged out of it, and nothing is left to it except faith alone.

Another nourishment of faith is to get before the mind that great faith of other people – to read the lives of those who have been sorely tried, and who have believed God against all odds. Faith kindles faith; by understanding how God has dealt with other souls enables us to interpret his dealings with us. Our faith is inspired by reading the trials of the Bible saints more than by reading the pleasant and easy things.

Another nourishment of faith is that mode of dealing with us by which the Lord is constantly changing the providential channels through which he sends blessings to us. If God's blessings flow on us in a certain way, for any length of time, we unconsciously fix our trust on the way the benefactions come, more than on the visible fountain. If the Lord gave the Jews water in the wilderness, sometimes it was from the rock, and sometimes it was from a well dug in the dry sand. (Num 21:16-18) When God sends us great spiritual refreshings, he will change the circumstances under which they come; when he sends temporal blessings in answer to prayer, he will change the channels through which they flow. He does not want us to become attached to any mode or phenomenon. He wants our faith perfectly united to himself, and not to *his mode of doing things*, and hence he will disappoint us on the old lines of expectation and reveal his favors from a new quarter, in a new way, and surprise us with some great and sweet device of his infinite wisdom. And as our faith is strengthened by disappointment, until it reaches such perfect union with God that it never looks to anybody, or anything, or any mode, or any old channel, or any circumstances, or any frame of mind, or any meeting, or any set of feelings, or at any time or season; but keeps itself swung free from all these things, and dependent on God alone. This degree of faith can never be disappointed, can never be jostled, because it expects nothing except what God wills, and looks to no mode except infinite wisdom. Its expectation is from God only.

Excerpted from *Soul Food, Being Chapters on the Interior Life*. Cincinnati, OH: M. W. Knapp, 1896. p. 11-14.

Record your insights, revelations, and meditations from this week. DATE:

_____

_____

_____

_____

_____

_____

_____

_____

_____

_____

_____

_____

_____

_____

_____

WEEK NINETEEN   *INSIGHT and ENCOURAGEMENT*   **DAY 1**

I Surrender

by Ronnie Floyd (1955-present)

I have just completed my final Easter experience with my Cross Church Family. This past weekend was very difficult for me personally. After thirty-three consecutive Easters with the same church family, Easter weekend will never be the same for me. When I preach my final Sunday here on May 19, I will enter into my new calling formally and wholly.

One morning a few weeks ago in the midst of immense personal struggle, God used a song in my life. The reason this song has so resonated with me again and again is because its words represent what God has already done in my heart in calling me. There was no plan to hear it, nor was it a song someone suggested I listen to.

One morning while my wife was playing a series of tunes by the Brooklyn Tabernacle Choir, this song came on. I had never heard it before, even though it has been around for a number of years. The song is called, "I Surrender."

Doing God's will is not easy; in fact, sometimes it is very difficult. The moment you rise up to submit to God and surrender your life to His will, you face reason upon reason not to do it. But while tempted to walk away and choose the road of personal comfort, sameness, and familiarity where risks are minimal and the future seems secure, God calls you again to surrender to Him. Yes, "Here am I Lord, send me."

Speaking of this song, *"I Surrender,"* perhaps the words of the first verse and chorus will minister to you as they have to me and still do today:

I know Lord Your plan for me is right   *I surrender I surrender*
I need You to fulfill   *Lord I surrender my life*
Your purpose in my life   *Give it all to You*
I submit to You my King   *I surrender I surrender*
Be my everything   *Lord I surrender my life*
I'm coming to You again   *Give it all to You*
Lord here I am

Until we surrender to Jesus fully, we will have little to no prospect of a revival in our hearts, limited to no stirring of the Spirit in our churches, and little to no spiritual awakening in our land. True revival is nothing less and nothing more than the manifest presence of God in our lives.

A surrendered Christian, a surrendered pastor, and a surrendered church will experience spiritual revival.

God does not will that our life and leadership are spiritually powerless, lukewarm, ineffective, and purposeless. He does will this for you and me:

1.   Give 100% of yourself to Jesus daily.
I often pray these words regularly and more often now, daily: *"Lord, I give 100% of me to 100% of You so that 100% of You will work through 100% of me."*

Spiritual power is not found in holding on to what you have; spiritual power is discovered and released when you release yourself to God. We will never choose to let God have His way with us if we continue to hang on to our own desires, our own dreams, and our own bondage. Just go ahead and pray it now, "Lord, I surrender."

2.   Trust God really knows what is best for you.

Surrendering to God is abandoning all that we have in order to receive all that God possesses and has for our future. When we enter God's gateway to supernatural power for living, we begin to learn what a surrendered life looks like. Right now in my life, I am trusting God really knows what is best for us. It is *not* easy; if fact, it is very *difficult.*

Back to the song again… I don't know how many times I have listened to it. In fact, Jeana remarks at times, "You have played the song several times today, are you okay?" I reply, "Yes, I just need to be reminded again and again what I have done in prayer already."

So, I guess I feel as if I am the one singing this second verse of its lyrics:

> *Humble and broken I come to You*
> *I'm trusting and waiting*
> *To see what You will do*
> *Lord You know what's best*
> *And at Your feet I find my rest*
> *I'm coming to You again*
> *Lord here I am*

Again and again, and yes, even again, I go to God and surrender. He does know what is best for me and that is why I keep coming to Him. I believe this is God's will for my life and ministry. Do you believe this regardless of your vocation? I hope so. Join me now: *"Lord, I surrender my life to you."*

https://blog.ronniefloyd.com/13775/pastors/i-surrender/

WEEK NINETEEN   *HYMNS and POEMS*   **DAY 2**

Lord Jesus Christ, My Life, My Light

by Martin Behm (1557-1622)

Lord Jesus Christ, my Life, my Light,
My Strength by day, my Trust by night,

On earth I'm but a passing guest
And sorely by my sins oppressed.

Tim Tremaine

Far off I see my fatherland,
Where through Thy blood I hope to stand.
But ere I reach that Paradise
A weary way before me lies.

My heart sinks at the journey's length,
My wasted flesh has little strength;
My soul alone still cries in me;
"Lord, fetch me home, take me to Thee!"

Oh let Thy suff'rings give me pow'r
To meet the last and darkest hour!
Thy blood refresh and comfort me;
Thy bonds and fetters make me free.

The blows and stripes that fell on Thee
Heal up the wounds of sin in me;
Thy crown of thorns, Thy foes' mad spite,
Let be my glory and delight.

That thirst and bitter draught of Thine
Cause me to bear with patience mine;
Thy piercing cry uphold my soul
When floods of anguish o'er me roll!

Thy Spirit cry within me still
When here my lips grow white and chill,
And help my soul Thy heav'n to find
When these poor eyes grow dark and blind!

Thy dying words let be my light
When death approaches as dark night;
Defend me in my dying breath
When then I bow my head in death.

Thy cross let be my staff in life,
Thy holy grave my rest from strife;
The winding sheet that covered Thee,
O let it be a shroud for me.

Lord, in Thy nail prints let me read
That Thou to save me hast decreed
And grant that in Thine opened side
My troubled soul may ever hide.

Since Thou hast died, the Pure, the Just,
I take my homeward way in trust.
The gates of heav'n, Lord, open wide
When here I may no more abide.

And when the last Great Day shall come
And Thou, our Judge, shalt speak the doom,
Let me with joy behold the light
And set me then upon Thy right.

Renew this wasted flesh of mine
That like the sun it there may shine
Among the angels pure and bright,
Yea, like Thyself in glorious light.

Ah, then shall I most joyful be
And with the angels sing to Thee
And with Thy blessed, chosen fold
Fore'er Thy gracious face behold.

https://hymnary.org/text/lord_jesus_christ_my_life_my_light

148

WEEK NINETEEN   **Confession about the "bigness" of God**   **DAY 3**

Read Isaiah 40

I confess and believe there is nothing and no one who can be compared to you, my God. How big is my God? You could hold the contents of all the oceans in the palm of your hand. The vast expanse of the heavens is as long as your hand is wide. You could lift the weight of all the mountains together. No one had to teach you, or instruct you, or enlighten you, or counsel you. All knowledge and understanding are yours. The power of all the nations combined is like a drop in the bucket or a piece of lint on the floor compared to you. There is nothing I could find, or make, or commission to be made, that has any value or worth compared to you. Your throne is in the heavens. I am like an insect compared to you. People who think they are important and powerful will dry up like a blade of grass in the heat and blow away like a piece of straw in the wind. I look to the stars in heaven. You made each one and gave it a name. Because of your great power, everyone is in its place and none of them are missing. How foolish of me to think you don't know my circumstances or have forgotten about me. You are the everlasting Creator who never tires and never grows weary. Your understanding is beyond comprehension. When I am weary, you give me strength. When I am weak, you give me power. Everyone who puts their hope in you will have their strength renewed. My soul will soar like an eagle on the wind. My God will give me strength to keep going, no matter what.

WEEK NINETEEN   *INSIGHT and ENCOURAGEMENT*   **DAY 4**

The Only Path to Blessing

by Andrew Murray (1828-1917)

There is a danger in our evangelical religion of looking too much at what it offers from one side, as a certain experience to be obtained in prayer and faith. There is another side which God's word puts very strongly, that of obedience as the only path to blessing. What we need is to realize that in our relationship to the infinite being whom we call God who has created and redeemed us, the first sentiment that ought to animate us is that of subjection: the surrender to His supremacy, His glory, His will, His pleasure, ought to be the first and uppermost thought of our life. The question is not, how are we to obtain and enjoy His favor, for in this the main thing may still be self. But what this Being in the very nature of things rightly claims, and is infinitely and unspeakably worthy of, is that His glory and pleasure should be my one object. Surrender to His perfect and blessed will, a life of service and obedience, is the beauty and the charm of heaven. Service and obedience, these were the thoughts that were uppermost in the mind of the Son, when He dwelt upon earth. Service and obedience, these must become with us the chief objects of desire and aim, more so than rest or light, or joy or strength: in them we shall find the path to all the higher blessedness that awaits us.

Just know what a prominent place the Master gives it, not only in this 15th chapter (of John), in connection with the abiding, but in the 14th, where He speaks of the indwelling of the Three – One God. In verse 15 we have it: "*If you* love me, *keep my commandments*, and the Spirit will be given you of the Father." Then verse 21: "He that hath *my commandments and keepeth them*, he it is that loveth me;" and he shall have the special love of my Father resting on him, and the special manifestation of myself. And then again, verse 23, one of the highest of all the exceeding great and precious promises: "If a man love me *he will keep my words*, and the Father and I will come and take up our abode with him." Could words put it more clearly that obedience is the way to the indwelling of the Spirit, to His revealing the Son within us, and to His again preparing us to be the abode, the home of the Father? The indwelling of the Three – One God is the heritage of them that obey. Obedience and faith are but two aspects of one act – surrender to God and His will. As faith strengthens for obedience, it is in turn strengthened by it: faith is made perfect by works. It is to be feared that often our efforts to believe have been unavailing because we have not taken up the only position in which a large faith is legitimate or possible – that of entire surrender to the honor and the will of God. It is the man who is entirely consecrated to God and His will who will find the power come to claim everything that his God has promised to be for him. (Emphasis his.)

With Christ in the School of Prayer. Old Tappan, NJ: Fleming H. Revell, Co., 1953. p. 128-130.

WEEK NINETEEN　　　　　**Confession in Despair**　　　　　**DAY 5**

Read Psalm 13

Lord, I have to confess sometimes it feels like you have forgotten me. I look for you everywhere but can't seem to find you. I'm constantly having to wrestle with my thoughts because the enemy seems to have the upper hand. I'm heartbroken because I cannot get the victory over this situation. How long, Lord? How long? I need to hear from you. Let me know you see my troubles and show me the truth about this situation. If I don't get help from you, I'm not going to make it. Without your help, the enemy will claim victory over me. Without your help, I won't be able to stand against this oppression. Nevertheless, I know you love me, and I will continue to believe in your unfailing love, even though I can't see it right now. I know you are my Savior, and I will be happy and rejoice in your salvation even though I don't know how you're going to bring it about. And most of all, I will continue to worship you. You are my God and you are worthy of all praise and glory. You have been good to me in the past and will be good to me again. I will rejoice in your coming goodness.

The Perfection of Consecration

by George D. Watson (1845-1923)

All believers are, in a measure, consecrated to God, just as all believers are, in a measure, sanctified. The spirit of consecration is a part of the new life imparted to the soul in regeneration; but in order to receive the full baptism of the Spirit, the principle of consecration must be carried to completeness. Just as long as consecration is defective on any point, or in any degree, the experience of complete cleansing and filling cannot be received. The fullness of salvation is conditioned on perfect trust in Jesus as a present Savior, and on the other hand this perfect truth is conditioned on the perfect yielding of self up to God. Hence, if there is any defect or shortage in consecration, it almost surely blocks the way to the entrance into full salvation. Every believer is consecrated, but not all in equal degrees. Some converted people, who were not fully sanctified, are much more yielding to God than others are, and have only a few more steps to take in order to reach the state of entire abandonment, whereas others are so slightly yielded, as to be a long way from it. Again, all believers are not equally yielded on the same points. Some will more readily yield on certain points than others. There are always one or two points which are the last to be yielded, and upon which the self life has a death struggle; but these points of death struggle are very different with different souls.

The three great lines of consecration are, to be anything the Lord wants us to *be*; to do anything the Lord wants us to *do*; to suffer anything the Lord wants us to *suffer*. These embrace the subjective, the active and the passive forms of our existence, and to consent to all these three things, willingly, without a reservation, is the perfection of consecration. As each soul passes through these three things, there will come up a panorama of possibilities and contingencies according to each one's condition, nature, work environment, upon which the principle of loyalty will be tested. Some will find their complete yielding the hardest on the willing to *be*, others, on the willing to *do*, and others, on the willing to *suffer*. Unless consecration reaches the point of entirety, the soul will slip back and be consecrated itself over and over again a thousand times, without gaining a distinct step of victory, or making any positive progress. We are a great deal about reconsecrating ourselves, and making a fresh consecration, which is mere delusive talk, and does not get the soul where positive results are brought to pass. When the soul is perfectly yielded to God on every point, and for all time and eternity as well, it can drive a stake down, and hold its position. It has then got to the end of making good resolutions, it is then done with going over the same ground of giving up, it has reached the place of anchorage, it can then truly say,

> "'Tis done, the great transaction's done,
> I am the Lord's, and He is mine."

The Secret of Spiritual Power. Boston: The McDonald & Gill Co., 1894. p. 65-67.

Tim Tremaine

Crucified with Christ My Savior

by A. B. Simpson (1843-1919)

Crucified with Christ my Savior,
To the world and self and sin;
To the death-born life of Jesus
I am sweetly ent'ring in:
In His fellowship of suff'ring,
To His death conformed to be,
I am going with my Savior
All the way to Calvary.

Refrain:
All the way to Calvary,
Where my Savior went for me,
Help me, Lord, to go with Thee,
All the way to Calvary.

'Tis not hard to die with Jesus
When His risen life we know;
'Tis not hard to share His suff'rings
When our hearts with joy o'erflow;
In His resurrection power
He has come to dwell in me,
And my heart is gladly going
All the way to Calvary.

If we die we'll live with Jesus,
If we suffer we shall reign;
Only thus the prize of glory
Can the conqueror attain;
Oh, how sweet, on that glad morning
Should the Master say to thee,
"Yes, My child, thou didst go with Me
All the way to Calvary."

https://library.timelesstruths.org/music/Crucified_with_Christ_My_Savior/

Record your insights, revelations, and meditations from this week. DATE:

_____

_____

_____

_____

_____

_____

_____

_____

_____

_____

_____

_____

_____

_____

_____

O Love That Will Not Let Me Go

by George Matheson (1842-1906)

O Love that wilt not let me go,
I rest my weary soul in thee;
I give thee back the life I owe,
that in thine ocean depths its flow
may richer, fuller be.

O Light that follow'st all my way,
I yield my flick'ring torch to thee;
my heart restores its borrowed ray,
that in thy sunshine's blaze its day
may brighter, fairer be.

O Joy that seekest me through pain,
I cannot close my heart to thee;
I trace the rainbow thro' the rain,
and feel the promise is not vain
that morn shall tearless be.

O Cross that liftest up my head,
I dare not ask to fly from thee;
I lay in dust life's glory dead,
and from the ground there blossoms red,
life that shall endless be.

https://hymnary.org/text/o_love_that_wilt_not_let_me_go

Keeping the Commandments

by Alexander MacLaren (1826-1910)

'Circumcision is nothing and uncircumcision is nothing, but keeping the commandments of God is what matters.' I Corinthians 7:19

In our text from the Epistle to the Corinthians we read, 'Circumcision is nothing, and uncircumcision is nothing, but the keeping of the commandments of God.' If we finished the sentence it would be, 'but the keeping of the commandments of God is everything.'

And by that 'keeping the commandments,' of course, the Apostle does not mean merely external obedience. He means something far deeper than that, which I put into this plain word, that the one essential of the Christian life is the conformity of the will with God's – not the external obedience merely, but the entire surrender and the submission of my will to the will of my Father in Heaven. That is the all-important thing; that is what God wants; that is the end of all rites and ceremonies; that is the end of all revelation and of all utterances of the divine heart. The Bible, Christ's mission, his passion and death, the gift of His Divine Spirit, and every part of the divine dealings in providence, all converge upon this one aim and goal.

For this purpose the Father worketh hitherto, and Christ works, that man's will may yield and bow itself wholly and happily and lovingly to the great infinite will of the Father in Heaven.

That is the perfection of a man's nature, when his will fits on to God's like one of Euclid's triangles superimposed upon another, and line for line coincides. When his will allows a free passage to the will of God, without resistance or deflection, as light travels through transparent glass; when his will responds to the touch of God's finger upon the keys, like the telegraphic needle to the operator's hand, then a man has obtained all that God and religion can do for him, all that his nature is capable of; and far beneath his feet may be the ladders of ceremonies and forms and outward acts, by which he climbed to that serene and blessed height, 'Circumcision is nothing, and uncircumcision is nothing, but the keeping of God's commandments is everything.'

That submission of the will is the sum and the test of your Christianity. Your Christianity does not consist only in a mere something which you call faith in Jesus Christ. It does not consist in emotions, however deep and blessed and genuine they may be. It does not consist in the acceptance of the creed. All of these are means to an end. They are meant to drive the wheel of life, to build up character, to make your deepest wish to be, 'Father! not my will, but Thine, be done.' In the measure in which that is your heart's desire, and not one hair's-breadth further, you have a right to call yourself a Christian.

Excerpted from, *Expositions of Holy Scripture. Vol. 13*. Grace-eBooks.com., (unk). p. 430-432.

WEEK TWENTY   *INSIGHT and ENCOURAGEMENT*   **DAY 3**

Finding God is Good

by Dr. Larry Crabb, Jr. (1944-)

Maintaining our faith in God's goodness in these times is not easy. Like Job, we will cry out in fear and despair. No one would conclude that God is good by studying life. The evidence powerfully suggests otherwise. Belief in the goodness of God and the worship that naturally flows from this confidence depends on the revealing work of the Holy Spirit. When He ushers us into the presence of ultimate goodness, when our darkest tragedy is pierced by one glimpse of invisible glory, then faith is born. And the faith given by God's Spirit makes self-concern laughably unnecessary. We know we're in good hands no matter what comes. And our manner of living reflects our knowledge. We relax and get on with the purpose of life on this earth -worshiping God and advancing His kingdom.

Every Christian has a relationship with Christ as savior, God as father, and the Holy Spirit as indwelling comforter and guide. With full right, each of us can therefore say, "I have found God" or better, "God has found me." But in a far richer sense, every Christian must also say, "I am still looking for Him." Even

Paul longed to know more of Christ, for he was aware that he had not yet apprehended all there was to know about Him (Phil 3:12-14).

The search for God will lead us through struggles, setbacks, and confusion. Confidence in a God who doesn't always make clear what He's doing at any given moment doesn't come easily. It's hard to believe that God fully takes into account our strong desire to be happy. This natural inclination is what's fundamentally wrong with us. If left to our own way of thinking, every one of us would conclude that God either is bad or doesn't exist, that no God in this universe is good enough to be trusted with the things that matter most. We may ask him to bless our food, but we won't continue to trust him when a loved one betrays us.

This doubt has been passed on like a virus to every human being – except One. And that Person, having lived a life of absolute confidence in the Father, gave us reason to replace our doubt with faith. Jesus Christ has made his Father known and delights in continuing to do so. We find God through Christ. There is no other way. The only way through our problems is to know Christ better and thereby to find God. Remember the principle: you know you're finding God when you believe that God is good no matter what happens. Finding God means to face all of life, with a spirit of trust. We have a higher calling than finding joy in good things and working through bad things: we must reflect confidence in God in all our relationships and activities, in all our joys and sorrows.

Excerpted from *Finding God*. New York: Walker and Company, 1994. p. 100-102.

WEEK TWENTY   **Confession in Defeat**   **DAY 4**

Read Psalm 56

O God have mercy. Lord, have mercy and be gracious to me. I feel like I have been chased for miles and run over by a truck. It seems in life; I have been in one 15-round heavyweight fight after another and I have lost them all. The other guy is laughing and mocking me the whole time. It's a scary thing to go through. But when I am afraid, I will put my trust in you. I have acknowledged your word as the truth and based on that truth, I have believed and trusted in you, God. Therefore, I will continue to trust according to your word. I will confess and declare that I will not be afraid. What can men really do to me? They can twist and distort my words, the can scheme and conspire evil against me, they can wait in the shadows to attack me when I stumble. But they cannot escape your anger. You have seen everything I have endured. You will come when I call, and my enemies will retreat and flee because I know God is for me. I will continually praise your word. I have put my trust in you. What can they really do to me? I will continue to obey your word. I will continually thank you for delivering me and keeping me from falling. I will walk before my God in the light of life. I have put my trust in you. I will not be afraid.

WEEK TWENTY *INSIGHT and ENCOURAGEMENT* **DAY 5**

A Bond-Slave of Jesus

by Oswald Chambers (1874-1917)

"I am crucified with Christ; nevertheless I live; yet not I, but Christ liveth if in me."
Galatians 2:20

These words mean the breaking of my independence with my own hand and surrendering to the supremacy of the Lord Jesus. No one can do this for me, I must do it myself. God may bring me up to the point 365 times a year, but He cannot put me through it. It means breaking the husk of by individual independence of God, and the emancipating of my personality into oneness with Himself, not for my own ideas, but for absolute loyalty to Jesus. There is no possibility of dispute when once I am there. Very few of us know anything about loyalty to Christ – *"For My Sake."* It is that which makes the iron saint.

Has that break come? All the rest is pious fraud. The one point to decide is – Will I give up, will I surrender to Jesus Christ, and make no conditions whatever as to how the break comes? I must be broken from my self-realization, and immediately that point is reached, the reality of the supernatural identification takes place at once, and the witness of the Spirit of God is unmistakable – "I have been crucified with Christ."

The passion of Christianity is that I deliberately sign away my own rights and become a bond-slave of Jesus Christ. Until I do that, I do not begin to be a saint.

[If you do a word search on "bond slave," it says this is a person who is a slave and subject to his master's authority, but not because they were made a slave. They are in servitude by indenture. They voluntarily enter into a lifetime of service. We are not slaves because of military conquest. We are bond slaves because we were conquered by God's love.]

My Utmost For His Highest. Barbour and Company, Inc., Westwood, NJ.; 1963. p. 228-229.

WEEK TWENTY *HYMNS and POEMS* **DAY 6**

Origin of a Hymn, by "Quite a Young Girl"

by Frances Ridley Havergal (1836-1879)

My Dear Unknown Friend in Jesus –

Mrs. S. asked me to write and answer myself your question about the hymn, "I Give My Life for Thee." Yes, it is mine, and perhaps it may interest you to hear how nearly it went into the fire, instead of nearly all over the world.

It was, I think, the very first thing I ever wrote which could be called by hymn, written when I was quite a young girl (1859). I did not half realize what I was writing about. I was following very far off, always doubting and fearing. I think I had come to Jesus with a trembling, hem-touching faith, but it was a coming in the press, and behind, never seeing His face, or feeling sure that He loved me, though I was clear that I could not do without Him, and wanted to serve and follow Him.

I don't know how I came to write it. I scribbled it in pencil on the back of a circular, in a few minutes, and then read it over and thought, "Well, this is not poetry, anyhow! I won't go to the trouble to copy *this*." So I reached out my hand to put it into the fire! A sudden impulse made me draw it back; I put it, crumbled and singed, into my pocket. Soon after I went out to see a dear old woman in an alms house. She began talking to me, as she always did, about her dear Savior, and I thought I would see if she, a simple old woman, would care for these verses, which I felt sure nobody else would ever care to read. So I read them to her, and she was so delighted with them that, when I went back, I copied them out, and kept them, and now the Master has sent them out in all directions. I have seen tears while they have been sung at mission services and have heard of them being really blessed to many.

Long, Edwin McKean, *Illustrated History of Hymns and Their Authors*, Philadelphia: P. W. Ziegler, 1876. p. 200-201.

WEEK TWENTY   **Confession of Praise**   **DAY 7**

Read Psalm 21

I am rejoicing in your amazing strength and the great victories you are bringing into my life. You are giving me the desire of my heart. You are answering prayers and continually pouring out Your rich blessings on my life. I asked You to preserve, protect, and extend my life and You are granting that request. I am experiencing new levels of glory because of the victories You are bringing into my life. The blessings are of an eternal quality and will last forever. I am filled with joy because I have been in Your presence. I trust You, Lord, and in Your unfailing love. I will not be moved from my position of faith, believing Your word. The source of the attacks on me are Your enemies and You will deal with them. When You show up in my situation, the enemies are defeated like being consumed by fire. When they plot evil against me and devise wicked schemes to defeat me, those plans will not succeed. Those schemes cannot stand against the power of Your word. I will lift up Your name and glorify You because of Your mighty power. I will sing Your praises, my God the Almighty One.

Record your insights, revelations, and meditations from this week. DATE:

_____

_____

_____

_____

_____

_____

_____

_____

_____

_____

_____

_____

_____

_____

_____

_____

_____

_____

WEEK TWENTY ONE   *HYMNS and POEMS*   **DAY 1**

Seek Ye First, Not Earthly Treasure

by Georgiana M. Taylor (1857-1914)

Seek ye first, not earthly pleasure,
Fading joy and failing treasure,
But the love that knows no measure
Seek ye first.

Seek ye first, not earth's aspirings,
Ceaseless longings, vain desirings,
But your precious soul's requirings
Seek ye first.

Seek Him first, then when forgiven,
Pardoned, with the peace of heaven,
Let your life to Him be given:
Seek this first.

Seek this first—Be pure and holy;
Like the Master, meek and lowly;
Yielded to His service wholly:
Seek this first.

Seek the coming of His kingdom;
Seek the souls around to win them,
Seek to Jesus Christ to bring them:
Seek this first.

Seek this first, His promise trying;
It is sure, all need supplying.
Heavenly things, on Him relying,
Seek ye first.

https://www.hymnal.net/en/hymn/h/667

WEEK TWENTY ONE   *INSIGHT and ENCOURAGEMENT*   **DAY 2**

The Secret of Effective Prayer

by Paul Billheimer (1897-1984)

The church, by virtue of her faithful use of prayer, wields the balance of power not only in world affairs but also in the salvation of individual souls. Without violating the free moral responsibility of any individual, the church, by means of persistent, believing intercession, may so release the Spirit of God upon a soul that he will find it easier to yield to the Spirit's tender wooing and be saved than to continue his rebellion.

God will not go over the church's head to do things in spite of her because this would abort His plan to bring her to full stature as co sovereign with the Son. He will therefore do nothing without her. To this John Wesley agrees when he says, "God does nothing but in answer to prayer."

In order to enable the church to overcome Satan, God entered the stream of human history in the Incarnation. As unfallen Man He overcame and destroyed Satan both legally and dynamically. All that

Christ did in redemption He did for the benefit of the Church. He is "head over all things *to the church*" (Eph. 1:22). His victory over Satan is accredited to the Church. Although Christ's triumph over Satan is full and complete, God permits him to carry on a guerrilla warfare. God could put Satan completely away, but He has chosen to use him to give the Church "on-the-job" training in overcoming. (emphasis his)

Prayer is not begging God to do something which is loath to do. It is not overcoming reluctance in God. It is enforcing Christ's victory over Satan. It is implementing upon earth Heaven's decisions concerning the affairs of men. Calvary legally destroyed Satan, and canceled all of his claims. God placed the enforcement of Calvary's victory in the hands of the Church (Matt. 18:18; Luke 10:17-19). He has given to her "power of attorney." She is His "deputy." But this delegated authority is wholly inoperative apart from the prayers of a believing Church. Therefore, prayer is where the action is. Any church without a well-organized and systematic prayer program is simply operating a religious treadmill.

A program of prayer without faith is powerless. The missing element that is necessary to energize prevailing prayer that binds and casts out Satan is triumphant faith. And the missing element that is necessary to energize triumphant faith is praise – perpetual, purposeful, aggressive praise. The secret of answered prayer is faith without doubt (Mark 11:23). And the secret of faith without doubt is praise, triumphant praise, continuous praise, praise that is a way of life. The secret of success and overcoming Satan and qualifying for the throne is a massive program of the effective prayer. The secret of effective prayer is a massive program of praise.

Destined For The Throne. Fort Washington: Christian Literature Crusade. 1975. p. 17-18.

WEEK TWENTY ONE   **Confession about Wickedness**   **DAY 3**

Read Psalm 10

Lord, it is my desire that all wickedness be cleansed from my character. If I am arrogant and think highly of myself, there is wickedness in my character. If I brag about all the things I'm going to have and am jealous of those who already have them, there is wickedness in my character. If I'm so proud of my accomplishments that in my mind, there is no thought of God, there is wickedness in my character. If I think I have everything figured out and have guaranteed myself a happy, trouble-free life, there is wickedness in my character. If every time I talk my words are full of cursing and lies and threats that cause trouble and strife, there is wickedness in my character. If I constantly take advantage of those who are helpless and vulnerable for my own profit, there is wickedness in my character. If I think God doesn't see what I'm doing or has forgotten about me or doesn't care what I do, there is wickedness in my character. If I believe I am not responsible to anyone and no one will hold me accountable for what I do, there is wickedness in my character. But according to Your word, God, You do see all, and You do hear, and You do know and You will call everyone to account. So reveal and expose every wicked thing in my character so that I can be pleasing in Your sight, my Lord and my God.

WEEK TWENTY ONE   *INSIGHT and ENCOURAGEMENT*   **DAY 4**

The Mystery of Prayer

by Paul Billheimer (1897-1984)

The mystery of the design of prayer is pointed up in Ezekiel 22:30-31. During a time of national apostasy, God looked for someone to stand in the gap, but found none. Here we see God seeking to avoid exercising just and deserved judgment but cannot do so without any intercessor. Why should God be "dependent" upon the prayers of a man to defend the nation from the judgments which He, Himself, wishes to withhold? Since God's will is supreme in all things, when He wills or plans certain divine purposes such as the salvation of a soul or a revival in a specific area, why doesn't He arbitrarily go over our heads and carry out His will? Why did He set up a system which made Him "dependent" upon a man? Is this not a baffling mystery? Evidently God can do nothing without our prayers.

The fundamental importance of this scheme of prayer in God's economy is further emphasized by God's binding himself unequivocally to answer. God's promises to answer prayer are so sweeping and categorical, over such a broad spectrum, as to constitute a veritable carte blanche, that is, a blank card bearing the authority of His own signature. (See John 14:13-14; 15:7; 16:23-24).

I call these categorical promises, meaning they are unqualified or unconditional. When I use that term I mean that no conditions are attached which constitute the hedge on God's part. In other words, there are no conditions which are not fair or which are not within the reasonable capacity of a truly dedicated child of God. The condition of the abiding in Him and His words abiding in us is possible for any ordinary, earnest, and sincere born-again believer. The entire responsibility for prayerlessness or effective prayer falls entirely upon us. The scheme of prayer, so far as God is concerned, is "watertight." His part is already done. While His promise to answer is always circumscribed by His will, this is in no sense a hedge since any truly yielded child of God never wills anything but God's will. There is no "fine print" in God's prayer contract.

God's offer of his scepter to redeemed humanity is, therefore, a bona fide offer. It is an offer in good faith. Through the plan of prayer God actually is inviting redeemed man into FULL partnership with Him, not in *making* the divine decisions, but in *implementing* those decisions in the affairs of humankind. Independently and of His own will God makes the decisions governing the affairs of earth. *The responsibility and authority for the enforcement and administration of those decisions He has placed upon the shoulders of His Church.* (See Matt. 16:18-18; Luke 10:19; John 20:21-23). (Emphasis his.)

Excerpted from, *Destined For The Throne*. Fort Washington: Christian Literature Crusade. 1975. p. 44-47.

WEEK TWENTY ONE   **Confession about God's Character**   **DAY 5**

Read Nehemiah 9

Bless your glorious name which is exalted above all things. You alone are the Lord who made the heavens and the earth and everything in the earth. You are the God of the covenant. You have kept your words because you are righteous. You have revealed yourself to your people down through history and given your word to your people that we might know you and obey your commandments and laws. You have revealed yourself to me and opened your word to me and helped me to see the truth of your word. And yet, I have acted no differently than the ancestors who acted proudly and stiffened their necks against your word. In rebellion they refused to obey your commandments and even plotted to return to their life of slavery. But you are God, ready to pardon, gracious and merciful, slow to anger, abundant in kindness, and you did not forsake me. In my rebellion and faithlessness, you have never forsaken me and sustained me in my wilderness wanderings. Despite my disobedience, when I called to you from my miserable state, you heard me and delivered me from my torment according to your abundant mercy. Though I have fallen time and time again, you have been patient with me for you are gracious and merciful. You keep your promises even when I do not keep mine. Thank you for forgiving me and restoring me in your faithfulness. Help me to walk in total surrender to your word and your will.

WEEK TWENTY ONE   *INSIGHT and ENCOURAGEMENT*   **DAY 6**

The Priority of Praise

by Paul Billheimer (1897-1984)

Praise is the most useful occupation and activity in enabling God to realize the supreme goal of the universe, that of "bringing many sons into glory." In recent years the subject of mental health among believers has received much attention. In the world at large, it is alleged, over half of the available hospital beds are occupied by victims of mental and nervous disorders. To deal with this problem great mental health institutions have been constructed and the profession of psychiatry has been developed. The quintessence of all of our mental and nervous disorders is over-occupation with personal ego; namely, self-centeredness. To make one's self his center is self-destructive. Jesus affirmed this principle when

He said, "Whosoever would save his life shall lose it, but whosoever will lose his life for my sake, the same shall save it" (Luke 9:24).

Here is one of the greatest values of praise: it decentralizes self. The worship and praise of God demands the shift of center from self to God. One cannot praise without relinquishing occupation with self. When praise becomes a way of life, the infinitely lovely God becomes the center of worship rather than the bankrupt self. Thus the personality becomes properly integrated and destructive stresses and strains disappear. This results in mental wholeness. Praise produces forgetfulness of self – and forgetfulness of self is health.

One may pay a psychiatrist seventy-five dollars an hour to listen and look wise, and come away poorer and no better. But when a born-again believer suffering with depression and other emotional stresses turns to the infinitely lovely and all-wise God and applies himself diligently to worship and praise, the healing process begins. Praise, therefore, is something more than a vacuous religious form. It is the most practical and rewarding of occupations.

The secret of overcoming faith, therefore, is praise. To be most effective, then, praise must be massive, continuous, a fixed habit, a fulltime occupation, a diligently pursued vocation, a total way of life. How can one offer this kind of praise? Hebrews13:15 gives us the key: "By him, therefore, let us offer the *sacrifice* of praise to God *continually*, that is, the fruit of our lips." In the "sacrifice of praise" it is the personal ego which must be slain. "The fruit of the lips" means that the sacrifice of praise is incomplete until it is expressed. *The only time one can offer this "sacrifice of praise" is when things seem to be going wrong,* for it is only then that he is called upon to die to his own opinions, choices, and judgment. In offering the "sacrifice of praise" one embraces the faith that God is both benevolent and supreme, the faith that can "be still and know that he is God" (Ps. 46:10).

Excerpted from, *Destined For The Throne*. Fort Washington: Christian Literature Crusade. 1975. p. 117-123.

WEEK TWENTY ONE   *HYMNS and POEMS*   **DAY 7**

Sometimes a Light Surprises

by William Cowper (1731-1800)

Sometimes a light surprises
The Christian while he sings;
It is the Lord, who rises
With healing in His wings:

When comforts are declining,
He grants the soul again
A season of clear shining,
To cheer it after rain.

In holy contemplation,
We sweetly then pursue
The theme of God's salvation,
And find it ever new:

Set free from present sorrow,
We cheerfully can say,
E'en let the unknown morrow
Bring with it what it may.

It can bring with it nothing,
But He will bear us through;
Who gives the lilies clothing,
Will clothe His people too:

Beneath the spreading heavens,
No creature but is fed;
And He who feeds the ravens
Will give His children bread.

Tozer, A. W. *The Christian Book of Mystical Verse: A Collection of Poems, Hymns, and Prayers for Devotional Reading.* Chicago: Moody Publishers, 2016. p. 124.

Record your insights, revelations, and meditations from this week. DATE:

_____

_____

_____

_____

_____

_____

_____

_____

_____

_____

WEEK TWENTY TWO   *HYMNS and POEMS*   **DAY 1**

Oh, to be Nothing, Nothing

by Georgiana M. Taylor (1857-1914)

Oh, to be nothing, nothing,
Only to lie at His feet,
A broken and emptied vessel,
For the Master's use made meet.
Emptied that He might fill me,
As forth to His service I go;
Broken, that so unhindered
His life through me might flow.

Refrain:
Oh, to be nothing, nothing,
Only to lie at His feet,
A broken and emptied vessel,
For the Master's use made meet.

Oh, to be nothing, nothing,
Only as led by His hand;
A messenger at His gateway,
Only waiting for His command;
Only an instrument ready
His praises to sound at His will,
Willing, should he not require me,
In silence to wait on Him still.

Oh, to be nothing, nothing,
Painful the humbling may be,
Yet low in the dust I'd lay me
That the world might my Savior see.
Rather be nothing, nothing,
To Him let all voices be raised:
He is the Fountain of blessing,
He only is meet to be praised.

https://hymnary.org/text/o_to_be_nothing_nothing

WEEK TWENTY TWO   *INSIGHT and ENCOURAGEMENT*   **DAY 2**

We are Nothing in Ourselves

by Johannes Tauler (1300-1361)

Know of a truth that if your own honor is of more importance to you and dearer than that of another man, you do wrongfully. Know this, that if you seek something that is your own, you seek not God only; and you will never find Him. You are acting as though you made of God a candle to seek for something and, when you have found it, you cast the candle away. Therefore, when you do this, that which you seek with God, whatever it may be, it is nothing; gain, reward, favor, or whatever it maybe, you seek nothing, therefore you will find nothing. There is no other cause for finding nothing but that you seek nothing. All creatures are absolutely nothing. I do not say that they are small or anything else, but that they are absolutely nothing. That which has no being is nothing. And creatures have no being, because they have their being in God; if God turned away for a moment, they would cease to exist. He who desired to have all the world with God would have nothing more than if he had God alone.

Know that of ourselves we have nothing; for this and all other gifts are from above. Therefore he who would receive from above must of necessity place himself beneath, in truth humility. And know of a truth that if he leave anything out, so that all is not beneath, he will have nothing and receive nothing. If you trust to yourself, or to anything else or anybody else, you are not beneath and will receive nothing; but if you have placed yourself beneath, then you will receive all things fully. It is God's nature to give; and He lives and moves that He may give unto us when we are humble. If we are not lowly, and yet desire to receive, we do Him violence, and kill Him, so to speak; and although we may not wish to do this, yet we do it as far as in us lies. That you may truly give Him all things, see to it that you cast yourself in deep humility at the feet of God, and beneath all created things.

Baillie, John. *A Diary of Readings*. New York: Macmillan Publishing Co., 1955. p. 227.

WEEK TWENTY TWO   *INSIGHT and ENCOURAGEMENT*   **DAY 3**

Is Self-Surrender Workable?

by E. Stanley Jones (1884-1973)

The predicament of modern man is confusion. Our doctor's offices and mental institutions are filled with people who are passing on their mental, emotional, and spiritual confusions to their bodies. They suffer from "cross-currentitus."

Being caught in cross-currents can be disastrous, but the further developments in this particular shipwreck can be more disastrous: "ran the ship aground, so that the bow stuck fast and remained immovable, while the stern was being pounded to pieces by the breakers." If modern man is free to maneuver amid the cross-currents he may make his way through, but if the bow of the ship is caught in fixed formulas, fixed and rigid dogmatisms, then the rest of his life is being pounded to pieces by the breakers.

If Jesus is the center of your faith and surrender to him is the center of your loyalty, then you have a maneuverable position. Cross-currents may strike you and breakers may pound you, but you do not go to pieces. But if you are stuck in the sands of fixed doctrines and dogmatisms, then you are pounded to pieces by the breakers.

Surrender to Jesus Christ as a person gives you something fixed and unfixed, static and dynamic. He is fixed in history, but He is dynamic and beyond history. When you belong to Him you belong to the unfolding. The more you see in Him, the more you see there is to be seen. You know you have arrived, and yet you are always setting out. It is an adventure in discovery. A surprise is around every corner. He can never be outgrown and outworn. You belong to the undecayable, the eternally fresh.

Is self-surrender workable? I would give an unqualified reply: Negatively, nothing else is workable. If you belong to anything less than God it will inevitably let you down without exception.

Positively, self-surrender is the most emancipating, the most universalizing thing imaginable. You don't have to belong to this group or that; you don't have to be in line with any apostolic succession; you don't have to attain a certain degree of goodness; you don't have to be educated, rich, or cultured; you don't have to be young, old, this color or that. You have to be willing to give you, the only thing you own – and that alone! You don't have to believe this doctrine or that – you have to be His.

Self-surrender is workable, for it works to the degree you work it. Nothing else does.

Victory Through Surrender. New York: Abingdon Press, 1966. p. 101-102.

WEEK TWENTY TWO   *INSIGHT and ENCOURAGEMENT*   DAY 4

According to the Working of His Power
by Andrew Murray (1828-1917)

'Him we preach, warning every man and teaching every man in all wisdom, that we may present every man perfect in Christ Jesus. To this end I also labor, striving according to His working which works in me mightily.' Colossians 1:28-29

'…the mystery of Christ… of which I became a minister according to the gift of the grace of God given to me by the effective working of His power.' Ephesians 3:4,7

In Philippians 2:12-13, Paul encourages the Philippians to work because it was God who worked in them. *'Therefore, my beloved, as you have always obeyed, not as in my presence only, but now much more in my absence, work out your own salvation with fear and trembling; for it is God who works in you both to will and to do for His good pleasure.'* This is one of the most momentous and comprehensive statements of the great truth that it is only by God's working in us that we can do true work. In the texts above, we have Paul's testimony about his own experience. His whole ministry was to be according to the grace which was given to him according to the working of God's power. He says that his labor was a striving according to the power of Him who worked mightily in him.

We find here the same principle we found in our Lord – the Father doing the works in Him. Let every worker who reads this pause and say – "If the ever-blessed Son and Paul could only do their work according to the working of His power who worked mightily in them, how much more do I need this working of God in me!" This is one of the deepest spiritual truths of God's word. Let us look to the Holy

Spirit within us to give it such a hold of our inmost life, that it may become the deepest inspiration of all our work. We can only do true work as we yield ourselves to God to work in us.

All goodness and holiness and power are only to be found in God and where He gives them. He can only give them to man, not as something He parts with, but by His own actual presence and dwelling and working. God can only work in his people as He is allowed to have complete possession of their hearts and lives. As the will and faith and love are yielded up in dependence and faith, and we wait on God as Christ waited on Him, God can work in us.

Excerpted from *How to Work for God*. Pittsburgh, PA: Whitaker House, 1983. p. 112-113.

MONTH SIX

Along the way, the Lord has allowed me to have many interesting and wonderful (and sometimes weird) encounters with people that turn into "God things." Years ago, I was working the midnight shift on the South Division and I was dispatched to a call concerning a suspicious person. That area is now a sprawling retail district but back them is was open fields. There was a car parked and blacked out off the highway access road. It was a young couple "parking." My shift commander at the time was the first on the scene. He walked up on the couple undetected and caught them in the act. The boy was just a few days outside the legal limit for an under-age relationship and the Lieutenant arrested him for it.

I was assigned the task of transporting him to jail and doing the paperwork. As you might imagine, the boy was devastated. I listened to him most of the long drive downtown, and then I saw an opportunity to ask him about his relationship to the Lord. I don't remember the exact conversation but, by the time we reached the jail sally-port, he was ready to receive Christ as his Savior. I walked around to the passenger side and knelt down so I could pray with him before taking him inside. It was a glorious time, and he was much relieved afterward.

I kept up with him for a few years after that. He joined a church and eventually worked in youth ministry. We lost touch for many years but not too long ago, we ran into each other in a convenience store. It was wonderful seeing him again. He owns a business and is married with children. Not everything is rosy, but the Lord will provide.

Just a few years back, I was having my morning devotional and felt like some breakfast. I drove to the local McDonald's and finished my reading there. A black man about my age went up to the condiment counter and said something that caught my attention. I responded and we struck up a conversation. I invited him to my table, and we talked casually for a bit. After a while, he noticed I was reading a Bible and we talked about church things. He was a believer. Soon he asked me what I did for a living and I told him. The expression on his face went totally blank. He could not believe I was a cop. In his 50-some years, he had never had a casual conversation with a police officer. That was enlightening to me.

We kept in contact. He was a little down on his luck at the time and was trying to find a new job while not losing his apartment. The Lord let us enjoy some good times together over meals and helping him find work. Rodney is now one my best friends. God has blessed him with a good job and a great place to live and blessed me by helping him find those things. Although he no longer lives close, he is still in the area and we communicate on a regular basis.

When you surrender to the Lord, you are open to opportunities you might not have seen before. You are constantly listening to His voice and seeking His will. More than likely, He will give you assignments that stretch you in the area of relationships. But it is during those times God expands your ability to hear and obey. He's preparing you for the bigger and better things He has in store as you continually surrender new areas of your heart to Him.

WEEK TWENTY TWO   *HYMNS and POEMS*   **DAY 5**

Self-Love

by Frederick William Faber (1814-1863)

Oh I could go through all life's troubles singing,
Turning earth's night to day,
If self were not so fast around me, clinging
To all I do or say.

My very thoughts are selfish, always building
Mean castles in the air;
I use my love of others for a gilding
To make myself look fair.

I fancy all the world engrossed with judging
My merit or my blame;
Its warmest praise seems an ungracious grudging
Of praise which I might claim.

In youth or age, by city, wood, or mountain,
Self is forgotten never;
Where'er we tread, it gushes like a fountain,
And its waters flow forever.

Alas! no speed in life can snatch us wholly
Out of self's hateful sight;
And it keeps step, whene'er we travel slowly,
And sleeps with us at night.

No grief's sharp knife, no pain's most cruel sawing
Self and the soul can sever:
The surface, that in joy sometimes seems thawing,
Soon freezes worse than ever.

Thus we are never men, self's wretched swathing
Not letting virtue swell;
Thus is our whole life numbed, forever bathing
Within this frozen well.

O miserable omnipresence, stretching
Over all time and space,
How have I run from thee, yet found thee reaching
The goal in every race.

Inevitable self! vile imitation
Of universal light,
Within our hearts a dreadful usurpation
Of God's exclusive right!

The opiate balms of grace may haply still thee,
Deep in my nature lying;
For I may hardly hope, alas! to kill thee,
Save by the act of dying.

O Lord! that I could waste my life for others,
With no ends of my own,
That I could pour myself into my brothers,
And live for them alone!

Such was the life Thou livedst; self-abjuring,
Thine own pains never easing,
Our burdens bearing, our just doom enduring,
A life without self-pleasing!

Tozer, A. W. *The Christian Book of Mystical Verse: A Collection of Poems, Hymns, and Prayers for Devotional Reading*. Chicago: Moody Publishers, 2016. p. 88-89.

WEEK TWENTY TWO   *INSIGHT and ENCOURAGEMENT*   **DAY 6**

Progressive Christlikeness

by J. Sidlow Baxter (1903-1999)

171

'Now the Lord is the Spirit; and where the Spirit of the Lord is , there is liberty. But we all, with unveiled face, beholding as in a mirror the glory of the Lord, are being transformed into the same image from glory to glory, just as by the Spirit of the Lord.'   II Corinthians 3:17-18

There is some question as to whether Paul here means (1) that *we* are the reflecting mirror, or (2) that our Lord Jesus is the mirror, reflecting "the glory of the Lord", or (3) that the gospel, as the "new covenant" (see verses 6-11) is the mirror, reflecting the glory of Christ. Perhaps number three best fits the context, but, yes or no, the central idea remains the same, namely, that we, beholding with "unveiled face," our glorious Lord, are "transformed into the same image." Like Romans 12:2, it certainly teaches a transfiguration of character. The phrase, here, "with unveiled face," means with unveiled eyes of the *mind.* There are four aspects of this character transfiguration which are here indicated and blended.

(1) It is transfiguration through *communion.* One of the things which we never dare forget, especially in teaching inwrought holiness through consecration and faith, is, that no matter what crisis we may experience or what spiritual elevation may come to us, *no* blessing of the Christian life ever continues with us unless there is continuous communion with Christ. Moreover, this "beholding" or "reflecting" is that kind of communion which we call the *adoring contemplation.*

(2) This transfiguration is *progressive.* The verb is in the present tense: "being transfigured." In these chapters we have emphasized that in no sense is inwrought holiness our reaching a fixed point of static sanctity. No, this deeper renewal within us marks a crisis-point of new departure into a *progressive* transfiguration of character.

(3) This transfiguration is inwrought by the Holy Spirit. It is "from the Lord the Spirit," that is, it is a result from His activity in the mind. He effects his transfiguration work through the believers adoring contemplation of "the glory of the Lord." In Romans 12:2, a transfiguration begins with "entire renewal of the mind." Here, it is developed through communion; through an adoring contemplation, which absorbs into itself the interests of the beloved heavenly Lord.

(4) This transfiguration is an approximating *likeness to Christ* – "transformed into the same image." That is the supreme goal of true, Christian sanctification: to become ever increasingly conformed in character to the sublime character of Christ. Entire sanctification, or restoration to holiness, according to the New Testament, is restoration from moral and spiritual disease to fullness of health, making possible therefrom an ever-developing likeness to the character and beauty of the Lord Jesus. The supreme purpose of the Holy Spirit's deeper work in us is transfiguration of character. (Emphasis his.)

Excerpted from, *A New Call to Holiness.* Grand Rapids: Zondervan, 1973. p. 169-171.

WEEK TWENTY TWO   **Confession about Forgiveness**   **DAY 7**

Read Psalm 32

I am so happy God has forgiven my sins and covered them over, hiding them from view. I am elated God does not hold to my account the sins I honestly confess and repent of. When I refuse to confess and repent, it makes me physically and emotionally sick and tired. But I have acknowledged my sin and I will not hide my transgressions from you. You have promised and you are faithful to forgive me and not find me guilty. I will be faithful to pray to you while you may be found so the flood of adversity does not sweep me away. You are my hiding place. You preserve me from trouble, and I will sing the songs of deliverance. Instruct me and teach me in the way I should go. Guide me based on what you can see. I will not be stubborn or refuse to accept Your instruction. I understand I am totally dependent on your guidance and leadership. Those who reject Your ways and follow their own wicked ideas find many sorrows. But mercy will continually surround me because I trust in the Lord. I will rejoice and be exceedingly glad. I will shout for joy because I am walking in righteousness and uprightness of heart.

Record your insights, revelations, and meditations from this week. DATE:

_____

_____

_____

_____

_____

_____

_____

_____

_____

_____

_____

_____

_____

_____

_____

_____

WEEK TWENTY THREE   *HYMNS and POEMS*   **DAY 1**

Once I Thought I Walked With Jesus
by Francis Augustus Blackmer (1855-1930)

Once I thought I walked with Jesus,
　Yet such changeful feelings had;
Sometimes trusting, sometimes doubting,
　Sometimes joyful, sometimes sad.

Oh, the peace the Savior gives!
　Peace I never knew before;
And my way has brighter grown
Since I've learned to trust Him more.

But He call'd me closer to Him,
Bade my doubting, fearing, cease;
And when I had fully yielded,
Filled my soul with perfect peace.

Now I'm trusting every moment,
　Nothing less can be enough;
And the Savior bears me gently
　O'er those places once so rough.

Now I'm trusting every moment,
　Nothing less can be enough;
And the Savior bears me gently
　O'er those places once so rough.

https://www.hymnal.net/en/hymn/h/573

WEEK TWENTY THREE   **Confession about the Statutes**   **DAY 2**

From Psalm 119

The statutes You have laid down are wonderful, righteous and fully trustworthy. I am trusting You to give me understanding so that I may obey them and live. I know I will be blessed when I keep Your statutes wholeheartedly. I do no wrong when I follow Your statutes and that makes me as happy as if I had just inherited a fortune. There is more to be treasured in following Your statutes than in all the riches of this world. In fact, I have set my affections toward Your statutes instead of purposing selfish gain because Your statutes are my eternal heritage. They are the joy of my heart. I will hold fast to Your statutes and love them greatly because in them I find You. I have considered doing things my way but have decided to base my choices and decisions on Your statutes and will not turn away from them. I will continuously ponder and meditate on Your statutes so that I do not turn away from them. Give me the discernment to understand Your statutes and live to faithfully obey them every day. Even in the face of persecution, I will steadfastly uphold and testify to the righteousness of Your statutes. I will confess Your statutes before the wicked and the powerful, no matter what may come for I trust You will not put me to shame. May those who also seek to understand and obey Your statutes find comfort and encouragement in me.

WEEK TWENTY THREE   *INSIGHT and ENCOURAGEMENT*   **DAY 3**

What is Faith?
by Charles S. Price (1887-1947)

Faith is a ladder up which we climb out of the world of things that seem to be into the realms of things as they really are. The transition might not be instantaneous, but the very fact that you climb the ladder proves that you have faith in the ladder to bear you and in the fact that there is something at the top.

The top is the thing that is hoped for-- every rung of the ladder is a promise of God--but it is faith that inspires to do the climbing. The top of the ladder might be beyond the vision of the brainiest and the most keen-sighted man. It has to be--for if they could see it there would not be the need to exercise faith to believe it was there.

My Greek Testament declares that faith is "a conviction of things not seen." What do we mean by this word conviction? In the larger and broader sense we mean a persuasion of the heart and mind--for both of them cooperate in the operation of faith. If the things that are not seen are at the top of the ladder and two men are sitting together on the ground at its foot, the man who starts to climb the ladder is persuaded that the thing he wants is at the top. The man who makes no attempt to climb does so because he refuses to believe what he cannot see. If you could see it and climb for it, it would not be faith. When you do not see it, and yet climb for it--that is faith. So faith is the conviction--the persuasion of heart and mind of things not seen.

But let me bring you again to our original statement that it must be based upon evidence. If a poor old tramp told you that there was a pot of gold at the end of the rainbow you would not believe it--because there would be no evidence. If a millionaire told you on his word of honor that there was a purse of gold awaiting you at his office you would immediately go after it. The act of going after it would be faith in operation following a persuasion of the mind that what he said was true.

Now then, when God says something--God, the eternal one; the Lord of Creation; the one who held the oceans in the hollow of His hand; the One whose fingers fashioned the mountains and traced the course of the rivers down their sides; when God says something and backs it by His authority--then, I submit, you have a basis for your faith. When that eternal One, clothed in glory and majesty and power-- before whom devils tremble and flee--before whose majestic words of command even nature suspends its operation--when that God speaks, then I maintain you have a basis, an evidence for the operation of your faith. When that wonderful Jesus--the Christ of Calvary who was clothed and filled with all the fullness of the Godhead and who bade the angry waves of Galilee be still--when that Jesus speaks and gives you a promise, then I maintain that you have a basis for your faith. He promises the unattainable and we receive it. He promises the impossible and we get it. An unbelieving world may scoff – but just the same, I maintain that faith can still remove mountains and that all things are possible to the man who believes.

Excerpted from *The Meaning of Faith*. Pasadena, CA: Charles S. Price Pub. Co., 1936. p. 245.

WEEK TWENTY THREE   *HYMNS and POEMS*   **DAY 4**

Jesus Calls Us

by Cecil Francis Alexander (1818-1895)

Jesus calls us; o'er the tumult
of our life's wild, restless sea,
day by day his clear voice soundeth,
saying, 'Christian, follow me; '

As, of old, Saint Andrew heard it
by the Galilean lake,
turned from home and toil and kindred,
leaving all for His dear sake.

Jesus calls us from the worship
of the vain world's golden store;

from each idol that would keep us,
saying, 'Christian, love me more.'

In our joys and in our sorrows,
days of toil and hours of ease,
still he calls, in cares and pleasures,
'Christian, love me more than these.'

Jesus calls us! By thy mercies,
Savior, may we hear thy call,
give our hearts to thine obedience,
serve and love thee best of all.

https://www.poemhunter.com/cecil-frances-alexander/

WEEK TWENTY THREE   **Confession of Obedience**   **DAY 5**

Read Psalm 85

I confess that You, Lord, have been very favorable to me and have rescued me from captivity to sin. You have forgiven the iniquity of my heart, the hidden things of darkness that drove me to sin. You have covered all my sin with blood of Your perfect sacrifice, Jesus my Savior. You have taken away Your wrath and turned away Your fierce anger. Instead of being angry at my forever, You have restored me, shown me mercy, and granted me salvation through Your Son. I will pay attention to Your voice and listen to what You have to say because You are speaking words of peace to my heart. I will not return to the foolishness of my past life of sin and disobedience. I will see Your glory in my life because I will continue to follow Your will and obey Your word. Your mercy will lead me to Your truth and Your righteousness will guide me to Your peace. What a blessing trusting You will be. Truth and righteousness shall surround me on all sides, above and below. You, the Lord, my Lord will supply everything that it is good. The portion you have assigned to me will grow and increase because of Your grace and mercy. Doing the right thing and acting the right way and having the right attitude will lead me in the right direction. I will follow in Your footsteps every moment of every day so Your glory and blessing will be evident to everyone I encounter.

WEEK TWENTY THREE   *INSIGHT and ENCOURAGEMENT*   **DAY 6**

Faith: How to Get It

by Charles S. Price (1887-1947)

Beloved, herein lies the secret of the attainment of faith. Get close to God. Get very close to God. Withdraw yourself from the noise and hubbub and clamor of a world of unbelief and sin--get alone with God. Close your ears to the whispers of evil men and plead the blood of Jesus as a barrier against the suggestions of the devil--get alone with God. Pray for the blood to cleanse from sin, and for the heart to be made clean and pure--get alone with God.

The Scripture tells us that the Word of the Lord is a power that sanctifies. With all my heart I cry unto you, "Faith cometh--faith cometh," but how does it come? "Faith cometh by hearing, and hearing by the Word of God."

How wonderful the contemplation of this truth! Are you in the dark? His Word is a light unto your feet and a lamp unto your pathway. Are you sick and suffering? He sent forth His Word and healed them. Are you hungry and crying out for that which satisfies? Men do not live by bread alone, but by every word that proceeds out of the mouth of God. Are you lost, groping in the darkness and slipping down the steeps of time toward eternity's night? He alone has the Word of eternal life.

Once again, I repeat--get alone with God if you would have faith. Again, let me remind you that if miracle-working, irresistible faith was to be possessed separate and apart from the presence and person of God, man might use it for evil and not for good. God withholds it from the man who desires to use it for his own glory and aggrandizement but imparts it to the man who wants to use it for the glory and the honor of the name of the Lord.

There have been many cases, as we travel down the corridors of history, of men who have lost their faith because they have lost their God. It is a well-known fact that the depth and sincerity of a man's belief is measured by his nearness to God. It is not so much what you know, but what you are. God has seen to it that the highways of Glory are open to the illiterate and the poor. It is that beautiful and intimate walk with the One who still will travel with you as he walked with Adam in the garden before sin separated them in the days of the long ago.

Get alone with God. He will not disappoint you. Get alone with God. He will not let you down. As you feel the sacred nearness of His presence, and as you listen to the tenderness and understanding tones of His voice, doubts and fears and unbelief will slink away and in their places He will impart the faith that you need. Not from your agony, not from your groanings, not from your struggles--but from the heart throbs of the Father's heart you will get your faith. You will get it not only because you need it, but because you believe Him. He will impart it. Get alone with God.

Excerpted from *The Meaning of Faith*. Pasedena, CA: Charles S. Price Pub. Co., 1936. p. 510.

WEEK TWENTY THREE   *HYMNS and POEMS*   **DAY 7**

Following Jesus

by Barney E. Warren (1867-1951)

Following Jesus, following Jesus,
Gently He leads me in the heavenly way;
Watching and praying, trusting, obeying,
He will restrain me from going astray.

Refrain:
Following Jesus, following Jesus,
Following Jesus by day and by night;
Watching and praying, trusting, obeying,
You is my helper in doing the right.

Following Jesus, following Jesus,
He who has suffered to redeem me from sin;

Oh, what a blessing, while I'm confessing,
You in Your fullness, come reign within.

Following Jesus, following Jesus,
I am delighted with Your wonderful love;
While I'm confiding, in You I'm hiding,
Soon I shall meet You in heaven above.

Following Jesus, following Jesus,
This is my duty for Your goodness to me;
Joyful in glory, telling the story,
How in Your favor I'm happy and free.

Modified from https://library.timelesstruths.org/music/Following_Jesus/

Record your insights, revelations, and meditations from this week. DATE:

_____

_____

_____

_____

_____

_____

_____

_____

_____

_____

_____

_____

_____

_____

_____

_____

WEEK TWENTY FOUR   *HYMNS and POEMS*   **DAY 1**

Sweet Will of God

by Lelia Naylor Morris (1862-1929)

My stubborn will at last hath yielded;
I would be Thine, and Thine alone,
And this the prayer my lips are bringing,
"Lord, let in me Thy will be done."

I'm tired of sin, footsore and weary,
The darksome path hath dreary grown,
But now a light has ris'n to cheer me;
I find in Thee my Star, my Sun.

Thy precious will, O conqu'ring Savior,
Doth now embrace and compass me;
All discords hushed, my peace a river,
My soul a prisoned bird set free.

Shut in with Thee, O Lord, forever,
My wayward feet no more to roam;
What pow'r from Thee my soul can sever?
The center of God's will my home.

https://www.hymnal.net/en/hymn/h/383

WEEK TWENTY FOUR   *INSIGHT and ENCOURAGEMENT*   **DAY 2**

Sanctification Simplified to a Child

by Mrs. Phoebe Palmer (1807-1874)

Said a pious mother to little daughter, who was on the eve of attending a special means of grace, "Daughter, you have been a professor of religion for some time, and you ought to expect to get much good in attending this meeting. Yes, you ought to expect to get much more religion. I do not see why you ought not to expect to be wholly sanctified."

The child listened attentively, and then rather earnestly exclaimed, "Why, Ma, I hardly know what you mean by that. If you mean to be so saved as never to sin again, that is what I *never could do*!" The latter was said with so much warmth, but the pious mother saw that her daughter had, like many other professors, imbibed the idea, that sin is not so exceedingly sinful as set forth in the Scriptures of truth. And though the mother imagined her daughter might not fully understand the meaning of the term "*sanctification,*" if merely spoken of as a doctrine, yet she was not prepared to see her shrink so instinctively from a state which she imagined might imply salvation from all sin. Said the mother in reply, - "Daughter, God hates sin now just as much as he hated it in the days of Adam. God is unchangeable in his nature. With him 'there is neither variableness nor shadow of turning,' 'the *same* yesterday, today, and forever.' Think of the effect of one sin in the days of Adam, - how it has been felt along down through time, even until the present hour! We are feeling it today, and its effect will be felt down to the end of time! Only think, all this the effect of one sin! Now, my daughter, if you knew that with the very next sin which you commit you would be ushered into the eternal world with the guilt, the stain of that sin, upon your garments, would you not be very careful how you sin?

The little daughter stood mute with astonishment. Probably she had never before had such perceptions of the exceeding sinfulness of sin, and the certainty with which it banishes the soul endlessly from God. And still she stood gazing upon the face of the earnest mother, while that mother still waited and repeated her importunate inquiry, "What would my daughter do if she *knew* that, while in the act of committing the next sin, she would be ushered into eternity. I can tell you, my dear daughter, what I think you would do. You would be every moment looking to Jesus. O how carefully you would be every moment watching against sin! And how truly you would this and every coming moment be casting yourself on Christ, and *trusting in Christ to save you from sin*! And while you are trusting in Him thus carefully to *save you from sin*, He *would* save you, - would He not?" The child's eyes brightened, for her spirit was relieved. She saw that there was a way in which she might be saved from sin *every moment*. And the simplicity of the process relieved and delighted her. (Emphasis hers)

Excerpted from, *Present to My Christian Friend on Entire Devotion to God*. London: William Nichols, 1857. p. 89-91.

WEEK TWENTY FOUR   Confession about Enlightenment   DAY 3

Read Ephesians 1

I will rejoice and give thanks for the faith and love you give. You are the God of our Lord Jesus Christ. You are the Father of Glory. You have given me the spirit of wisdom and revelation and are increasing my knowledge of you. You are the source of wisdom and revelation. My only hope of getting to know you more is through what you reveal to me of yourself. You have opened my spiritual eyes and enlightened my spiritual understanding. You want me to know and make it possible for me to know, the hope of your calling on my life, the riches of the glory of my inheritance in the saints, and the exceeding greatness of your power given and made available for those of us who believe in you. That power, that resurrection power, is the same mighty power worked in Jesus Christ when you raised Him up from the grave and seated Him at your right hand in the heavenlies. Jesus, the Risen King, is right now seated far above all principalities, all other powers, all other might, all other dominion and anyone else that I could possibly think of to mention. He is seated there now, and he will be seated there for eternity. You have made him the head of his church and you have put all things under his feet which means that since I am part of the body of Christ, all things are under my feet as well.

WEEK TWENTY FOUR   *INSIGHT and ENCOURAGEMENT*   DAY 4

How is the Blessing of Sanctification to be Retained?

by Rev. Jeremy Boynton (1824-1883)

We know one way only in which to retain the blessing of holiness and that is this, - just as you attained it so are you to retain it. "As ye have received Christ Jesus the Lord, so walk ye in him," said Paul: so we say, "As you attained the blessing of sanctification, so you are to holding fast; or, in other words, as ye received Christ in the sanctification of your heart, so walk ye in him." If our position, then, be correct, as we think it is, in order to ascertain how to retain the blessing, we must inquire how we received or obtained it. In making this inquiry, we learn that four things are essential to the attainment of perfect love or holiness: they are –

First, the belief that the blessing is attainable. If you would retain it, stand firm in this faith; for, notwithstanding your rich experience, there is danger of being led into unbelief. You will need to watch much, and always be on your guard, lest the temptations of Satan, the scoffs of the world, or the opposing influence in the Church, may shake your faith in the doctrine. It is absolutely necessary, that we stand firm in the belief that holiness is attainable, in order to obtain and retain the great blessing.

Second, conviction. This we have already defined to imply not merely a persuasion that holiness is necessary; but it is so to feel its necessity as to lead us to groan after it. So we are to feel in order to retain the blessing. He that is living in the enjoyment of the comforts of full redemption is constantly "hungering and thirsting after righteousness." We must so feel the necessity of purity and holiness, as to say, "I cannot rest till pure within."

Third, perfect consecration. If we enjoy sanctification, we are not only to look back to some time when the great work is wrought; but we are momentarily saved from all sin, and filled with the fullness of Christ. When sanctified, we enjoyed a continual cleansing. In order to attain the blessing, we had to make an unreserved and unconditional consecration of all we have and are to God; so are we to retain the blessing. We are to possess always a spirit of perfect consecration.

Fourth, faith. It was by faith we obtained the blessing of sanctification, and it is by faith that we are to retain it. It was when we grasped the promises of God, and believed, as we prayed, that we received the things we desired, that our hearts were washed in the blood of Jesus, and we rejoiced in the witness of sanctification. When for a time, clouds and darkness are round about us, those who walk by sight give up due to despair, but those who walk by faith, and not by sight, hold on to God with an unyielding grasp. They know by faith that the clouds will soon disperse, and the Sun of Righteousness will again shine upon them.

Excerpted from, *Sanctification Practical*. New York: Foster & Palmer, 1867. p. 77-83.

WEEK TWENTY FOUR   Confession about Learning Obedience   DAY 5

From various verses in Psalm 119

The earth is filled with your love, Lord. You are good, and what you do is good; teach me your decrees. Oh, that my ways were steadfast in obeying your decrees! I will obey your decrees; do not utterly forsake me. May my lips overflow with praise, for you teach me your decrees. Uphold me, and I will be delivered; I will always have regard for your decrees. Salvation is far from the wicked, for they do not seek out your decrees. But I delight in your decrees; I will not neglect your word. When I recount my ways, you respond by teaching me Your decrees. Teach me, Lord, the way of your decrees, that I may follow it to the end. I search for your commands, which I love, so that I may meditate on your decrees. Your decrees are the theme of my song wherever I live. I will wholeheartedly follow your decrees, for when I do, I know I will not be put to shame. It was good for me to be afflicted so that I might learn your decrees. Though my body shrivels away from affliction, I will not forget your decrees. You reject all who stray from your decrees, for their delusions come to nothing. Deal with your servant according to your love and teach me your decrees. Make your face shine on your servant and teach me your decrees. My heart is set on keeping your decrees to the very end.

WEEK TWENTY FOUR   *INSIGHT and ENCOURAGEMENT*   DAY 6

The Necessity of Sanctification

by Adam Clarke (1762-1832)

The life of a Christian is a growth; he is at first born of God, and is a little child: becomes a young man and a father in Christ. Every father was once an infant; and, had he not grown, he would never have been a man. Those who content themselves with the grace they received when converted to God are, at best, in a continual state of infancy; but we find, in the order of nature, that the infant that does not grow, and grow daily, too, is sickly, and soon dies; so, in the order of grace, those who do not grow up into Jesus Christ are sickly, and will soon die – die to all sense and influence of the heavenly things. There are many who boast of the grace of their conversion; persons who were never more than babes, and have long since lost even that grace, because they did not grow in it. Let him that readeth understand.

In order to get a clean heart, a man must know and feel its depravity, acknowledge and implore it before God, in order to be fully sanctified. Few are pardoned, because they do not feel and confess their sins; and few are sanctified and cleansed from all sin, because they do not feel and confess their own sore and the plague of their hearts. As the blood of Jesus Christ, the merit of his passion and death, applied by faith, purges the conscience from all dead works, so the same cleanses the heart from all unrighteousness. As all unrighteousness is sin, so he that is cleansed from all unrighteousness is cleansed from all sin. To attempt to evade this, and plead for the continuance of sin in the heart through life, is ungrateful, wicked, and blasphemous; for, as he who says he has not sinned makes God a liar, who has declared the contrary through every part of his revelation, so he that says the blood of Christ either cannot or will not cleanse us from all sin in this life gives also the lie to his Maker, who has declared the contrary, and this shows that the word, the doctrine of God, is not in him. Reader, it is the birthright of every child of God to be cleansed from all sin, to keep himself unspotted from the world, and so to live as never more to offend his Maker. All things are possible to him that believeth, because all things are possible to the infinitely-meritorious blood and energetic Spirit of the Lord Jesus.

To every believer the new heart and the right spirit are offered in the present moment; that they may, in that moment, be received. For as the work of cleansing and renewing the heart is the work of God, his almighty power can perform it in a moment, in the twinkling of an eye. And as it is this moment our duty to love God with all our heart, and we cannot do this till he cleanse our hearts, consequently he is ready to do it at this moment, because he wills that we should in this moment love him.

Sanctification. Kansas City: The Publishing House of the Pentecostal Church of the Nazarene, 1907. pp. 51-52, 60-61.

WEEK TWENTY FOUR   *HYMNS and POEMS*   **DAY 7**

The Remembrance of Mercy
by Frederick William Faber (1814-1863)

Why art thou sorrowful, servant of God?
And what is this dullness that hangs o'er thee now?
Sing the praises of Jesus, and sing them aloud,
And the song shall dispel the dark cloud from thy brow.

For is there a thought in the wide world so sweet,
As that God has so cared for us, bad as we are,
That He thinks of us, plans for us, stoops to entreat,
And follows us, wander we ever so far?

And is it not wonderful, servant of God!
That He should have honoured us so with His love,
That the sorrows of life should but shorten the road
Which leads to Himself and the mansion above?

Oh then when the spirit of darkness comes down
With clouds and uncertainties into thy heart,
One look to thy Savior, one thought of thy crown,
And the tempest is over, the shadows depart.

That God hath once whispered a word in thine ear,
Or sent thee from heaven one sorrow for sin,
Is enough for a life both to banish all fear,
And to turn into peace all the troubles within.

The schoolmen can teach thee far less about heaven,
Of the height of God's power, or the depth of His love,
Than the fire in thy heart when thy sin was forgiven,
Or the light that one mercy brings down from above.

Then why dost thou weep so? For see how time flies,
The time that for loving and praising was given!
Away with thee, child, then, and hide thy red eyes
In the lap, the kind lap, of thy Father in heaven.

Adapted from Tozer, A. W. *The Christian Book of Mystical Verse: A Collection of Poems, Hymns, and Prayers for Devotional Reading.* Chicago: Moody Publishers, 2016. p. 134-135.

Record your insights, revelations, and meditations from this week. DATE:

_____

_____

_____

_____

_____

_____

_____

_____

_____

_____

_____

_____

_____

_____

_____

WEEK TWENTY FIVE   *HYMNS and POEMS*   **DAY 1**

Just as I Am, Thine Own to Be

by Marianne Hearn (1834–1909)

Just as I am, Thine own to be,
Friend of the young, who lovest me,
To consecrate myself to Thee,
O Jesus Christ, I come.

In the glad morning of my day,
My life to give, my vows to pay,
With no reserve and no delay,
With all my heart I come.

I would live ever in the light,
I would work ever for the right;
I would serve Thee with all my might;
Therefore, to Thee I come.

Just as I am, young, strong, and free,
To be the best that I can be
For truth, and righteousness, and Thee,
Lord of my life, I come.

With many dreams of fame and gold,
Success and joy to make me bold,
But dearer still my faith to hold,
For my whole life, I come.

And for Thy sake to win renown,
And then to take the victor's crown,
And at Thy feet to cast it down,
O Master, Lord, I come.

Published in *The Voice of Praise* in 1887 according to http://www.hymntime.com/

WEEK TWENTY FIVE   **Confession of a Young Fool**   **DAY 2**

Read Psalm 14

What a fool I was when I was young. I lived every day with not a single thought about God. No one I hung out with ever gave God a thought. If they did, they never said so or ever acted like it made a difference. What a bunch of losers we were. It was nothing to steal, if there was something we wanted and couldn't have. Fights were commonplace. They set the pecking order. The top third was merciless on the bottom third, but they had to take it because there was no place else to go. The middle third was so afraid they would do anything but to be treated like the lower boys. I was in the top third. You always had to watch your back. No one could be trusted. No one told the truth when it mattered. Everyone had an angle. Everyone was on the make. And everyone was angry, especially the older boys. Then came Ernest. A clumsier kid you've never seen. We were ruthless. It was brutal. I can't count the number of jokes and pranks that were played at his expense. But he never got mad, he never got angry, he never fought back, he never spoke an ill word. He would just pick himself up, dust himself off, then go on. Sometimes he would laugh along and complement us saying, "That was a good one." This went on for months until one day, I accidentally found Ernest in the park, sitting alone, crying and talking to himself. I hid behind a tree, thinking of how I could take advantage of the opportunity. As I was planning my next move, I realized Ernest wasn't talking to himself. He was having a conversation, as if someone were sitting beside him.

My conniving turned into curiosity. I began to listen. Then my curiosity turned into confusion. I heard my name. Ernest was praying and he was praying for me. I heard him thank God for me and ask God to bless me and forgive me. My heart broke. All this time, I had been heaping abuse on a righteous man who was probably the closest thing to a real friend I have ever had. From then on, I didn't want to beat Ernest, I wanted to be Ernest. Thank God for Ernest.

WEEK TWENTY FIVE   *INSIGHT and ENCOURAGEMENT*   **DAY 3**

Breathings from His Spirit

by Isaac Pennington (1617-1680)

Friend, it is a wonderful thing to witness the power of God as it reaches to the heart and demonstrates to the soul the pure way of life. Surely the person who partakes of this power will be favored by the Lord. Therefore, we ought to wait diligently for the leadings of the Holy Spirit in everything we do thus we will be able to travel through all that is contrary to God and into the things that are of God.

It is also a wonderful thing to witness God's preservation that keeps us from sliding backwards and being entangled in the traps of the enemy. For the enemy has many ways and uses many devices to ensnare our minds and draw it away from the Truth. There our souls are lulled to sleep with false hopes and we lose the feeling and enjoyment of the true life and power.

O friend, do you not have a sense of the way to the Father? Then you must press your spirit to bow daily before God and wait for breathings to you from his Spirit. Pray that he will continue his mercy to you and make his way more and more clear before you every day. Yes, and also pray that he will give you strength in all the trials which may come your way. By his secret working in your spirit, giving you assistance from time to time, you will advance nearer and nearer towards the kingdom.

And do not pay careful attention to the desires of the body, but instead, trust the Lord. Though you are weak and small, and though you may fall into the company of those who are more clever than you and are able to trick you by their reason, you know and can feel God's pure Truth in your spirit. Desire only to have that life brought forth in you and to have your spirit renewed and changed by God's power.

O dear heart, it is in this that you are accepted by God, and here his love and tender care will be all over you. His mercy will reach out to you daily and you shall have true satisfaction in your heart. Hold that Truth in your heart where all the devices of the devil and the reasoning of false teachers shall not be able to reach it. You will be able to feel the strength of the Lord helping his child during times of trial, and you will feel the joy of praise during the seasons of his good pleasure.

And you shall experience the truth of God's promise that the gates of hell will not prevail against you. Therefore, remember, do not look to others or to the reasonings of the wise, but keep yourself where you have felt the Lord visit you that he may visit you again and again – every day – teaching you more and more the way to his dwelling place, drawing you near to the place where there is righteousness, life, rest, and peace – forever!

Foster, Richard J. and Smith, James Bryan. *Devotional Classics*. New York: Harper One, 2005. p. 124-125.

WEEK TWENTY FIVE *HYMNS and POEMS* **DAY 4**

Take Me As Thy Tool, O Lord

by Josiah Carley (1996-present)

Take me as Thy tool, O Lord;
Use me as thou wilt.
Wash me with Thy cleansing power,
Thy blood so freely spilt.

I ask no other thing,
No other fervent plea,
But this one thing I ask, O Lord:
Let me be ruled by Thee.

Take me as Thy tool, O Lord;
Sanctify my all.
Take my life, my love, my will,
Tune me to hear Thy call.

My life is lived in vain,
If it is not for Thee;
So let me die to self today,
And come Thou, live in me.

Take me as Thy tool, O Lord;
Purge me in Thy flame.
Use me by Thy skillful hand,
Bring glory to Thy name.

No work do I desire,
No thing in all the earth,
But that which Thou dost give to me,
Of true, eternal worth.

Take me as Thy tool, O Lord;
Mold me for Thy tasks.
Here I lie, to wait to do
All that Thy service asks.

Lord, I am not mine own,
For Thou hast purchased me;
So take control of all I am,
And so I shall be free.

Take me as Thy tool, O Lord;
Lead me to the skies;
Make my life all that Thou seest
As best in Thine own eyes.

If I should live or die,
It matters not as long
As my whole life makes Thee smile,
A sweet and pleasing song.

Take me as Thy tool, O Lord;
When my work is done,
Let my life be well to Thee,
And let the prize be won.

For Thee I live today,
For Thee I glad shall be
Laid down, if I may one day sing
Thy praise eternally.

http://www.hymntime.com/tch/htm/t/a/k/e/takemeas.htm

WEEK TWENTY FIVE   *INSIGHT and ENCOURAGEMENT*   **DAY 5**

The Spirit of Holiness: Our Sanctification

by A. J. Gordon (1836-1895)

"According to the Spirit of holiness" Christ "was declared to be the Son of God in power by the resurrection from the dead" (Rom 1:4). How striking the antithesis between our Lord's two natures, as revealed in this passage, son of David as to the flesh, Son of God as to the Spirit. And "as he is so are we in this world." We who are regenerate have two natures, the one derived from Adam, the other derived from Christ, and our sanctification consists in that double process of mortification and vivification, that deadening and subduing of the old and the quickening and developing of the new. In other words, what was wrought in Christ who was "put to death in the flesh but quickened in the spirit" is rewrought in us through the constant operation of the Holy Ghost, thus the cross and the resurrection extend their sway over the entire life of the Christian.

Mortification is not asceticism. It is not a self-inflicted compunction, but a Christ-inflicted crucifixion. Our Lord was done with the cross when on Calvary he cried: "It is finished." But where he ended each disciple must begin: "If any man will come after me let him deny himself and take up his cross and follow me. For whosoever will save his life shall lose it, and whoever will lose his life for my sake shall find it" (Matt 16:24, 25). These words make it clear that the death-principle must be a realized within us in order that the life-principle may have final and triumphant sway. It is to this truth which every disciple to solemnly committed in his baptism (Rom. 6:3, 4). Baptism is the monogram of the Christian; by it every believer is sealed and certified as a participant in the death and life of Christ; and the Holy Spirit has been given to be the executor of the contract thus made at the symbolic grave of Christ.

The scriptures clearly distinguish that there are three deaths in which we have a part:

Death in sin. (Eph 2:1; Col 2:13) This is the condition in which we are by nature, as participants in the fall and ruin into which the transgression of our first parents has plunged the race. It is a condition in which we are under moral insensibility to the claims of God's holiness and love; and under the sentence of eternal punishment from the law which we have broken.

Death for sin. (Rom. 7:4) This is the condition into which Christ brought us by his sacrifice up on the cross. This condition of death for sin having been affected for us by our Savior, we are held legally or judicially free from the penalty of a violated law, if by our personal faith we will consent to the transaction.

Death to sin. (Rom. 6:11) This is the condition of making true in ourselves what is already true for us in Christ, of rendering practical what is now judicial; in other words, of being dead to the power of sin in ourselves as we are already dead to the penalty of sin through Jesus Christ. It is this condition which the Holy Spirit is constantly effecting in us if we will have it so. "If ye through the Spirit do mortify the deeds of the body ye shall live" (Rom. 8:13).

Excerpted from *The Ministry of the Spirit*. Philadelphia: American Baptist Publication Society, 1894. p. 96-97.

WEEK TWENTY FIVE   *HYMNS and POEMS*   **DAY 6**

Thy Will Be Done

by John Greenleaf Whittier (1807-1892)

WE see not, know not; all our way
Is night, — with Thee alone is day:
From out the torrent's troubled drift,
Above the storm our prayers we lift, Thy will be done!

The flesh may fail, the heart may faint,
But who are we to make complaint,
Or dare to plead, in times like these,
The weakness of our love of ease? Thy will be done!

We take with solemn thankfulness
Our burden up, nor ask it less,
And count it joy that even we
May suffer, serve, or wait for Thee, Whose will be done!

Though dim as yet in tint and line,
We trace Thy picture's wise design,
And thank Thee that our age supplies
Its dark relief of sacrifice. Thy will be done!

And if, in our unworthiness,
Thy sacrificial wine we press;
If from Thy ordeal's heated bars
Our feet are seamed with crimson scars, Thy will be done!

If, for the age to come, this hour
Of trial hath vicarious power,
And, blest by Thee, our present pain,
Be Liberty's eternal gain, Thy will be done!

Strike, Thou the Master, we Thy keys,
The anthem of the destinies!
The minor of Thy loftier strain,
Our hearts shall breathe the old Refrain:, Thy will be done!

https://www.poemhunter.com/poem/thy-will-be-done-6/

WEEK TWENTY FIVE   *HYMNS and POEMS*   **DAY 7**

Spirit

by Anne Bradstreet (1612-1672)

Be still, thou unregenerate part,
Disturb no more my settled heart,
For I have vow'd (and so will do)
Thee as a foe still to pursue,
And combat with thee will and must
Until I see thee laid in th' dust.
Sister we are, yea twins we be,
Yet deadly feud 'twixt thee and me,
For from one father are we not.
Thou by old Adam wast begot,
But my arise is from above,
Whence my dear Father I do love.
Thou speak'st me fair but hat'st me sore.
Thy flatt'ring shews I'll trust no more.
How oft thy slave hast thou me made
When I believ'd what thou hast said
And never had more cause of woe
Than when I did what thou bad'st do.
I'll stop mine ears at these thy charms
And count them for my deadly harms.
Thy sinful pleasures I do hate,
Thy riches are to me no bait.
Thine honours do, nor will I love,

For my ambition lies above.
My greatest honour it shall be
When I am victor over thee,
And Triumph shall, with laurel head,
When thou my Captive shalt be led.
How I do live, thou need'st not scoff,
For I have meat thou know'st not of.
The hidden Manna I do eat;
The word of life, it is my meat.
My thoughts do yield me more content
Than can thy hours in pleasure spent.
Nor are they shadows which I catch,
Nor fancies vain at which I snatch
But reach at things that are so high,
Beyond thy dull Capacity.
Eternal substance I do see
With which inriched I would be.
Mine eye doth pierce the heav'ns and see
What is Invisible to thee.

https://www.poemhunter.com/poem/spirit/

Record your insights, revelations, and meditations from this week. DATE:

_____

_____

_____

_____

_____

_____

_____

_____

_____

_____

_____

_____

_____

_____

WEEK TWENTY SIX   **Being Filled with the Holy Spirit**   **DAY 1**

Few things have troubled the body of Christ in the past century more than the doctrine of being filled with the Holy Spirit. If you are not familiar with the issue, there is plenty of information online for you to look at to learn about the holiness movement, the advent of Pentecostalism, and the rise of the Charismatic movement. As I document elsewhere in the book, this issue was of great interest to me in the 1990s as I sought to learn how to live a life of total obedience to the Lord. The emphasis this week will be on this doctrine. I believe the Lord gave me a way to look at the doctrine that would not be offensive to those who are not active in the Charismatic movement. To do so, we are going to look at seven questions:

> What does the Bible say we can be filled with negatively?
> What does the Bible say we can be filled with positively?
> Who does the Bible say was filled with the Spirit?
> Why do we need to be filled with the Holy Spirit?
> What is the evidence of not being filled with the Holy Spirit?
> What is the evidence we are filled with the Holy Spirit?
> How are we filled with the Holy Spirit?

I.   What does the Bible say we can be filled with negatively?   This will be a Scripture-heavy study because I want you to see everything the Bible says about the concept of being filled with something. You may not be cognizant of being filled with these negative things but, I argue that, if these things are coming out of you, at least in that moment, you are filled with that thing. Being filled with these negative things is not limited to evil people. The Biblical idea of being filled with something involves overflow. You are not really full of something until it is flowing out of you. Read these verses and see if you can find any of your behaviors reflected therein.

Proverbs 12:21	**filled with evil.**
Esther 3:5; Luke 4:28	**filled with wrath,**
Esther 5:9	**filled with indignation**
Job 9:18; Lamentations 3:15	**filled with bitterness.**
Psalms 123:3	**filled with contempt.**
Proverbs 14:14	**filled with (your) own ways**
Jeremiah 51:5	**filled with sin**
Ezekiel 23:33	**filled with drunkenness and sorrow**
Ezekiel 28:16	**filled with violence**
Habakkuk 2:16	**filled with shame**
Matthew 23:32	**filled with guilt**
Luke 6:11	**filled with rage**
Luke 5:26	**filled with fear**
Acts 13:45	**filled with envy**
Acts 19:29	**filled with confusion**
Acts 5:3	**Satan filled your heart**

Romans 1:29 and Galatians 5:19-21 have a longer list of negative things that can fill us. As you meditate on these verses in the context of absolute surrender to the Lord, let the Holy Spirit reveal the times you let something other than Him fill you. You may need to confess, repent, and receive His forgiveness. This important part of the sanctification process cannot be ignored or overlooked. Journal what He reveals to you and obey what He tells you to do.

WEEK TWENTY SIX   **Being Filled with the Holy Spirit**   **DAY 2**

II.   What does the Bible say we can be filled with positively? Yesterday we looked at all the things we can filled with negatively because I wanted to establish a foundation that the idea of a person being filled with something is pervasive throughout the Bible. Today we will look at the things we can be filled with positively. This may not be an exhaustive list, but it's pretty close.

Exodus 28:3	**filled with the spirit of wisdom**
Psalms 126:2	**filled with laughter, our tongues with songs of joy**
Isaiah 33:5	**filled Zion with justice and righteousness.**
Matthew 5:6	**filled with righteousness**
Luke 2:40	**filled with wisdom**
Acts 3:10	**filled with wonder and amazement**
Romans 15:14	**full of goodness, filled with all knowledge**
II Corinthians 7:4	**filled with comfort**
Ephesians 3:19	**filled with all the fullness of God.**
Philippians 1:11	**filled with the fruit of righteousness**
2 Timothy 1:4	**filled with joy.**
Acts 13:52	**filled with joy and with the Holy Spirit.**
Colossians 1:9	**filled with the knowledge of His will**

Ephesians 5:18 is the primary Scripture referenced as a divine commandment to be filled with the Holy Spirit: "Do not get drunk on wine, which leads to debauchery. Instead, **be filled with the Spirit.**"

Just as we pointed out two Scriptures with long lists of negative things, there is a list of positive things, in Galatians 5:22, that the Bible refers to as the fruit of the Holy Spirit: "But the fruit of the Spirit is love, joy, peace, longsuffering, kindness, goodness, faithfulness, gentleness, self-control. Against such there is no law." If you compare this verse to the list above, you will see many similarities. In fact, I would argue the list above is almost describing the Holy Spirit. How can you have the fulness of God without the Holy Spirit? He is called the Comforter. He is the source of wisdom, knowledge, and righteousness, etc.

I like to think of the fruit of the Holy Spirit as the attributes of the Spirit. All these nine things, as well as the list above, describe the way the Holy Spirit acts. Most everyone teaching on the fruit of the Spirit points out that "fruit" is singular. The Holy Spirit doesn't come to you or to me missing any of His attributes. If you are filled with the Spirit, all of who He is available to all of who you are. Again, this is not a thing we are referring to but a person. If I come into your home, I cannot leave my emotions outside, or my opinions, or my attitudes. I may not express them, but I am not without them. So it is with the Holy Spirit.

This is different than what we call the gifts of the Holy Spirit. There are four major passages that talk about the gifts of the Spirit (Eph 4:11-16; Rom 12:4-8; 1 Cor 12:7-11, 28-30) I refer to these as the abilities of the Holy Spirit. All these things are what the Spirit can do. He dispenses these gifts or does these certain things in each of us differently, as Scripture clearly says. When you are filled with the Spirit, all His attributes are available to you but not all His abilities will present themselves. Any ability could present at any time, but no one person has all of them. Think about how the fruit and the gifts are demonstrated in your life. Does your life overflow with the attributes and abilities of the Holy Spirit?

WEEK TWENTY SIX   **Being Filled with the Holy Spirit**   **DAY 3**

III.   Who does the Bible say was filled with the Spirit? Now that we have a picture of what can fill our lives, both positively and negatively, let us examine who in the Bible demonstrated being filled with the Spirit. Surely, we can learn something of what this means by their examples.

Exodus 35:30-33   **Bezalel** … (was) filled … with the Spirit of God, in wisdom and understanding, in knowledge and all manner of workmanship, to design artistic works … (Bezalel is the first person in the Bible described as filled with the Holy Spirit. He was filled to produce the articles for the Tabernacle. He may not have been the only one, according to Exodus 28:3.)

I Kings 7:13-14   **Huram** … was filled with wisdom and understanding and skill in working with all kinds of bronze work. So he came to King Solomon and did all his work … (Although it does not say Huram was filled with the Spirit, everything else mirrors Bezalel so I am confident Huram was filled with the Spirit to do the work for the Temple just like Bezalel was for work in the Tabernacle.)

Luke 1:67	**Zacharias** was filled with the Holy Spirit, and prophesied …
Luke 1:41-42	**Elizabeth** was filled with the Holy Spirit
Luke 1:15	He (**John the Baptist**) will also be filled with the Holy Spirit
Luke 4:1	**Jesus**, full of the Holy Spirit, left the Jordan and was led by the …
Acts 4:8	**Peter**, filled with the Holy Spirit, said to them …
Acts 13:9	**Paul**, filled with the Holy Spirit, looked straight at Elymas and said …
Acts 6:3	seek out from among you seven men (**Deacons**) full of the Holy Spirit
Acts 7:55	but (**Stephen**) being full of the Holy Spirit …
Acts 11:24	For (**Barnabas**) was a good man, full of the Holy Spirit and of faith …

Acts 1:5 says there were about 120 disciples gathered in the upper room on Pentecost. Acts 2:4 says, "All of them were filled with the Holy Spirit and began to speak in other tongues as the Spirit enabled them." If you count the names of the people we know were there, you come up with around 20. So, there were

around 100 disciples that were filled with the Holy Spirit on Pentecost that we never hear about by name. We might call them ordinary Christians. They may have preached and pastored, done miracles, signs and wonders, but all that is lost to history. Nevertheless, they were also filled. And not once but twice!

Acts 4:31 states, "And when they had prayed, the place where they were assembled together was shaken; and they were all filled with the Holy Spirit, and they spoke the word of God with boldness." We do not know the exact time between Pentecost and this event. Some speculate it could have been up to two years later. Certainly, some or many of those original unknown disciples were still a part of the Church and experienced this "second Pentecost," as it were.

Later in the week, we will look a little further at three other incidents recorded in Scripture were groups of ordinary Christians were filled with the Holy Spirit; the church in Antioch, the household of Cornelius, and the disciples at Ephesus. The point is the filling of the Holy Spirit was not, and is not, limited to any certain class of individuals. Jesus needed the filling of the Holy Spirit for ministry, as did Peter, as did Paul, as did the Seven Deacons, and as did the scores of ordinary Christians then and now. That is the witness of Scripture. It is also the testimony of countless believers down through the ages, as I have attempted to illustrate in the pages of this book. The filling of the Holy Spirit is for you. Next, we examine, why?

WEEK TWENTY SIX　　　　**Being Filled with the Holy Spirit**　　　　**DAY 4**

IV.　Why do we need to be filled with the Holy Spirit? So far, we have learned what we can filled with negatively and positively, and who was filled with the Holy Spirit, according to the Bible. Next, we need to discover why it is so important to be filled with the Spirit. Those who teach on the subject often point to the verb tense in Ephesians 5:18. The word translated "be filled" can also carry the sense of continuous action, "be being filled." Do not continue to be filled with wine but continue to be filled with the Spirit. If so, why is it important for the Christian to continuously be filled with the Holy Spirit?

First, we were designed for fullness. I Corinthians 6:19-20 says, "Or do you not know that your body is the temple of the Holy Spirit who is in you, whom you have from God, and you are not your own? For you were bought at a price; therefore, glorify God in your body and *in your spirit*, which are God's." (Emphasis mine.)

In Exodus 40:34, the glory of the Lord filled the tabernacle. In II Chronicles 7;1, the glory of the Lord filled the temple. Isaiah, Ezekiel, and the Apostle John saw similar things. Clearly, as His temple, the Lord through His Spirit wants to fill all of us. We can live without fulness, but we were designed for it. The late evangelist to Africa, Reinhart Bonnke, illustrated the difference between the two as the difference between having power steering in your car and not having it. Without power steering, you can still drive but it is much more difficult. With power steering, it is much easier to keep the car going in the right direction.

Second, we don't automatically get fullness or always keep fullness. Being filled with the Spirit is not the same as being born again. According to Peter in Acts 2:38, salvation comes through repentance, being baptized for the remission of sins, and receiving the gift of the Holy Spirit. Paul amplifies this in Titus 3:5 by explaining God saved us "through the washing of regeneration and renewing of the Holy Spirit." You can be renewed by the gift of the Holy Spirit without being filled. It is possible to be so, but Scripture, history, and personal experience bears witness that it rarely happens that way.

There are three Biblical examples of salvation and filling coming at different times. In Acts 8:14-17, Philip led a revival in Samaria where many received the word of God and were baptized. But only after Peter and John came did they receive the Holy Spirit. In Acts 10:44-46, during Peter's sermon, the household of Cornelius received the Holy Spirit and were later baptized. You could refer to this event as the "Gentile Pentecost." In Acts 19:1-2, believers in Ephesus received the Holy Spirit by Paul's hand. We even have an example of two men we know were filled with the Spirit and lost that fulness. Peter and Barnabas in Antioch (Gal 2:11-13) fell into hypocrisy because they were filled with the fear of man.

Third, we need fullness because without it, we can resist the Holy Spirit. In Acts 7:51, Stephen points out that people always resisted the Holy Spirit. We do that by not letting the Holy Spirit be and do in us what He wants to do. You cannot be committed to the Lordship of Christ and not be committed to being filled with the Holy Spirit. They are inseparable. In Ephesians 4:30, Scripture enjoins us not to grieve the Holy Spirit. We do that by doing things we know we are not supposed to do. This has to do with purity of character. In I Thessalonians 5:19, it states we should not quench the Holy Spirit. We do that by not doing the things we know we are supposed to do. This has to do with the power of obedience.

Next, we will examine what the Bible says is the evidence of being filled with the Holy Spirit but, as we did in the beginning, we will look at the negative side first. What is the evidence we are not filled?

WEEK TWENTY SIX   **Being Filled with the Holy Spirit**   **DAY 5**

Today, we will look at two questions that address two sides of the same coin.

V.   What is the evidence of not being filled with the Holy Spirit?   In the previous session, we mentioned an example from Scripture where two men we know were filled with the Spirit later lost that fullness because they let something else fill them, at least temporarily – the fear of man. Fewer things give Christians more trouble than what other people think of them. In that moment, Peter and Barnabas were not being led by the Spirit or acting in accordance with Jesus' teachings because they were afraid of what the disciples from Jerusalem were going to think. Paul called them out on this.

We can do the same thing with any of the negative things we looked at in the first session. If anything the Bible says we be can be filled with negatively comes from us, we are not filled with the Holy Spirit.

If anything comes from us that the Bible calls a "work of the flesh," (Gal 5:19-21) we are not filled with the Holy Spirit. If anything comes from us that is opposite of the "fruit of the Holy Spirit," we are not filled with Him. "Does a spring send forth fresh water and bitter from the same opening?" (Jam 3:11).

VI.   What is the evidence that we are filled with the Holy Spirit? What does the Bible say about those we know were filled with the Spirit and about being filled with the Spirit in general?

First, the Bible refers to walking in the Spirit. We find this phrase at the end of the passage on the fruit of the Spirit in Galatians 5:22-25. The Bible uses the imagery of walking to refer to one's lifestyle or way of life. "If (or since) we live in the Spirit, let us also walk in the Spirit." The fruit should be evident in our walk, in our way of life.

Second, we learn from the Old Testament saints that the fullness of the Spirit can help you become the best you. Bezalel and Huram were artisans before being filled with the Spirit for the work in God's house but the Spirit gave them greater abilities that enhanced or augmented what they did.

Third, and I believe most importantly, fullness enables us to speak with boldness. Many who teach on this subject would here point to speaking in tongues as an evidence of being filled. Certainly, that did and does happen; however, the evidence for speaking with boldness is more compelling.

Luke 1:67   Now his father Zacharias was filled with the Holy Spirit, and *prophesied* …

Luke 1:41-42 Elizabeth was filled with the Holy Spirit. *In a loud voice she exclaimed* …

Luke 1:15   What was John sent to be? *"The voice* of one crying in the wilderness" Luke 3:4

Acts 4:8   Then Peter, filled with the Holy Spirit, *said to them* …

Acts 13:9   Paul, filled with the Holy Spirit, looked straight at Elymas *and said* …

Acts 4:31   …they were all filled with the Holy Spirit, and *they spoke the word of God with boldness.*

Acts 6:8-10   …they were not able to resist the wisdom and the Spirit *by which he* (Stephen) *spoke.*

Acts 19:6   … the Holy Spirit came upon them, and they spoke with tongues *and prophesied.*

What does the Bible say we are primarily supposed to be? Jesus said in Acts 1:8, "But you shall receive power when the Holy Spirit has come upon you; and you shall be *witnesses* (i.e.. bold speakers) to Me in Jerusalem, and in all Judea and Samaria, and to the end of the earth." How many of you know it is easier to witness with the power of the Holy Spirit than without? Speaking with boldness is the primary evidence you have been filled with the Holy Spirit. Next, how do we get the filling?

WEEK TWENTY SIX   **Being Filled with the Holy Spirit**   **DAY 6**

VII.   How are we filled with the Holy Spirit?

First, we are filled by our choice. Remember earlier we said it is possible not to be filled. We have been commanded to be filled and the fullness is available to all so what makes the difference? It starts with your choice. We see this in the foundational text we have referenced from Ephesians 5:18. "And do not be drunk with wine … but be filled with the Spirit. There is your choice. There is always a choice. With Adam and Eve there was a choice between two trees. In Deuteronomy 30:19, the children of Israel had a choice between life and death, blessing and cursing. There has always been a choice.

Second, we are filled when we obey. Acts 5:32 says, "And we are His witnesses to these things, and so also is the Holy Spirit whom God has given to those who obey Him." We cannot receive the fullness of the Holy Spirit apart from obedience.

Third, we are filled through faith. Galatians 3:14 states, "that the blessing of Abraham might come upon the Gentiles in Christ Jesus, that we might receive the promise of the Spirit through faith." We are saved through faith and we are filled through faith. Everything in the Christian life comes through faith.

Fourth, we receive the fullness in believing. Romans 14:17 says, "for the kingdom of God is not eating and drinking, (here is the choice again) but righteousness and peace and joy in the Holy Spirit. Later in Romans 15:13, Paul continues, "Now may the God of hope fill you with all joy and peace *in believing*, that you may abound in hope *by the power of the Holy Spirit*." I make this distinction between believing and faith because here is the act of faith not just the fact of faith. Not only must be have faith but we must act in faith to receive the fullness of the Holy Spirit. We don't just believe what the Book says, we do what the Book says. That makes all the difference.

Finally, we receive the filling of the Holy Spirit by prayer, preaching, and/or the laying on of hands. Let's revisit the record of the filling events recording in Samaria, with Cornelius, and in Ephesus. There appears to be no prescription for helping someone to receive the fullness but neither does it happen in a vacuum. Something was going on; either preaching, praying, laying on of hands, of a combination of these. My point is this does not happen unconsciously or haphazardly like walking through a door from one room to the next. The Holy Spirit will be at work through preaching or prayer or a Bible study like this one, and you can be filled when you choose to ask for His fullness believing, through faith in His word and in obedience to His command.

The late Baptist evangelist and teacher J. Edwin Orr told a story about a man from Europe who wanted to join his father in America after WW1. He scrimped and saved just enough to buy a ticket. Since the boat trip in those days lasted almost a week, his mother made a sack of cheese sandwiches. He ate those sandwiches for three days on the deck because he couldn't stand to smell the wonderful food in the dining room. Finally, he had enough and went to the chef and offered to wash dishes if allowed to eat the gourmet food. With a smile, the chef accepted. He worked like a dog but ate like a king. Only when he arrived to America did he learn that the food was included in the price of the ticket. Don't starve as a Christian for want of the Holy Spirit. As you surrender yourself to the Lord, pray now and every day to be filled with the Holy Spirit. If you spring a leak, ask Him to fill you again. This is your birthright in Christ.

INSIGHT and ENCOURAGEMENT

Being Filled with the Spirit – Ephesians 5:18

by J. Oswald Sanders (1917-1992)

What does this apostolic injunction in Ephesians 5:18 mean? It is not an invitation to realize a privilege but a command to fulfill an obligation. There is probably no more frequent prayer petition than: "Lord, fill me with Thy Holy Spirit." Yet there seldom appears to be equal assurance that the prayer has been answered. What do we expect to happen when we offer that prayer? Is it something mystical and mysterious? The clear teaching of Scripture is that we are filled with the Spirit when our human spirit is mastered and controlled by the Holy Spirit. The idea behind the command "Be filled with the Spirit" is not so much that of an empty vessel passively waiting for something to be poured into it, as water into a glass. It is rather the concept of a human personality voluntarily surrendered to the domination of the Holy Spirit.

If we look at the manner in which "filled" is used on other occasions, we will get light on this point. "They … were filled with fear" (Luke 5:26). When the Lord was breaking the news to His disciples that He was going to leave them, He said: "Because I have said these things unto you, sorrow hath filled your heart" (John 16:6). What does it mean to have hearts filled with fear or sorrow? Thayer says in his lexicon, "That which wholly takes possession of the mind is said to fill it." To have hearts filled with fear or sorrow means that these emotions so take hold of and possess and control heart and mind that other things become of only secondary importance. To be filled with the Spirit, then, means to be controlled by the Spirit.

Perhaps the imperfect illustration of hypnotism may be of some help here. A hypnotized person speaks and acts at the behest of another person to whom he has yielded control of his will. In hypnotism, the subject is passive and allows his mind to go blank, giving himself up to the hypnotist—a very dangerous attitude. But in being filled with the Spirit there is no passivity. Every faculty and power of the Spirit-filled person are constantly in the fullest exercise. The Spirit's control is not automatic but voluntarily and constantly conceded. If the surrender of the personality to the Spirit is withdrawn, His control is thereby broken, and His power short-circuited.

The Holy Spirit will exercise this control from the center of the yielded believer's personality. He will enlighten the intellect *so* that ever-deepening spiritual truth can be apprehended. As the Spirit of truth, He leads into all truth. He will purify the *affections* and fix them on Christ, for His ministry is always Christocentric. He will reinforce the will, weakened by sinful indulgence, and empower it to do the will of God. Thus from the very inner citadel of the heart He carries on His gracious ministry.

The fullness of the Spirit does not obliterate personality, as does hypnotism. In fact, the person who is filled with the Spirit only then realizes and discovers his true personality. It is not obliterated but released. We will never know the possibilities of our redeemed personality until we definitely yield ourselves in full and unreserved surrender to His control.

Cultivation of Christian Character. Chicago: Moody Publishers, 2017. p. 51-52.

Record your insights, revelations, and meditations from this week. DATE:

_____

_____

_____

_____

_____

_____

_____

_____

_____

_____

_____

_____

_____

EPILOGUE

Congratulations on reaching the end of your first six months of walking with the Lord in full surrender. As you reflect on this time, what have you learned about this way of living? Hopefully, you can look back over your journaling and see how the Holy Spirit has lead you and taught you about this life with His insight and revelation. For me, this life is more peaceful and not as frenetic as living out of my own mind and resources. It is costly, in the sense of what the Lord asks us to part with, but it is so much more satisfying. This life is filled with more blessings and more opportunities. There are still challenges but the ability to meet those challenges is inherent in the deeper relationship with Him. I have experienced a greater desire to be generous and an enhanced ability to be so through more resources and less waste. There is more waiting, but less pressure. I have seen more revelation, more insights, more answers to prayer, and greater boldness in witnessing. Placing yourself completely at the disposal of the Lord requires radical obedience that only the surrendered life can supply. I leave you with one last poem that has encouraged me these last forty years of ministry.

Don't Quit

by John Greenleaf Whittier

When things go wrong as they sometimes will,
When the road you're trudging seems all up hill,
When the funds are low and the debts are high
And you want to smile, but you have to sigh,
When care is pressing you down a bit,
Rest if you must, but don't you quit.

Life is strange with its twists and turns
As every one of us sometimes learns
And many a failure comes about
When he might have won had he stuck it out;
Don't give up though the pace seems slow—
You may succeed with another blow.

Success is failure turned inside out—
The silver tint of the clouds of doubt,
And you never can tell just how close you are,
It may be near when it seems so far;
So stick to the fight when you're hardest hit—
It's when things seem worst that you must not quit.

This is my prayer of benediction and blessing over you from Hebrews 13 and Ephesians 4.

Now may the God of peace who brought again from the dead our Lord Jesus,
the great shepherd of the sheep,
by the blood of the eternal covenant,
equip you with everything good that you may do his will,
working in us that which is pleasing in his sight,
through Jesus Christ, to whom be glory forever and ever.

I, therefore, the prisoner of the Lord,
beseech you to walk worthy of the calling
with which you were called.
Amen.

Together, we are **Prisoners of Grace**.

INDEX OF AUTHORS

Antoinette Bourignon (1616-1680)
Mary Brown (1856-1919)
John Burton, Jr. (1803-1877)
Josiah Carley (1996-present)
Catherine Booth-Clibborn (1858-1955)
Thomas O. Chisholl (1793-1847)
Josiah Conder (1789-1855)
William Cowper (1731-1800)
Sister Eva of Friedenshort (1866-1930)
Emily May Grimes Crawford (1864-1927)
Frederick William Faber (1814-1863)
B. M. Franklin (1882-1965)
William H. Foulkes (1877-1961)
Christian F. Gellert (1715-1769)
Thomas Hornblower Gill (1819-1906)
Paul Gerhardt (1607-1676)
Ann Griffiths (1776-1805)
Homer W. Grimes (published 1934)
Jeanne Marie De La Motte-Guyon (1648-1717)
Ada Ruth Habershon (1861-1918)
Frances Ridley Havergal (1836-1879)
Marianne Hearn (1834–1909)
George Herbert (1593-1633)
Grace W. Hinsdale (1833-1902)
Oliver Holden (1765-1844)
Mildred E. Howard (unknown)
Mary Dagworthy James (1810-1883)
Calvin W. Laufer (1874-1938)
Witness Lee (1905-1997)
Karl Friedrich Lockner (1634-1697)

Henry F. Lyte (1793-1847)
George Matheson (1842-1906)
John S. B. Monsell (1811-1875)
Lelia Naylor Morris (1862-1929)
Charles W. Naylor (1874-1950)
Watchman Nee (1903-1972)
John Henry Newman (1801-1890)
John Newton (1725-1807)
Anna Olander (unknown)
J. Edwin Orr (1912-1987)
Mary Bowley Peters (1813-1856)
Jean Sophia Pigott (1845-1882)
Christina Rossetti (1830-1894)
Nikolaus Selnecker (1532-1592)
Sharla Sensenig (unknown)
A. B. Simpson (1843-1919)
Walter Sheely (1725-1786)
Alfred C. Snead (1884-1961)
Nahum Tate (1652-1715)
Georgiana M. Taylor (1857-1914)
Anna Laetitia Waring (1820-1910)
Barney E. Warren (1867-1951)
Isaac Watts (1674-1748)
Charles Wesley (1707-1788)
Ernest G. Wesley (1847-1929)
John Greenleaf Whittier (1807-1892)
Daniel W. Whittle (1840-1901)
Gertrude E Worthington (unknown)
Katharina A. von Schlegel (1697-1768)
Nicolaus Ludwig Von Zinzendorf (1700-1760)

INDEX OF WEEKLY THEMES OR FEATURED AUTHORS

BIBLIOGRAPHY

Allestree, Richard.   *The Whole Duty of Man*. London: Society for Promoting Christian Knowledge, 1841.

Arndt, Johann.   *True Christianity*. Philadelphia: Smith, English, & Co., (unk).

Baillie, John.   *A Diary of Readings*. New York: Macmillan Publishing Co., 1955.

Baxter, J. Sidlow.   *A New Call to Holiness*. Grand Rapids: Zondervan, 1973.

Beasley, Manley.   *Adventures in Faith*. Kindle Edition, 2013. (Originally a self-published workbook.)

Billheimer, Paul.   *Adventure in Adversity*. Wheaton: Tyndale House, 1984.
Destined for The Cross. Wheaton: Tyndale House Publishers, Inc. 1982.

Blackaby, Henry.   *Holiness*. Nashville: Thomas Nelson, 2003.

Boch, Fred.   *Hymns for the Family of God*. Nashville: Paragon Associates, Inc. 1976.

Bonhoeffer, Dietrich.   *The Cost of Discipleship*. New York: Simon & Schuster, 2018.

Boynton, Jeremy.   *Sanctification Practical*. New York: Foster & Palmer, 1867.

Brother Lawrence.   *The Practice of the Presence of God*.   New Kensington, PA: Whitaker House, 1982.

Chambers, Oswald.   *If Thou Wilt Be Perfect*. Fort Washington, PA: Christian Literature Crusade, 1941.
My Utmost For His Highest. Barbour and Company, Inc., Westwood, NJ.; 1963.

Clarke, Adam.   *Sanctification*. Kansas City: The Publishing House of the Pentecostal Church of the Nazarene, 1907.

Crabb, Jr., Dr. Larry.   *Finding God*. New York: Walker and Company, 1994.

Culpepper, Sr., Charles L.   *The Shantung Revival.* https://www.gospeltruth.net/shantung.htm.
1968. (Based on the book of the same name by Mary K. Crawford ,1933.)

de Sales, Francis.   *Introduction to the Devout Life.* Mineola, NY: Dover Publications, Inc.,

Eitel, Lorraine, ed.   *The Treasury of Christian Poetry.* Old Tappan, NJ: Revell, 1982.

Fénelon, François.   *Christian Perfection.* New York and London: Harper & Brothers, 1947.

Francke, Augustus Hermann. *Memoirs of A. H. Francke.* Philadelphia: American Sunday School
Union, 1831.
The Prayer of Faith Answered, or An Encouragement to Live by Faith, In the Promises and Faithfulness of God. Plymouth Dock: Printed by J. Heydon. 1705.

Foster, Richard J. and Smith, James Bryan. *Devotional Classics.* New York: Harper One, 2005.

Gordon, A. J.   *The Ministry of the Spirit.* Philadelphia: American Baptist Publication
Society, 1894.

Gordon, S. D.   *Quiet Talks on Power.* New York: Fleming H Revell Co, 1903.

Hayford, Jack, ed.   *The Spirit-Filled Bible.* Nashville: Thomas Nelson, 2018.

John of the Cross.   *Dark Night of the Soul.* Start Publishing eBook edition: 2012.

Jones, E. Stanley.   *Victory Through Surrender.* New York: Abingdon Press, 1966.

Jorgensen, Johannes. *Saint Francis of Assisi: A Biography.* New York: Longmans, Green, and
Co., 1912.

Kolenda, Daniel.   *Slaying Dragons.* Lake Mary FL: Charsima House, 2019.

Law, William.   *A Serious Call To A Devout and Holy Life* (1729). New York: Scriptura
Press, 2015.

Lewis, C. S.   *Mere Christianity.* Westwood, NJ: Barbour and Co., Inc. 1952.

MacLaren, Alexander.   *Expositions of Holy Scripture. Vol. 13.* Grace-eBooks.com., (unk).
The Secret of Power. London: Macmillan and Co., 1882.

Marshall, Walter. *Sanctification; or The Highway of Holiness.* London: James Nisbet & Co., 1884.

McIntyre, David. *The Hidden Life of Prayer.* Originally 1891. https://www.scribd.com/document/176950429/The-Hidden-Life-of-Prayer

Morgan, G. Campbell. *Discipleship.* Pathos Publishers EBook, 2015.

Müller, George. *The Autobiography of George Müller.* Dallas: Gideon House Books, 2017.

Murray, Andrew. *Abide in Christ.* Readaclassic.com, 2010.
Absolute Surrender and other addresses. Chicago: Moody Press, (unk).
Divine Healing. Fort Washington, PA: Christian Literature Crusade, 1971.
Holy in Christ. Minneapolis: Bethan Fellowship, [original 1887].
How to Work for God. Pittsburgh, PA: Whitaker House, 1983.
Growing in Christ. Westchester, IL: Good News Publishers, 1979.
Living the New Life. Springdale, PA: Whitaker House, 1982.
Living to Please God. Pittsburgh, PA: Whitaker House, 1984.
The Believer's Secret of Holiness. Minneapolis: Bethany House, 1984.
The Holiest of All. Old Tappan, NJ: Fleming H. Revell Co, 1978.
The School of Obedience. Chicago: Moody Press, no date.
Waiting on God. Chicago: Moody Press. (reprint from 1905).
With Christ in the School of Prayer. Old Tappan, NJ: Fleming H. Revell, Co., 1953.

Nee, Watchman. *Love Not the World.* Philadelphia: Christian Literature Crusade, 1973.

Orr, J. Edwin. *Full Surrender.* London: Marshall, Morgan & Scott, 1951.

Palmer, Phoebe. *Present to My Christian Friend on Entire Devotion to God.* London: William Nichols, 1857.

Price, Charles S. *The Meaning of Faith.* Pasadena, CA: Charles S. Price Pub. Co., 1936.
The Real Faith. Self-published, 1941. Jawbone Digital, Kindle ed.

Pughe, George R. G. trans. *The Hymns of Ann Griffiths.* Blackburn: Geo. H. Durham, Exchange Works, 1900.

Ryle, J. C. *Holiness.* Dublin, CA: FirstLove Publication, 2017.

Sanders, J. Oswald. *Cultivation of Christian Character*. Chicago: Moody Publishers, 2017.
Spiritual Discipleship: principles of following Christ for every believer. Chicago: Moody Publishers, 1994.

Sheldon, Charles M. *In His Steps*. Nashville: Broadman Press, 1935.

Shepperd, John. *Chosen Words from Christian Writers*. London: Hodder & Stoughton, 1869.

Silvoso, Dr. Ed. *Anointed for Business*. Ventura, CA: Regal Books, 2002.
Ekklesia. Bloomington, MN: Chosen Books, 2018.
Strongholds. Bloomington, MN: Chosen Books, 2018.
That None Should Perish. Ventura, CA: Regals Books, 1994.
Transformation. Ventura, CA: Regal Books, 2007.

Smith, Hannah Whithall. *The Christian's Secret of a Happy Life*. Grand Rapids: Revell, 1952.

Smith, James. *Handfuls on Purpose II*. London: Pickering & Inglis, 1923.

Thomas, W. Ian. *How to Work for God*. Pittsburgh, PA: Whitaker House, 1983.
The Mystery of Godliness. Carnforth, Great Britain: Capernwray Press, 1981.
The Indwelling Life of Christ. Colorado Springs: Multnomah Publishers, 2006.

Tozer, A. W. *The Crucified Life*. Minneapolis: Bethany House, 2017.
The Christian Book of Mystical Verse: A Collection of Poems, Hymns, and Prayers for Devotional Reading. Chicago: Moody Publishers, 2016.

Watson, Charles D. *Soul Food, Being Chapters on the Interior Life*. Cincinnati, OH: M. W. Knapp, 1896.
The Secret of Spiritual Power. Boston: The McDonald & Gill Co., 1894.

Wesley, John. *Sermons on Several Occasions, Vol. 1*. Digireads.com Publications, 2012.
Christian Perfection. Franklin, TN: Seedbed Publishing, 2014.

Westcott, B. F. *Social Aspects of Christianity*. London: Macmillan and Co., 1900.

Wigglesworth, Smith. *Smith Wigglesworth on Healing*. New Kensington, PA: Whitaker House, 1999.

CPSIA information can be obtained
at www.ICGtesting.com
Printed in the USA
FSHW022215040321
79194FS

9 781648 302640